To all who seek peace and fellowship amid the
lofty peaks of the Canadian Rockies.

Mrs. Charles Schäffer. Courtesy Whyte Museum, V653.

No Ordinary Woman

THE STORY OF MARY SCHÄFFER WARREN

JANICE SANFORD BECK

RMB

RMB | Rocky Mountain Books Ltd.
rmbooks.com
@rmbooks
facebook.com / rmbooks

Cataloguing data available from Library and Archives Canada
ISBN 13: 978-0-921102-82-3 (paperback)

Printed and bound in Canada by Friesens

Distributed in Canada by Heritage Group Distribution and in the U.S. by Publishers Group West

For information on purchasing bulk quantities of this book, or to obtain media excerpts or invite the author to speak at an event, please visit rmbooks.com and select the "Contact Us" tab.

RMB | Rocky Mountain Books is dedicated to the environment and committed to reducing the destruction of old-growth forests. Our books are produced with respect for the future and consideration for the past.

We acknowledge the financial support of the Government of Canada through the Canada Book Fund and the Canada Council for the Arts, and of the province of British Columbia through the British Columbia Arts Council and the Book Publishing Tax Credit.

Contents

Acknowledgements

The six-year journey that brought this book into being would not have been possible without the assistance of many, many people. I thank my parents for exposing me to the mountains and mountain culture, for my first fateful introduction to Mary Schäffer Warren and for the innumerable forms of assistance they have provided along the way.

I am also grateful for the financial support of two Mount Allison University Junior Research Fellowships, which allowed me to research, write and begin to edit the work. I thank Dr. Heather Jones for supporting my initial research and encouraging me to create a book of it, and Dr. Raymond Blake for picking up where she left off, reviewing early drafts and refining my style.

Many archives and library staff have patiently endured my enquiries and guided me through their collections. I appreciate the assistance of those at the Provincial Archives of Alberta, the University of Alberta Archives, the Glenbow-Alberta Archives, the West Chester Historical Society, the Archives of the Philadelphia Academy of Natural Sciences, the Chester County Archives and Records Services, and the Friends Historical Library at Swarthmore College.

I am especially indebted to the Whyte Museum of the Canadian Rockies in Banff for permission to print Mary Schäffer Warren's previously unpublished manuscripts. Special thanks go to Lena Goon, Mary Andrews, Elizabeth Kundert-Cameron and Don Bourdon of the Whyte Museum of the Canadian Rockies in Banff, and to Ted Hart for his editorial advice.

Hart's research and writing about Mary's life—and that of PearlAnn Reichwein and Cindy Smith—were also of tremendous assistance. Although only direct quotations from primary sources are acknowledged within the text, the work of these historians—and others listed in the bibliography—contributed significantly to my own.

Also facilitating my research was the incredible hospitality of Phil and Barb Bowes of Canmore and the Sisters of Saint Malachy's in Philadelphia. Thank you. Thanks as well to everyone at Rocky Mountain Books for bringing this project to fruition. And last but certainly not least, I thank my partner, Shawn, for his tremendous contributions to this project and to my life over the past years.

A final note: In the quoted material in this book, I have remained as true to the original manuscripts as possible without straining or confusing readers. I have also chosen to retain the First Nations names in use at the time of Mary's explorations and writings.

The Average American Girl?

I HATE DOING THE ORDINARY THING.[1]
When 72-year-old Mary Schäffer Warren penned these feisty words, she was neither writing a manifesto of her beliefs nor defending an impetuous deed. She was simply comforting a troubled friend. Young Humphrey Toms was feeling alienated from a society whose standards he could not bring himself to uphold. Mary understood. As she pondered her young friend's dilemma, memories of all the times she had violated society's unwritten codes flooded her mind, along with troublesome recollections of the censure that had often resulted. She remembered her defiant teenage years during which, much to her chaperone's dismay, she had insisted on mingling with the indigenous people they had encountered on their travels. She recalled the painful period after her husband and parents had passed away, when her social circle had shunned her for not keeping up with the latest fashions. She remembered the opposition she had encountered while engaging in scientific activities deemed more suitable for men. Above all, she remembered the summer of 1907 when she had committed the greatest transgression of her 72 years. That was the summer she had put aside the protestations of her family, friends and society in order to follow her dreams. She and her friend Mollie became the first non-Native women to travel through much of the Canadian Rocky Mountain wilderness that today makes up Banff and Jasper national parks. In so doing, they had found true peace. Carry on, Mary advised her discouraged friend, dare to be different. You will not regret it.

The foundations of Mary's life were infused with just the courage Humphrey Toms needed. The paternal branches of both her parents' families trace back to John and Jane Sharpless, refugees who fled from Britain to America in 1682. The Sharplesses were members of the Society of Friends, or Quakers, as they are better known, who could no longer endure the persecution they were suffering for their religious beliefs. There was simply no place for them in British society. So they packed a few belongings and with their young children journeyed across the Atlantic to a new life.

The Sharplesses settled along Pennsylvania's Ridley Creek, where they grew to prosperity through farming and a successful mill industry. Their faith no longer an obstacle to their well-being, the family thrived. Many of the descendants of John and Jane Sharpless were prominent residents of Chester County, heavily involved in religious and community life. Mary's great-grandfather was the first Chief Burgess of the borough of West Chester and her uncle Philip divided his energies between tending to the affairs of West Chester's High Street Friends' Meeting, bringing public education to West Chester, serving on boards of directors for the local bank and railroad company and studying local history.

Yet even in Chester County, Pennsylvania, where Quakers were in the majority, their spirituality set them apart from many of their neighbours. The four Quaker testimonies of Equality, Peace, Simplicity and Community influenced both their world view and their actions. Initially, their external manifestations of simplicity, most notably their plain dress, were a strong visual reminder of their difference. More important, they approached their fellow human beings with a spirit of love and respect. Believing God's light to be present in every person, Friends had heightened concern for the marginalized people of their world, including Aboriginals, slaves, and women. Quakers were involved in early philanthropic work among Natives and played a key role in the abolition of slavery and the operation of the underground railroad. Both women and men could be Quaker ministers, and, although the men's meetings had more clout than the women's, women in the Society did conduct their own business meetings.

The story of Rachel Price, Mary's great-grandmother, is a prime example of what the Quakers' heightened respect for women could mean. Rachel's relationship with her husband, Philip, was almost two hundred years ahead of its time. Even before being recommended as a Quaker minister of the gospel in 1802, Rachel was travelling with other women to make religious visits in Delaware and Maryland. After 1802, she expanded her travels to include New Jersey, Ohio and Virginia. While she was away, Philip would care for their ten children. When she returned, she would take her turn at home while he pursued his ministerial duties.

Of course, such freedom was rare and was qualified by strict Quaker disciplines. The expanded range of activities a Quaker vocation could open up was accompanied by strict beliefs about what it meant to live out the testimonies of equality, peace, simplicity and community. Some of these beliefs had such power over the Quaker conscience that they created expectations even of non-members. Friends working with North American Aboriginals, for example, sought to instil in them their own Protestant work ethic. Aboriginal peoples were expected to embrace a sedentary agricultural lifestyle, European-style education and the Christian religion, all of which were foreign to their traditional way of life.

Imagine, then, what impact Quaker beliefs would have had on members. When Mary's parents, Alfred and Elizabeth Sharpless, decided to marry, they quickly discovered the power of strong convictions regarding proper comportment. Both had grown up in Quaker families on Chester County farms. As a young adult, Alfred left the area for Philadelphia, where he worked with his brother William as a wholesale commission agent and took an active interest in the management of the West Chester Railroad. During this time he began to court Elizabeth Sharpless. The problem was, his family belonged to the Hicksite branch of the Society of Friends, hers to the Orthodox. Neither branch approved of their marriage; each of Mary's parents was officially chastised for marrying an "outsider." Yet marry they did, in 1857, and they settled down in Chester County. Not long thereafter, Alfred became superintendent of transportation for the Schuylkill Navigation Company, a position he maintained until 1870, when the lease of the canal to the Reading Railroad prompted him to return to his farming roots and dabble in local politics.

It was in the area their ancestors had been farming for close to two hundred years that Alfred and Elizabeth began a family of their own. Elizabeth gave birth to their first two sons, Henry Lewis and Joseph Townsend, in 1858 and 1859. Frederick Fraley and Herman Hoopes joined them in 1866 and 1871. In between, on October 4, 1861, Alfred and Elizabeth Sharpless became the proud parents of a beautiful baby girl. They named the infant Mary, which was both a family name and very popular at the time. But a hint of their daughter's future unconventionality was carried by her middle name. Although Townsend was also a family name, it was chosen in honour of Elizabeth's former fiancé!

The hint of eccentricity borne by this name took some time to surface. Mary Townsend Sharpless's early life proceeded much as one would have expected for the daughter of an upper-middle-class American Quaker family. A live-in nurse cared for her and her brothers, carefully ensuring they did not learn too much about the world beyond their lovely home. Although Mary was born in a town seized by Civil War fervour, little awareness of the conflict would have penetrated her sheltered existence. In fact, the Sharpless children were so spoiled that Mary, although responsible for supervising her younger brothers, had not learned how to make a bed by the age of 18. Such skills were not required in a well-staffed home like the Sharplesses'.

Still, not all was blissful in the Sharpless household. Eight months before Mary's birth, the family was struck by the loss of little Henry, not yet three years old. Death again visited the household eight years later, when 11-year-old Joseph succumbed to scarlet fever. And Mary was but a young girl when first afflicted with neuralgia, a painful disease of the nerves. She learned early the harsh reality of the human condition, developing an inner strength that would serve her well in trials to come.

From a young age, Mary struggled with the narrow confines of behaviour expected from girls in privileged Quaker families. Alfred and Elizabeth Sharpless demanded strict obedience from their children. But young Mary was a rebel. She enjoyed the challenge of tricking her wise mother, avoiding punishment, and appearing sweet and innocent enough to be showered with gifts of candy from unsuspecting relatives. Typical as these antics might seem, they were symptoms of a much deeper malaise with conventional behaviour in one who "always had a sense of stepping out beyond what was expected or tolerated by [her] very prim relatives."[2]

Mary's discomfort with conventional roles, particularly those assigned to young girls, led her to spend a great deal of time with her father. This father-daughter time proved to be extremely enriching. The history of formal education in West Chester ran through Alfred Sharpless's blood, his father and grandparents having built and superintended various local boarding schools and his brother, Philip, having helped spearhead public education in the borough. He taught Mary to read before she even set foot in a school, then saw her through her primary and secondary education at local public and private schools.

Even so, Mary always felt that her formal education was inadequate. The strength of her training was not in school subjects like math and Latin, but in the extracurricular enrichment she received. After-school lessons with George Lambden, a renowned American flower painter, were a crucial component of this additional training, as was the time Mary spent with her father exploring the great outdoors.

A well-known amateur geologist, mineralogist, and archaeologist, Alfred Sharpless eagerly shared his Victorian enthusiasm for detailed observation and the cataloguing of nature with his young daughter. In part, this sharing consisted of taking her on drives with his close friend, Dr. Joseph Leidy, one of the greatest figures in nineteenth-century American science. A kind and popular gentleman, Leidy did not let his prestige keep him from enjoying visits with friends like Alfred. The time he, Alfred and Mary spent together had a profound influence on the young girl. Mary later declared that Leidy's "language was simple enough for even a child of 6 to understand and tho I never grew brainy I did understand the story of stones, of grasses and so many wee things which most people attach no attention to."[3]

The study of natural history, though a fairly recent phenomenon, was already becoming a family tradition. Alfred's father had been interested in all branches of science, and Mary's younger brother Fred followed suit with a career in mineralogy. They were not alone. Concerned about the practicality of their leisure pursuits, many Quakers were delighted to find a hobby that was empirical, accessible and utilitarian. They were also attracted to natural history's spiritual dimension: its veneration of nature as an awe-inspiring example of God's creative and sustaining powers. Through her father's influence, Mary learned to see her environment as God's creation, worthy of honour and respect.

She was also intrigued by the attention natural historians devoted to studying the indigenous peoples of North America. Pennsylvanian Quakers had long been involved in efforts to mitigate the results of Euro-Americans' disregard for the dignity and human rights of indigenous peoples. Among natural historians this concern took the form of meticulous documentation of Aboriginal cultures believed to be on the brink of extinction. In fact, one of Pennsylvania's largest private collections of Native artifacts was held by none other than Mary's uncle Philip. For a young girl already fascinated by stories of the wild west, these authentic stone tools, leather work, baskets, whips, pipes and wampum belts were most intriguing.

But the spark that set Mary's fascination with Aboriginal peoples ablaze was a visit from "Cousin Jim," an American army officer involved in the western Indian raids. Young Mary was spellbound by this handsome, uniformed visitor. His countenance spoke to her of the unknown world beyond her sheltered home. She could not take her eyes off him, nor divert her ears from one word he spoke. She was so captivated that when her parents sent her to the nursery so they

Alfred Sharpless, ca. 1890. Courtesy Chester County Historical Society.

could speak with Jim alone, the daring young girl surreptitiously hid in a corner of the veranda to eavesdrop on the conversation.

Little did Mary know this small act of defiance would profoundly alter her outlook on life, paving the way for many more rebellious deeds. Her imagination was set afire by Jim's tales of buffalo hunts, expansive prairies, forts and soldiers. Images danced through her mind, drawing her further and further into a fantasy world of the Wild West. Then came the shock of her short life when Jim, oblivious to the young eavesdropper's presence, described the trauma of overturning a corpse only to stare into the blood-smeared face of the woman's live baby. Having heard more than she ever wanted or expected to, Mary could not help but cry out. She was promptly ushered to bed, but images from Jim's story were permanently seared in her mind. From that day forward she requested "Indian stories," scoured the Pennsylvania hills for old arrowheads, and let her imagination run wild with fantasies of Native life. The stereotypical Indian as a wild and free individual unwilling to adopt the mores of Euro-American society appealed immensely to a young girl feeling trapped by the rules and expectations that governed her life.

Years passed before Mary was able to compare the fantasy world she

11

had developed with the reality of the western states. Finally, during her adolescence, she had the opportunity to interact with the Natives of the American West. Tourism, which Briton Thomas Cook had spearheaded in the 1860s with his working-class excursions to the country and seaside, had spread to the upper-middle and gentried classes, then crossed the Atlantic to the wealthier residents of the northeastern United States.

Rail technology was the crucial link that made this new leisure activity possible. West Chester had been connected to Philadelphia by rail in 1833, and Alfred Sharpless, then a boy of eleven, made the trip even before the link was complete. His experience as one of the first local children to see the world beyond their farms and the borough of West Chester was forever engraved in his memory. Nothing was more natural than to endeavour to give his daughter the same experience almost half a century later, when the technology was in place to link their state with the rest of the country.

Early travel on the new American railways was quite the adventure. Wood fuel created sparks and sometimes even fires that threatened the well-being of travellers and their possessions. Comfort was also impaired by the use of jerky hand brakes until 1860, and by the frequent train changes that were necessary until standardized tracks were introduced in 1882. Even so, the economy, speed and reliability of rail travel endeared it to the American people—including 14-year-old Mary Sharpless, whose adventurous spirit was at last to find an outlet.

Of course, a young woman with so active an imagination and so little experience beyond her own backyard was poised for disappointment. All across the great plains Mary searched for Natives and their tipis, only to find signs of Euro-American colonization—ranches, wheat fields and cow after cow. As she and her chaperone crossed the Mohave desert, she "continued to look for her beloved Indians, but when they appeared she was forced to confess to herself they were not up to standard, or at least not as her fancy had proclaimed them."[4] The danger her reading had encouraged her to expect was nowhere to be found. Mary managed "a few thrills and shivers when [she] saw Indians wrapped in their gay blankets at various little stations and watching the 'dude' traveller with hardened and critical eye,"[5] but was almost disappointed that the small revolver she had packed for protection proved to be quite unnecessary. In place of the wild and free life of the fictional West, Mary witnessed the saddening spectacle of tainted meat being tossed from the railway cars into the hands of poverty-stricken Aboriginal women.

Finding the West so different from what she had come to expect did not, however, dampen Mary's enthusiasm for its indigenous peoples. Where many would have retreated from the situation before them, further embedding themselves in their imaginations, Mary not only accepted reality, but was an eager participant. When a fellow passenger poked a Native woman with his cane, "Mary's heart ... bounded ahead of all action toward her Indian friend (as she would have loved to call her)."[6] With a combination of Quaker respect and the paternalism that often results from sympathy ungrounded in genuine relationship, Mary caressed the woman's shoulder, gently handing her a few coins. As she later reflected, "Prosaic enough was the young girl's first contact with the race over whom she had wept in her baby days but she had proven to herself that even without knowledge she was able to carry her message of affection and understanding to a very misunderstood people."[7]

Despite the burden of her own very limited understanding, Mary persevered in her desire to befriend the friendless and defend the defenceless. When her fellow passengers began to throw money at a Native woman from whom they wished to purchase a basket, Mary was enraged. She could not bear to see others insulting the people she so longed to know. Without a second thought, she descended from the stagecoach, picked up the coin and handed it apologetically to the Native woman. As she later explained, "The squaw looked at the dollar then at the bills so temptingly held out to her from the other aspirants for her one cooking utensil. Without one sound, just that look which loving women the world over understand, she waved her hand contemptuously at the larger money and smilingly bent from her saddle, handing the treasure to the young girl who had won her by her look of true sympathy which was more to her than dollars."[8]

Once young Mary Sharpless had begun to explore her vast continent via its ever-expanding network of railways, there was no holding her back. Perhaps it was her desire to escape from suffocating relatives that spurred her on; perhaps her longing for adventure. Or perhaps she was simply trying to keep pace with globe-trotting friends. Regardless, she enthusiastically ventured to whatever destinations were offered her, consistently insisting on interacting with her new surroundings more profoundly than most tourists.

The 1880 steamer trip she made along the Alaskan coast was no exception. Against her chaperone's wishes Mary took every opportunity to explore Native settlements. Having understood that the Wild West was no more (if it ever had been), she instead began searching for middle-class, Europeanized Natives. Again, she found that reality did not coincide with her expectations. She brashly peered into various homes only to be put off by their bare and dirty appearance and the lack of warmth in their inhabitants' response to her friendly smile. Blind to her class bias, with no sense that people might not appreciate having her peek into their homes, Mary persevered in her quest.

At last, she found what she was looking for: a dainty Native woman in a neat house with bright wildflowers bordering its walk. Yet even this lovely home was not enough to impress Mary's chaperone. Fearing for Mary's health and safety—not to mention her own—she begged her to return to the boat. But Mary was not to be deterred. She defiantly retorted, "Go back to the boat if you wish. She may have had the smallpox and every other evil, but I am 18 and I think I would prefer to manage this call myself and alone!'"[9]

The older woman wisely stepped back as Mary proceeded to befriend her new acquaintance. She discovered that the woman had been living alone for two years—ever since her husband, a white sailor, had run out of money and gone off to hunt seals. She maintained her home as he had liked it, but with each passing day her hope that he would soon return grew more difficult to maintain. Mary listened intently as her new friend choked back tears, struggling to describe how her community scoffed at the possibility of her husband's return, ridiculed him and urged her to remarry among her own kind.

Whatever her biases, Mary was a beacon of hope to this troubled soul. She consoled her new friend, assuring her that she was right to wait for her husband. Before long, her chaperone angrily summoned her back to the boat, disrupting a brief connection neither young woman would ever forget. The next morning, just as the boat was to lift anchor, the lonely Alaskan appeared at its side with a pair of doe-skin moccasins in appreciation of Mary's sympathetic ear.

The themes that emerge from Mary's early travel experiences were to remain prominent throughout her life. Her readiness to shun her less courteous fellow travellers and to enter an Alaskan woman's home contrary to the demands of her chaperone were early signs of a persistent reluctance to let societal pressures stand in her way. At the same time, her choice of which Alaskan home to visit reflects her inability to completely abandon certain pervasive societal values. As eager as Mary was to reach out to people with whom she felt an affinity, she had few qualms about shunning those whom she found either too rough or too snobbish.

Mary moved into young adulthood full of confidence and passion. Yet she lacked a real channel for her energies. She enjoyed her summer travels, but the rest of the year remained distinctly empty. Where a young man might have gone to university and embarked upon a career, as her brother Frederick had, Mary was at a loss. Her family history of accomplished men and women encouraged her to act, but also reminded her that her desires often violated her relatives' sense of propriety. She was caught in a bind. Her strong foundation of education, study of natural history and travel supported her; her headstrong nature prodded her forward, but none of the paths open to her was entirely satisfactory. She was a bright, enthusiastic young woman searching for a mission.

Westward Bound

T HE 1885 COMPLETION OF the Canadian Pacific Railway's transcontinental line was a much-heralded feat of engineering. For Canadians it meant relatively rapid transportation of people and goods from one end of the country to the other. It was the line of steel that was to bind the country together. For better-off Americans little concerned about the state of Canadian unity, the railway's significance lay in the vast new pleasure ground it opened up. Wealthy tourists, tempted by the CPR's promises of richly upholstered seats, luxurious sofas, polished mahogany berths and gourmet dining, began flocking to western Canada in droves. Little did Mary Sharpless know that her future awaited her amidst the splendour of the Canadian Rockies.

As in her childhood travels, she was to be accompanied on her Canadian journey by an older escort. But Dr. Charles Schäffer was no overbearing matron. A physician by profession, the handsome Philadelphian's true passion lay in the study of natural history. His devoted participation in the Philadelphia Academy of Natural Sciences, presided over by Alfred Sharpless's old friend, Dr. Joseph Leidy, could only have endeared him to the family. Indeed, the more he and Mary conversed, the more connections they uncovered, and the more their mutual attraction grew. The fact that he was 23 years older and already twice widowed had little bearing on the growing romance. A Quaker ceremony at the Sharplesses' home united Mary and Charles in marriage on July 24, 1889.[1]

Mary's West Chester wedding marked a fond farewell to the borough where she had spent her first 28 years. Though she would often visit her childhood home, her residence was now 1309 Arch Street, Philadelphia, where Charles Schäffer had lived since childhood. The home, since torn down to make room for a parking lot across from Philadelphia's Convention Centre, had been built according to a standard plan. It bore a distinguished pressed brick front complemented by white marble steps and trimmings and solid white wooden shutters. The front door opened into a

15

Dr. Charles Schäffer. Courtesy The Academy of Natural Sciences, Philadelphia Library, #06573.

wide hall leading to the parlour, the dining room, the kitchen and most likely a summer kitchen as well. On the second floor were a sitting room, bedrooms and a bathroom. The third floor was devoted to spare bedrooms and the servants' chambers. A furnace in the cellar kept the house warm, gas lighting brightened the evenings, and both hot and cold water flowed through the taps. Three live-in servants kept the house clean and its residents fed.

It was not, however, until fall that Mary was to see much of her new home. From the first months of their marriage, Charles Schäffer's scientific interests proved most conducive to indulging Mary's passion for travel. Unaware of the extent to which this seemingly insignificant decision would affect her life, Mary agreed to accompany her new husband to an 1889 scientific gathering in Toronto. There, she came across a series of images of majestic Lake Louise. Mary was awestruck. Nothing in all her travels had prepared her for the feast before her eyes. She had no inkling that sights so spellbinding were to be found on the North American continent. She simply had to see them for herself.

Mary Schäffer did not have long to wait. Before the week was out, she was presented with the opportunity to witness for herself the glories of the Canadian Rockies. Not yet having fully absorbed the lessons of her travels in the American west, Mary was convinced that she would be risking her life travelling through recently ceded Native territory. She briefly considered declining the trip, but her spirit of adventure prevailed. Bearing a small pistol to assuage her fears, she boarded the westbound Canadian Pacific train that was to carry her across the continent in comfort and style.

The trip, though relatively brief, was altogether pleasurable. Far from being consumed by the desire to see her destination, Mary was eager to take in all the sights along the way. Dismissing the complaints of those who found the prairie scenery monotonous, she was fascinated by the opportunity to witness history in the making. Mary noted the abandoned boats of Colonel Garnet Wolseley's men, brought from the east in a belated show of Canadian opposition to the 1869 Riel Rebellion. She purchased polished buffalo horns from Natives posted at various stations throughout the west. And, most exciting of all, she met the brother of Sitting Bull, who had fled north after the infamous Custer Massacre of 1876. Intrigued by both his link with celebrity and the unusual affection he displayed toward his wife, Mary sought permission to photograph the striking couple. Sadly, competing egos prevented the photo from being shot. Mary responded to the man's request of a five-dollar fee by haughtily turning her back and departing. Only later did she turn back in spirit, declaring, "I have often wished I had pocketed my pride, unloosed my purse and kept for the future a replica of that storm-beaten old face and his apparent affection for his squaw."[2]

A 4:00 a.m. stop at the tiny station of Gleichen, Alberta, pushed all regrets to the back of Mary's mind. For it was from there that she first saw the stunning mountain range that was to dominate her consciousness forever after. "That one glimpse paid for the whole trip," Mary later declared, "and I dreamed not that more and more were to come."[3] Though that first cross-Canada voyage offered little opportunity to make deeper contact with the Rockies, Mary and Charles' journey home was dominated by plans for a lengthier stay in the mountains that had so captivated her imagination.

When the Schäffers returned to the Rockies two years later, they chose Glacier House, which Mary described as "a tiny picturesque chalet cuddled close to the railroad track as though to shield her from the dark forests behind her,"[4] as their base. This Swiss-style restaurant/hotel, established to avoid carrying dining cars over the steep mountain passes, provided ample opportunity to indulge a hunger for adventure and a passion for natural history. The combination of Charles' financial standing and his enthusiasm for the flora of the Canadian mountains enabled the Schäffers to enjoy the best of both worlds—Philadelphia society in the winter, mountain scenery in the summer.

While Charles kept busy through the winter with his medical practice and involvement in such organizations as the Academy of Natural Sciences, the Geographical Society of America, the Historical Society of Pennsylvania, the Art Club and the Orpheus Club, Mary could not take her mind off the mountains. She later explained: "In spite of the fact that I had entree in the east to art circles, musical circles—all that goes to make a city life adored by those who are willing to endure the black dust of rail-roads, clanging of cars twenty-four hours of the day, puddles of mud on rainy days, broiling heat of summer, etc., my heart turned ever to my memory pictures of the Rockies and open spaces. No sweltering heat was there, where by pure accident, I had found my first 'location,' only the distant toot of a train at odd moments, only the singing birds, the chatter of busy squirrels, an occasional deer passing fleet and frightened into the brush beside the trail, and if we were specially lucky, at times a perfectly live and frightened bear would go tumbling out of sight at the pace of a race horse."[5]

The summers Mary and Charles spent in the Rockies were undoubtedly her favourite time of year. Accompanying Charles on his botanical investigations, Mary was reminded of her childhood excursions with her father.

But delightful as these memories were, she was no longer a child, and she despised the moments when she was made to feel like one. She was mortified, for example, when her efforts to impress a famous botanist with a stunning water lily resulted in a crushing: "You had better keep it for my mind is entirely engaged with a much higher type of plant life."[6] Charles' gentle explanation that the most beautiful flowers are not necessarily the most scientifically valuable scarce soothed her bruised ego.

Charles likely anticipated doing a great deal of such fatherly explaining; he did not expect his wife to be a learned botanist. Nor did he expect her to have artistic talent, though in this he was sorely mistaken. Mary stunned him with the revelation that she was a skilful painter capable of significantly enhancing his work. Yet even in this domain she had a few lessons to learn. She tended to focus on the aesthetics of grouping, while Charles insisted on the accuracy of every detail. Before they could begin their highly successful program of gathering flowers together for her to press, dry, paint and photograph and for him to identify and study, she had to elevate her work to his standards. Frustrated, she explained that "many a sketch had to be destroyed for what to me, was a mere kink. But I learned my lesson and any sketch that passed his eagle eye, simply HAD to be correct. In this way I really learned to know right from wrong and the Dr. began to appreciate his much younger wife."[7]

His appreciation was well deserved. While it was quite common for women of Mary Schäffer's generation to assist their husbands with their scientific work, she was more enthralled than most. She experimented with photographic methods to take the most accurate photos possible, then created colour slides by hand-painting the negatives with transparent pigments. Her efforts to support Charles' botanical work led to photographs of such quality that they were exhibited in international shows.

The first organization to acknowledge Mary's contribution to the study of nature was the Philadelphia Academy of Natural Sciences. Charles Schäffer was heavily involved in the Academy, serving as recorder of the Botanical Section for over a decade, as recorder and secretary of the Mineralogical and Geological Section for almost as long, and as corresponding secretary of the Biological and Microscopial Section for several years. With Mary's increasing involvement in the field, her name was put forward as a potential member in 1896. Fortunately, threats of strong opposition failed to materialize, and on March 31, 1896, Mary Schäffer was granted life membership.

Her contributions to the Academy were primarily behind the scenes. Although it was she who donated a wide variety of specimens acquired on their travels, it was always Charles who was elected a councillor and asked to chair meetings. As a dutiful wife keen to support her husband's interests, Mary wrote up minutes for Charles when he was ill, but never aspired to such a position for herself. Very few women were elected officers of the male-dominated Academy.

Operating in a milieu in which her much older husband was the uncontested expert and in which she was considered a novice, Mary's childhood confidence dissipated. Unlike the daring teenager who traipsed through Alaskan villages in quest of friendly Natives, Mary Schäffer, like the majority of her peers, was quite unadventurous in her early travels through the Rockies. She considered herself "a delicate girl, not staunch enough to attempt some of the 'first climbs' of which [she] was hearing daily or to penetrate some of the 'new' valleys of which others spoke."[8] She mostly stuck beside her husband, whose heart trouble prevented him from travelling far from the railway, and assisted him with his botanical work.

The one exception was an 1893 camping trip to Lake Louise. Tom Wilson, Rocky Mountain pioneer and guide, arranged the trip. As a railway packer and scout under Major A.B. Rogers, engineer-in-charge of the Mountain Section of CPR construction, Wilson had been the first non-Native to discover the beauty of Lake Louise and Emerald Lake. Since the end of his railroad days, guiding, outfitting and trail-cutting had been his passion. The mountain veteran was keen to share his finds with the ever-increasing number of visitors making their way across the continent on the CPR.

The excursion to Lake Louise was the first time the Schäffers ventured away from the luxurious Canadian Pacific hotels, and the prospect of spending a night on the shores of the renowned lake inebriated them. Delighting in the fresh mountain air, they and their friends agreed to travel the forty miles between their hotel and Laggan Station (now Lake Louise) on top of a box car. Although she later wondered who had dreamed up this scheme, at the time Mary felt so accustomed to trying new things that she "had no qualms whatever she could sit on top of a wabbling freight car without sliding off, providing she could master the horrid little iron ladder whereby to reach that lofty perch."[9] After lengthy delays, the train at last set out, excellent views compensating for the shower of soot that enveloped the enthusiastic travellers.

Their means of transportation from Laggan Station to the lake itself was even more outlandish, but again the party was blind to the absurdity. They saw nothing odd in the fact that Stoney Indians William and Joshua Twin travelled eighty miles, accompanied by their wives and children, to bring the eastern tourists horses with which to travel a mere three miles to Lake Louise! Mary, for one, was far too concerned about the horses' vicious appearance to question how far they had come. As her nervous energy intensified, she decided to bribe one of the Twins fifty cents to point out the horse most likely to carry her safely to her destination.

The appearance of the horse thus selected did little to inspire confidence. Mary questioned the wisdom of her bribe, wondering if her selfish plan would backfire. All doubts were put to rest, however, when the party began its trek, and Mary discovered hers to be the only horse travelling a straight line. While the others struggled to stay on the trail, she was able to soak in the delightful scenery. When spectacular Lake Louise came into view, she "could have fallen off [her] horse with surprise, so suddenly had the great experience come to an end!"[10]

Or so she thought. Relaxing into the prospect of spending the rest of the day enjoying the view, Mary and her companions were startled to hear their guide summon them to further explorations. Mary was even more surprised to spy another woman attempting to mount "her" horse. But the interloper was not counting on the loyalty of William Twin, who promptly returned the horse to its original rider. Thanks to his efforts, Mary greatly enjoyed the excursion to the Beehive, Mirror Lake and Lake Agnes. Her first trail ride was a success.

However, the night of camping was yet to come—and Mary was no more experienced with camping than with horses. Glorious as the prospect of a night beneath the stars had seemed from afar, the lakeshore turned out to be "a dismal, stump-filled swamp, a breeding place for myriads of mosquitoes."[11] Had they come a year earlier, a log hut would have provided some protection, but it had burned down. Mary had no choice but to tough it out in a tent. Exhausted by her day's adventure, she gave up supper, opting rather to collapse into the first tent in sight. Chilled to the bone, she drew up the blankets, struggling to ignore their decidedly horselike odour. Harder to ignore were the successive fits of shivers and sneezes contorting Mary's petite frame. The camping neophyte grew increasingly convinced she was suffering from typhoid fever.

Utter misery consumed her, relieved only by the arrival of a friend. The considerate trailmate, suspecting Mary's chill, had brought a hot stove lid to warm her. She announced her presence at the door of the tent, then proceeded to convey her gift to Mary. It was not as simple a journey as it appeared. Undoubtedly fatigued by the day's efforts, the woman stumbled over the planks carefully laid to protect the mattresses from the soggy ground and careened headfirst toward Mary, banging her friend's head with the stove lid as she landed.

Far from compounding Mary's misery, the accident was just what she needed to regain her positive outlook. She laughed heartily, then with the warm lid judiciously placed between her and her friend, fell into a deep sleep. Nevertheless, the following morning they peeked out of their tent "upon that magnificent scene with chattering teeth and shivering bodies, and vowed never again to camp in the Canadian Rockies."[12]

For a time, Mary steadfastly adhered to this promise. By staying in the CPR hotels, she was able to enjoy the mountain scenery without abandoning her creature comforts. Assisting her husband with his botanical work, studying local wildlife and researching the history of the region, she had plenty to keep her occupied. But before long Mary's interest in the area was so keen that she had little choice but to summon the courage to broaden her wilderness experience.

Mary had seen climbing enthusiasts Samuel Allen and Walter Wilcox attempt the peaks around Glacier House in 1893. She had heard of their 1894 exploration of the Lake Louise area, the most thorough to date by non-Natives. She was not far away when Professor Charles Fay, president of Boston's Appalachian Club, first climbed Mounts Lefroy and Victoria, then led a group of 20 climbers, many of them women, to the Lake Louise area in 1895. She was fascinated to hear of Walter Wilcox's exploration of the upper Bow Valley and areas farther north; captivated by his and Professor Norman Collie's efforts to locate the famed Mounts Hooker and Brown. The more tales about the Rocky Mountain wilderness Mary absorbed, the more motivation she developed to stray from the comfort of the railway tracks and CPR hotels.

Mary was not yet ready to imitate the exploits of her inspirers, nor to mournfully declare that her "secret haunts [had been] laid bare to all who came"[13] and lament that "the little tents on the shores of Lake Louise, with their balsam-bough beds and an atmosphere reeking with health and strength to those weary with the city's life, were banished, and only found again by the determined few who had heard of the recently discovered Moraine Lake, Lakes O'Hara and McArthur, and Ptarmigan and Yoho valleys. Point by point we fled to them all, each one of them a stronghold at civilization's limits, each one of them a kindergarten of the at-first-despised camping life."[14] But she was ready to give camping another try.

With Mary's youthful pluck reviving, the summer of 1898 proved to be one of significant personal growth. She and Charles began the season by accompanying fourteen members of the Philadelphia Photographic Society across the continent from Philadelphia to British Columbia in a private railway car. Their guide, Jimmy Simpson, met them in Field to lead them to

The Schäffers' 1893 camp at Lake Louise. Courtesy Whyte Museum, NA 66-1401.

Emerald Lake by horseback. It was a momentous trip for all involved. The enthusiastic photographers had the distinction of being both the first tourists in the yet unnamed Yoho Valley and the first group guided by Simpson, a man soon to be renowned for his exploits as guide, hunter, outfitter and lodge operator.

Another first came later that summer, when Mary had her "first baptism in the sadness and the wildness and the beauty of the Canadian Alps."[15] The occasion was a trip to the Big Bend of the Columbia River, the first time the Schäffers' travels extended beyond the range of the ever-present train whistle. They hired a driver to transport them from Revelstoke to the Big Bend in a horse-drawn wagon. There began a somewhat treacherous hike, following a narrow path between the wild river and high canyon walls. The area's rugged beauty set Mary's imagination aflame. As she walked she reflected upon the gold-seekers of 1865 and '66 whose steps she was retracing. She nervously remembered those who had met their death attempting the passage, all the while vicariously experiencing the excitement of their hope-filled journey.

All in all, it was a delightful afternoon—until it came time to return to the hotel. Filled with the satisfied fatigue that marks the end of a pleasant jaunt in the great outdoors, the Schäffers began to make their way back to the spot where the horses had been tied. Darkness was falling; an evening chill penetrated the air. At last, the weary hikers caught a glimpse of their destination, then drew close enough for a good look. Something was not right. The field was empty! Search as they might, the horses were nowhere to be found. Mary and Charles had no choice but to trudge the remaining three miles to Revelstoke. Their tired legs protested, but the couple knew they had to hurry if they wished to arrive before dark. Their foul tempers only grew fouler when the driver insisted on collecting his pay for the ride. Making matters worse, Mary discovered that the horses had not run away, but rather had been removed by one of the driver's practical-joking friends. Exhausted, and filled with a "righteous though smothered wrath,"[16] she could do nothing but try to forget the whole aggravating incident.

The familiar surroundings of Glacier House, where the Schäffers spent the remainder of the summer, eased this task. All unpleasant memories were quickly erased, and, unlike five years earlier, Mary did not allow her trying experience to push her back into less adventurous pursuits. She still spent time painting and photographing wildflowers with Charles, but could no longer limit herself to botanical work. She started leaving her husband at Glacier House while she joined her friend Mary Vaux in exploring the mountains.

Mary Vaux had been among the first to discover the Canadian Alps' potential for scientific research. Hers was a prominent Philadelphia Quaker family taken with more than the typical dose of scientific enthusiasm. She and her brothers George and William spent their summer holidays making detailed observations of glacial activity. Their winters were spent spreading news of their fabulous retreat. Their dedication to the task was remarkable; their enthusiasm for the mountains contagious. Mary Schäffer could not have dreamed of better companions or mentors.

She began by accompanying the Vauxes on a hike to Bear Creek falls. The journey was a slow and difficult one through uncut bush, but spirits were high, and the challenge only intensified their sense of adventure. They travelled farther than the trainmen at Rogers Pass were willing to believe, and were so exhilarated that they could not bear to wait several hours for the next train. In an ironic counterpoint to Mary's experience at the Big Bend, they opted to walk back to Glacier House, where they arrived at 7:30 p.m.

Mary enjoyed the outing so much that she resolved to join the Vauxes on one of their climbing expeditions. Her first attempt fell through when she failed to respond to the 4:00 a.m. wake-up call, but she succeeded in joining them on their August 28 ascent of Mount Abbott. Filled with trepidation, Mary followed the more experienced mountaineers, determined not to make a fool of herself. William Vaux does not specify whether she was one of those who attained the summit that day, but her experience was rewarding enough that she joined the Vauxes on their trek to Glacier Crest several weeks later.

As she and Charles returned to the mountains summer after summer, Mary's interests steadily diversified. Always delighted by the scenery and enthusiastic about mountain flora, she had greatly improved her photographic and illustrative skills and begun to develop a taste for camping, riding and hiking. And having grown up in a family of amateur local historians, she could scarce help but become "an American citizen absolutely enthralled with any data [she] could obtain of those who had gone before in the most beautiful land of the world—the Canadian Rockies."[17]

Unfortunately, Mary's health did not keep up with her ever-increasing passion for the Rockies. The intermittent debilitating pain of the neuralgia she had suffered since childhood kept her from working on her photographic printing during the winter of 1899. Her health was so uncertain in February that Charles could not say whether she would be able to make the trip to Lake O'Hara that summer, though she had great hopes of doing so. Again in May 1903, Charles wrote to their outfitter, Tom Wilson, that "Mrs. Schäffer will not be strong enough yet to make camping safe for her, though her heart is set on it."[18] With her mother's ill health further restricting their travels that summer, a westward journey looked unlikely.

Unlikely, but not impossible. Their trip was shorter than usual, but Mary and Charles did travel to Glacier House for a visit they would never forget. Mary had met numerous celebrities before, but her most inspiring encounter took place on a summer day in 1903. The meeting was pure chance. As Mary rested in Glacier House one afternoon, her reveries were interrupted by the arrival of a distinguished-looking gentleman. Careful listening revealed he was none other than Sir James Hector, surgeon to the famous Palliser Expedition.

Before Mary's very eyes was a man who had spent three years exploring the Canadian West under Captain John Palliser. The British government had backed the expedition as an investigation into the settlement potential of the area, but for Hector it was more an opportunity to try his mettle in the wilderness while studying the geology and scenery of the Canadian Rockies. He had travelled between Fort Edmonton and Rocky Mountain House, delighted in the peaks surrounding present-day Banff, crossed Kicking Horse Pass and explored northward along the North Saskatchewan and Athabasca rivers—almost three decades before the completion of the CPR!

Mary could hardly contain her excitement. She struggled to maintain a cool appearance, pretending to mind her own business while desperately hoping to be introduced to this remarkable explorer. When she could no longer restrain herself, she made her way to his side and apologetically asked permission to listen in. Well acquainted with Mary's passion for exploration, the manager of Glacier House graciously introduced the two.

Swarms of people were eagerly awaiting Sir James' arrival, but fate had it that Mary and Charles Schäffer, who had "only climbed the most mediocre mountains at that time or followed very poor trails,"[19] were the only North American mountain enthusiasts to meet him—and even their encounter was cut short. The following morning, Sir James' son took ill. Accustomed to doctoring ailing adventurers, Dr. Schäffer agreed to have a look. He diagnosed appendicitis and recommended immediate hospital attention. Unfortunately, such orders were not easily followed at railroad stops like Glacier House. The boy arrived at Revelstoke's hospital too late for a successful operation. Unable to bear staying away from home any longer, Sir James returned to New Zealand in grief.

Short as his stay in Canada was, it profoundly touched the Schäffers' lives. Charles was so moved that he began constructing a monument to Sir James on the Great Divide. Mary later wrote several articles about the famous explorer and her encounter with him. Most important, her conversations with Sir James and other mountaineers, along with her extensive reading on their activities, considerably increased her desire to know and experience more of the Rockies. These men were Mary's inspiration, pushing her to grow beyond her fears. Together with the Vaux family, they encouraged her to recover some of the intrepid courage of her youth, gradually putting aside the insecurities that had developed during her adult life. They reminded her how powerful dreams could be.

From House Plant to Wildflower

L ESS THAN A YEAR AFTER HER meeting with Sir James Hector, Mary Schäffer's happy world of mountain touring in the summer and stylish Philadelphia living in the winter collapsed. Within a few short months, she lost her mother, her husband, and her father. Forty-two-year-old Mary Schäffer was rapidly transformed from the doted-upon wife of a wealthy Philadelphia doctor into a childless, parentless widow. Deprived of her former sources of consolation, she scarce knew where to turn. She felt set adrift, alone and full of grief. Struggling to carry on with her emptied life, Mary could scarcely have imagined the exciting new directions that were to emerge from the trauma.

At the time, she understood only that life as she knew it was over. Her sources of support, both moral and financial, were gone, and not much money remained. Charles, whom she described as "the most wonderful scientist of [her] acquaintance,"[1] was also a generous soul who could neither resist lavishing expensive gifts upon his wife nor deny those who requested his assistance. Unfortunately, the combination of his generosity and significant stock market losses left Mary feeling very vulnerable when he passed on. Her parents had fared little better. She described them as "dear people but absolutely the most impractical ones you could conceive."[2] Much to Mary's dismay, their pocketbooks were always open to poor relatives and her father was prone to racetrack speculation. Their charitable hearts and entrepreneurial spirits had depleted the family fortune. Thankful as Mary was that her loved ones, so accustomed to living luxuriously and holding prominent positions, did not live to bear the burden of their financial losses, she could not help resenting having been "left to stare the future in the face with very little."[3]

It was an extremely challenging time for her. The society in which she had always lived shunned her; she was "banned from parties as [her] clothes were not correct."[4] She garnered some comfort from what family she had left, but tensions developed there too. Never as disposed to family charity as her husband and parents, Mary's precarious situation left her even more cautious. Relatives accustomed to receiving generous assistance intensified her strain by pressuring her into giving far more than she felt able to. A word of thanks might have consoled her, but the utter absence of gratefulness aggravated an already tense spirit. In this period of terrible sorrow and alienation, Mary learned the "bitter lesson, to count the pennies, to lean on no one and make the best of the crumbling fortunes."[5]

Fortunately, she had long been recognized as one able to keep a level head in any crisis. Spoiled as she may have been until that dreadful winter of 1903, Mary Schäffer was not the type to sit at home and mope. She firmly believed that "one must really carve their own lines and not depend on our ancestors."[6] She resolved to make the best of her new-found independence. Fulfilling this resolution involved a certain level of pretence—maintaining the appearance of her former lifestyle although the money behind it was largely gone—and a good deal of sound financial management. In the latter task, she was fortunate to receive assistance from R.B. Bennett, a Calgary lawyer, member of the legislative assembly of the North-West Territories and future prime minister of Canada, who shared her love for the Rockies. The two must have rubbed shoulders one summer in Banff, and in her time of grief, Mary boldly called upon this extremely wealthy man. His investment advice—and the assistance of friend and lawyer George Vaux Jr.—eased her efforts to "make the best of the crumbling fortunes."

But simply regaining financial security was not enough to relieve Mary Schäffer of her sorrows. Her problems were more social and emotional than financial. She had lost her companion of fourteen years and been shunned by her Philadelphia social circle. Her summer activities were equally disrupted. No longer could she ramble through alpine meadows "studying botany in a rather desultory way."[7] Without Charles, her former centre, she needed a purpose, an activity around which her new life could revolve.

In some ways, the early twentieth century was a terrible time for a woman searching for a purpose other than marriage and motherhood. For the most part, women were still expected to content themselves with the domestic sphere, and if they entered the public sphere it was to represent the interests of a devoted wife and mother. Those women bold enough to engage in non-traditional activities were confronted with new medical theories "proving" women's biological inferiority. Unquestioning acceptance of the status quo was expected.

Even so, many women were challenging this conservative vision of womanhood. Increasingly, they sought an education and began to insist upon their rights. Their efforts created several new domains in which wealthier women could acceptably participate, including travel and, to a lesser extent, sport. It was a time of confusion and contradiction, not unlike the situation Mary had encountered growing up among Quakers: certain doors were swinging open to women, but others remained solidly locked and barred.

Had Mary's situation been less desperate, she might have been intimidated by the authorities determined to keep women from exploring new possibilities. But Mary had always been one to embrace any window of opportunity, however small, if it would lead her toward her goal. She had seen how her parents and husband had been hurt by their dreamy, impractical natures and resolved that it was time to act—but how?

One activity in which she could conceivably have immersed herself was mountain climbing. In 1906 Winnipeg's Elizabeth Parker helped found the Alpine Club of Canada, and by 1917 half of its members were women. Mary herself had tried some climbing in her excursions with the Vaux family. But much as she loved the Rockies, Mary was "scared stiff at rocks and precipices"[8] and announced that "mountain climbing for the sake of saying [she] was the first person on a certain peak, had no charms."[9] She would have to find something else.

Gentle nudging from her dear friend Mary Vaux led her to embrace the ideal project. Through it she could honour her husband's memory, work through her feelings of loss, continue to spend her summers in the Rockies and even potentially earn some money! She would write the guide to the flora of the Canadian Rockies that she and Charles had dreamed about, but never begun.

To her, it was the challenge of doing "something of which you are perfectly certain you have but the merest rudiments."[10] She knew that completing a thorough botanical study would require collecting specimens from farther afield than she and Charles had been able to travel. She would have to augment her minimal experience with horses and camping. To ease her into camping after ten years of resistance, she asked her old friend Tom Wilson to recommend someone who could teach her "to keep warm in the open … to live and be happy as the Indians of the past."[11] Wilson assigned her to the care of Billy Warren, a young, well-educated veteran of the Boer War who had recently arrived from Britain. Completely unaware of the impact his decision would have on the lives of both his client and his packer, Wilson prophetically assured Mary that she would be in good hands.

In spite of her long connection with natural science, Mary also felt handicapped by her "terrible ignorance."[12] She needed to compensate for her lack of technical botanical knowledge. At a time when travelling with a man other than a husband, father or brother was considered more dangerous for a woman than encountering a bear, a woman scientist seemed the obvious choice. The most likely candidates were Eastern American women who, like Mary, could afford to travel and were not restricted by family commitments. Accordingly, she teamed up with three single educators: Miss Farr of the University of Pennsylvania and Misses Day and James of Philadelphia High School.

The women spent the summer of 1904 gathering specimens from Moraine Lake and the Yoho Valley. In September, Billy Warren guided Mary and four friends (including a five-year-old girl) on a week-long trip into

Billy Warren (rt.) and fellow guide Joe Barker. Courtesy Whyte Museum, V527 NG10-162.

the Ptarmigan Valley to continue the research. Mary was discovering that "work, and hard work at that, is a great panacea for broken threads in life."[13] Having realized how much conceding to timidity had restricted her horizons, she was now growing in both confidence and determination. In the case of one attempt to photograph some exquisite gentians below the Banff Springs Hotel, one might even say she learned these lessons too well!

Mary marched along the banks of the Spray River toward the coveted flowers, eager to add these beauties to her growing collection. Full of her age-old determination, topped by new-found feminine confidence, she was shocked to see a shouting man violently waving his arms as if to send her back. Incensed, Mary thought: "Be turned out of my own garden? And by a man? No indeed!"[14] She was determined to get her gentians. The closer she drew to her foe, the more resolved she was to hold her ground. Then, having almost reached her destination, she was able to discern the man's words, "You'd better go back! There's a small-pox camp here."[15] Thoroughly embarrassed, Mary abandoned her quest and "retreated with what small dignity [she] could muster."[16]

Maintaining dignity was a perpetual concern. Mary's upbringing as one of society's finest, whom all should look up to as an example, made her unable to bear appearing the "tenderfoot" that she was. During her early lessons with Billy Warren, she attempted to mask the heavy beating of her

heart as her horse made his way up treacherous inclines or took an unexpected leap across a stream. She knew little of the capability of horses or
how to manage them, but refused to show her ignorance and fear. Were it
not for her eagerness to learn, Warren's constructive criticism would have
been unbearable.

As it was, his guiding hand combined with Mary's dedication led to
quick improvement. Her love for horses increased daily, and before long
her confidence was such that she trusted her horse completely—sometimes
even when she had good reason not to! On one occasion, she was placidly
riding down a mountain confident that her horse, Eva, could get her down
as easily as she had got her up when suddenly she noticed herself drawing
awfully close to Eva's ears. Just as she opened her mouth to ask if there
was a problem, she tumbled over Eva's head and onto the ground—her
left spur still caught in the large wooden stirrup! Looking around from her
frog-like position, she found that the horse had collapsed to her knees, her
head covered by the blanket. Her friends stared on in silent amazement.
But Mary, who once would have been mortified by this undignified position, was self-assured enough to simply laugh at her predicament as she
patiently waited for the guide to release her.

Just one season of lessons enhanced Mary's wilderness skills immeasurably. Her taste for adventure was growing stronger, her emotional
scars healing and her financial position improving. She was learning
"the secret of comfort, content, and peace on very little of the world's
material goods ... to value at its true worth the great un-lonely silence of
the wilderness, and to revel in the emancipation from frills, furbelows,
and small follies."[17]

Mary's transformation into a seasoned mountain enthusiast did not go
unnoticed. Less than two years after her distressing losses, local trapper
and prospector Charles Deutschman asked Mary Schäffer and Mary Vaux
to be the first women to enter a series of caves he had discovered in the
Selkirks. The three trekkers set out for the Nakimu Caves at 7:30 a.m. on
July 31, 1905, accompanied by Deutschman's Swiss guide, Edward Feuz.
The main purpose of the trip was to see the caves, but Mary Schäffer did not
overlook its potential contribution to her work. Her decision to carry two
cameras (one large 8x10 and one small 4x5) and a vasculum for gathering
rare plants paid off. She was delighted to discover that Cougar Valley, en
route to the cave, was full of rare plants for her collection.

After a successful day of travel, the foursome retired into the most comfortable tents either woman had ever seen. Exhausted as they were, they
were not able to enjoy the delightful tents for long—their expedition into
the cave required a 4:00 a.m. wake-up call. This time, Mary Schäffer rose
to the challenge, and soon discovered that the trip held demands far more
intimidating than an early breakfast. Glad as she was "to have seen [the
cave] still fresh and undimmed from the years of silence,"[18] the fact that
"there were no guard rails, a very little known of the whole place and all

kinds of dangerous places for those who have too many nerves or perhaps too much imagination"[19] troubled her.

With ropes around their waists, she and Mary Vaux descended the first ladder into a chamber called the Auditorium, then moved through a corridor that consisted of a series of holes, decreasing in size, through which they had to squeeze themselves. Mary found the last, known as the Big Hole, the most frightening. "She wriggled through minus the sinuous grace [of the guide] and plus a goodly amount of soil, and tumbled gently into a pot-hole, another gentle slide, a pay-out of rope, another pot-hole, still another tug of rope, a sensation of growing into the waist like proportions of a wasp, and she found herself in a taller pot-hole with a tiny river running gently down her back, while before her lay nothing."[20] The knowledge that she was absolutely safe provided little comfort. Standing on a narrow ledge surrounded entirely by darkness unnerved her. She had never been so happy to see sunlight as when she emerged from those caves.

Yet the benefits of the trip far outweighed Mary's discomfort. Not only had she viewed the newly accessible caves and collected a number of valuable plants, but this novel experience, available to so few women, encouraged her to develop another of her talents—writing. Several local newspapers published her account of the trip, the beginning of a series of articles intended to convince others that they, too, were capable of experiencing all the joys of mountain travel.

Later that summer, after studying the flora at Glacier House, Banff, and Field, Mary had Billy Warren escort her and another group of friends to the Red Deer River. She was becoming so enthusiastic about wilderness travel that they even tried to extend the trip into the Pipestone Valley. Unfortunately, foul weather interfered. En route to the valley, Mary and her friends encountered a weather-beaten group attempting to transport emergency food supplies to the Stoneys. Their horses were in such poor shape that Mary's party obligingly lent theirs to the cause, cutting their own journey short.

The disappointment Mary experienced was nothing, however, compared to the blow she was dealt that winter when her "botanist women ... played false."[21] But Mary had come too far to give up. Since Charles' death, she had maintained her relationship with the Philadelphia Academy of Natural Sciences, donating the shells, worms, skinned birds, and Native artifacts she collected each summer. It was time to see if the Academy might now assist her.

She knew that Charles had served on the executive committee of the Academy's Botanical Section with Stewardson Brown, curator of the Academy's Herbarium, and that Brown deeply respected Charles' work. She proposed that Brown complete her husband's project by writing scientifically accurate yet readily understood descriptions of the flora of the Canadian Rockies. She, in turn, would illustrate the work, pay his expenses—including a two-month stay in the Rockies—and provide any research notes, advice or other assistance that might benefit the project.

Stewardson Brown accepted; he and Mary Schäffer both headed west in the spring of 1906. By then, Mary was thoroughly enamoured with life on the trail and was travelling extensively through the Rockies.

She began the season with a trip to the valley of the North Saskatchewan River, having decided to retrace the return journey of Walter Wilcox's 1897 expedition. The party left Field on June 8 and followed the Emerald Lake Road and Beavertail (Amiskwi) Creek to Baker (Amiskwi) Pass, then continued northward over Howse Pass—with a detour to Glacier Lake—into the main valley of the North Saskatchewan. From there they followed the river east to the Kootenay Plains, known to the Stoneys as "'Kadoona-tinda'—'the valley where the wind blows always.'"[22] Previously the camping ground of the Kootenay Indians who guided fur trader David Thompson's men across the mountains in 1806, the area had become a common meeting place for tourist-explorers and the Stoney people. As Mary approached the Plains, she was perhaps reminded of her first contact with the Natives of the Canadian Rockies.

On one of her early visits, Mary Schäffer had been en route from Banff to Lake Minnewanka when a group of Native men appeared by the side of the road. In spite of her experiences in the American Southwest, Mary had not yet learned the difference between real Aboriginal people and

Mary Schäffer (lt.) in camp with friends. Courtesy Whyte Museum, V527 NG-95.

Expeditions in 1906 to
the Kootenay Plains
and Wilcox Pass

the Indians of American folklore. Observing her naïveté, the wagon driver decided to have some fun at her expense. As they approached the Stoneys, he ordered Mary to jump. Terrified, she threw herself out of the vehicle. When at last she was able to look up, she saw that "the Indians took in the situation, politely dropped down into the gully, grunted 'how,' laughed and the incident was closed."[23] Thoroughly embarrassed, Mary declared that "never again had the Indian any terror for the easterner, the smiles made us friends, a friendship which continues to this day."[24]

Unfortunately, the same could not be said of many of her relationships with the group of women with whom she made her second trip in July 1906. Having travelled in a larger group before, Mary did not anticipate trouble when she allowed New York geology teacher Mollie Adams, accomplished mountain climber and flower enthusiast Henrietta Tuzo, Dorothea Sharp, and Zephine Humphrey to join her on another trip to visit the Stoneys on the Kootenay Plains. It was an unfortunate assumption.

The problems began the very first morning as they travelled up the Pipestone River. When Mary and Mollie heard their guides beating the pan for breakfast, they promptly rose, dressed and headed out to eat. The others opted to remain in their tent giggling, thus delaying the entire party. Enjoying their moment of relaxation, they felt that Mary was uptight and domineering. She, in turn, complained that they were slow and foolish. Mary discovered their camping styles to be so incompatible that she advised: "O ye who think five women, no matter how excellent they be, can all be of one mind on the trail, take a tip from me. In three days from starting, the little woman and I were occupying one tent while the other three had the second. I do not think one unkind word was ever uttered by any one of the five, but we had separated as oil and water."[25]

It seemed that this separation would be sufficient to salvage the journey—until Mary discovered that one of the others was so desperate for a warm bath that she planned to shorten the trip by three days! She could not believe her ears. She had been planning this trip for over a year and

Leah, Frances Louise and Sampson Beaver. Courtesy Whyte Museum, V527 PS-5.

would not have it ruined. She had intended to stay out for two weeks and she was going to stay out for two weeks. Her childhood ruse rekindled, she and Mollie began plotting ways to extend the journey. Before long, they had the perfect plan. Drawing on their religious background, they refused to travel on Sundays, thus restoring the trip to its intended length.

Even so, Mary and Mollie had not yet had their fill of backcountry life. On August 28 they left Laggan for another trip to the North Saskatchewan. They took the same route as on the previous trip—Pipestone River, Pipestone Pass and the Siffleur River to the Kootenay Plains, then turned west. After a side trip to Glacier Lake they followed the North Fork to Wilcox Pass. There the weather turned wintry and reluctantly they retraced their steps to the confluence of the Nashan (Alexandra) River where they headed east into new territory: over Pinto (Sunset) Pass to Pinto Lake and down the Cline River.

Before heading back to Laggan via Bow Pass, the two women made yet another visit to the Kootenay Plains. Upon arrival in this piece of paradise, where "the air is sweeter, dryer, and softer than anywhere,"[26] Mary and Mollie dug out their cameras and headed over to the Native camp. They began to meet and photograph the various families present, particularly the women and children. By presenting young Frances Louise

33

Beaver, granddaughter of Chief Job Beaver, with a homemade doll, Mary won herself a lasting friendship with the Beaver family.

Although the two American women's positions as photographers and gift-bearers separated them from the Stoneys, the gap was not as large as one might have expected. Just as Mary was fascinated by the novelty of visiting a Native camp, so the Stoneys were intrigued to be visited by foreign women. Having seldom been visited by white women, they were so taken by the enthusiasm that had brought Mary Schäffer to their camp three times in one season the Stoneys named her Yahe-Weha, or Mountain Woman. They saw that she had a style all her own and respected it.

By the end of the summer, Mary Schäffer had essentially completed her mountain education. She had spent the three years since her husband's death learning more about botany, "considerably more about Indian ponies and … a GREAT deal more about the people who lived three thousand miles from what [she] had always held sacred as civilisation."[27] Her experience was broadening; her attitudes shifting. No longer did she cling tenaciously to the developed parts of the Rockies. Perhaps even more important, she had learned the invaluable lesson of travelling with companions who shared her new-found conviction that "nature meant us all to be wild flowers instead of house-plants!"[28]

Into the Unknown

B Y THE FALL OF 1906, Mary Schäffer had accomplished her mission. The botanical guide to the flora of the Canadian Rockies that she and Stewardson Brown had been completing was ready for publication. The motivation behind the project had also been fulfilled. Mary had not only weathered the most significant crisis of her life, but in so doing had discovered true peace. Yet far from wishing to retire to Philadelphia society, Mary was more devoted to the mountains than ever before. Her love for the wilderness had become all-encompassing; her appetite for adventure ravenous.

For years, she had been eagerly swallowing up the tales of the hunters and trappers whom she described as "the true pioneers of the country,"[1] while herself making short trips to more accessible areas. Captivated by their stories of adventure through unmapped terrain, she too began to long "for wider views and new untrammelled ways."[2] But in 1906 this was not an appropriate feminine ambition. Women could certainly take short trips, as she and several others had been doing, but heading out for more than a few weeks was virtually unthinkable. The media of the day insisted that outdoor life "would have little appeal to the average woman whose time is divided between her dressmaker's, her clubs and the management of her maids"[3] and proclaimed that "the ordinary woman travels much better in a Pullman than with a pack train, and is much more efficient in parlor adventures than on long hard trails; for a trail appears much more flowery and poetic in print and picture than in reality. A wild country is an inhospitable country, and tries the intruder's mettle in a thousand unexpected ways. While only a small percentage of seemingly sturdy men are fit for wild places, there are a hundred men to one woman who could possibly 'make good' in wilderness expeditions. With men, the fault is in 'the yellow streak' which civilized life does not readily betray; with women, it is the natural timidity, fastidiousness and love of ease."[4]

Mary Schäffer crossing stream on log. William Warren watching. Courtesy Whyte Museum, V439 PS-3.

For a time, Mary Schäffer and her friend Mollie Adams submitted to the force of such arguments. They meekly "bowed [their] heads to the inevitable, to the cutting knowledge of the superiority of the endurance of man."[5] Meanwhile, energetic men were busily discovering valleys unknown to Euro-Canadian society, exploring them, and leaving a trail of blazed trees and discarded tin cans. They cut new trails and cleared old ones, domesticating and defiling the wilderness that Mary and Mollie so longed to experience.

But as time went on, the two ambitious women found it increasingly difficult "to sit with folded hands and listen calmly to the stories of the hills [they] so longed to see, the hills which had lured and beckoned [them] for years before this long list of men had ever set foot in the country."[6] Even the horror stories of dreadfully harsh conditions and close encounters with death only fuelled their desire to travel. They longed to assess for themselves the veracity of these claims.

Mary Schäffer's adherence to the feminine virtue of patience could only last so long. Sooner or later, she was bound to rebel. Her parents had stressed the importance of obedience when she was growing up, but this spirited woman had never been one to let anything stand between herself and her goal. Having moved as far as she had from the life of a typical upper-middle-class Pennsylvanian woman, it was only a matter of time before she and Mollie "looked into each other's eyes and said: 'Why not? We can starve as well as they; the muskeg will be no softer for us than for them; the ground will be no harder to sleep upon; the waters no deeper to swim, nor the bath colder if we fall in,'—so—we planned a trip."[7]

Their fellow easterners were not impressed. Relatives and friends alike declared them mad and tried everything in their power to stop the trip from proceeding. But Mary had suffered social rejection before and was not afraid to risk it again. She knew that Philadelphia society could offer nothing to compare with the peace to be found in the wilds, and was certain that once the skeptics heard her stories, they too would long to explore the unknown reaches of the Canadian Rockies. For her, the fact that few men, let alone women, had travelled far north of Laggan was more of an incentive than a deterrent. She and Mollie trusted fully in their guide, Billy Warren, whose willingness to lead their expedition assured them that they were experienced enough to complete it.

Throughout the winter of 1906 they busied themselves making the necessary preparations. Deciding on travelling companions was easy. Their experience in the Pipestone Valley had taught them the value of limiting the size of their party, so they restricted the 1907 expedition to themselves, two guides and as many horses as necessary. They asked Billy Warren to choose an assistant packer and cook, and were pleased with his selection. Sid Unwin, like Warren, was a well-educated British veteran of the Boer War who left post-war employment as a London clerk to seek new adventure in Canada. His backcountry credentials were also strong: besides

Sid Unwin in guiding outfit. Courtesy Whyte Museum, V25 PA-1.

summer guiding he kept a winter trapline, his great speed on the trail earning him the name Mustiyah Nahounga, the Running Rabbit, from the Stoneys.

Selecting a destination was slightly more complicated. It was not for any one particular place that Mary and Mollie had become so enthused, but rather for the privilege of abandoning city life and the increasing tourist traffic along the CPR line to explore a wilderness known only to the Natives. They found it rather strange that they were expected to "announce some settled destination, that the very fact of its being a wilderness was not enough."[8] Still, they realized they needed a travel plan—and whisperings of a hidden lake near the Athabasca had caught their attention. When curious minds enquired, the women declared, in the language expected of those undertaking such an expedition, that their "chief aim was to penetrate to the head waters of the Saskatchewan and Athabaska rivers."[9]

Hidden lake or none, the North Saskatchewan Valley had captured the two women's imaginations in 1906, kindling their desire to explore the area further. What better destination for an entire summer on the trail? An avid reader of mountain literature, Mary began to search for any maps or accounts of travel through the region that might guide her party. Several such narratives had been published, but the only one she was able to obtain before the trip was *Climbs and Explorations*, an account of the various adventures of Dr. Norman Collie and Hugh Stutfield. After reading it thoroughly, she packed the valuable article and accompanying map in her gear and soon took to describing them as "our bible, our library for the summer."[10]

A substantial yet lightweight food supply was also vital to the success of the expedition. Having heard stories of food shortages curtailing the journeys of previous parties, Mary and Mollie spent many winter hours experimenting with various forms of dried foods. Their tests proved that dried cabbage, dried milk, dried eggs and granulose all left much to be desired, and they ended up packing the standard fare—flour, baking-powder, cocoa, coffee, tea, sugar, dried fruits, evaporated potatoes, beans, rice and bacon. They later discovered that the true delights were the berries, mushrooms, fish and game they procured along the trail.

Just as important as what to eat was what clothing to bring. Mary and Mollie's previous trips had taught them that ease of movement and protection against the elements were far more important than fashion or femininity. Mary filled her duffel bag with a buckskin jacket, three skirts—two thick woollen ones for camp and a short riding skirt—riding breeches, a sweater, a yellow rain slicker, a kerchief, a sou'wester and another hat. For footwear she carried both sturdy hob-nailed shoes and low rubber-soled canvas ones.

The women's personal luggage was rounded out by their photographic and other scientific equipment, including a geologist's hammer for Mollie and a plant press and paper for Mary. At first, Mary felt guilty asking to bring along the bulky plant press. She knew the importance of limiting her gear, and found that "there were days on the earlier part of the journey when we would have been glad to get rid of the cumbersome, troublesome thing, and leave it hanging on some tree till we should return in the fall."[11] Of course, they did not, and their perseverance was rewarded when Stewardson Brown, now working on his own botanical study, was able to use the material Mary gathered.

After almost eight months of preparation and increasingly impatient anticipation, Mary and Mollie boarded the train for Laggan early in June, 1907. Upon arriving in the Rockies, they were relieved to find their guides' preparations proceeding as smoothly as their own. At last they were able to set a precise date for their departure into the wilds: June 20. The closer the day drew, the more Mary and Mollie's excitement intensified. Then, with only two days to go, they made a shocking discovery that jeopardized the entire summer's plan. Their trunk was not in Laggan!

Tempting as it may have been, sitting around and lamenting their loss was simply not an option. Having finally decided to defy society's expectations and make their coveted expedition into the Rockies, these two women of action were not going to be stopped by the disappearance of their gear. They approached numerous officials at Laggan Station, but to no avail. Evidently, no help was to be had there, so they returned to Calgary to replace what items they could. There, they also informed the baggage master of their troubles, and, much to their surprise, he quickly set to work on the case. He found that the luggage had indeed passed through Calgary and must therefore be somewhere between there and Laggan. Eager to assist these frequent customers, he boarded the train with them, descending at every stop to search for the missing luggage. As they drew ever nearer to Laggan, it seemed his much-appreciated efforts would come to nought. The trunk was nowhere to be seen.

But the baggage master's determination matched that of the women he was attending to. Unwilling to give up prematurely, he made one final investigation that led to an astounding revelation—the missing

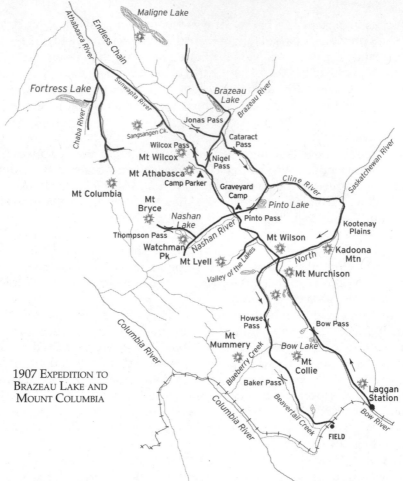

1907 EXPEDITION TO
BRAZEAU LAKE AND
MOUNT COLUMBIA

baggage had been at Lake Louise Chalet all along! Relieved to have recovered the missing valuables, Mary joked that "at least there was one cause for thankfulness, that none of the searchers had fallen over it and broken a bone, as it was found in a most dangerously conspicuous place."[12]

Any frustration the railway employees' blunder might have caused was quickly brushed aside in the four adventurers' haste to get out on the trail. Billy Warren and Sid Unwin, whom Mary referred to as Chief and K., saddled up four horses and loaded seven others with the party's gear. The long-awaited morning of June 20 had finally arrived; the great adventure for which Mary Schäffer had yearned so long was beginning.

The excitement of this significant moment was quickly replaced by frustration with the terrible travelling conditions. The sky threatened snow that fateful morning and there was a decisive chill in the air. The foursome briefly considered waiting out the bad weather, but decided against it. They knew crossing the North Saskatchewan River would become more dangerous with each passing day, and, of more immediate concern, that they risked losing some of their horses if they camped too close to the railway. They had no choice but to follow the difficult trail, slowly picking their way over fallen timber and trudging through thick muskeg.

It did not take long to realize that a wild country is indeed "an inhospitable country, and tries the intruder's mettle in a thousand unexpected ways." Conditions were such that Mary, Mollie and Billy could scarce believe this was the same trail they had used to return from the Kootenay Plains the previous summer. The spring melts were certainly taking their toll. Nevertheless, the spectacular scenery around Bow Lake reawakened certain fond memories and the view from Bow Pass was a photographer's dream. They followed the Mistaya River, spellbound by its beauty, but could not forget that the North Saskatchewan was still a day away and that each sunny day raised the water level, making their crossing that much more treacherous.

When at last they reached the river, Sid headed across on the most reliable horse. The others waited with bated breath while he rode into the water, picking his way across from one sandbar to the next. Fifteen minutes later, he waved from the far bank, signalling for the others to follow. It was an intimidating task, particularly on green horses, but all made it across without having to swim. And none too soon, for within days the water had risen so high there was no turning back.

Bow Lake. Courtesy Whyte Museum, V527 PS-8.

Wilcox Pass. Courtesy Whyte Museum, V439 PS-16.

Knowing oneself to be trapped in the wilderness, unable to return to town without severe risk, is enough to send a shiver down the spine of even the most enthusiastic explorer. For the briefest of moments, Mary and her friends were seized by the loneliness of their situation. Then a swarm of mosquitoes invaded their camp, allowing them scarcely a moment to think of anything else. In the following days the hardship of the trail below Mount Wilson afforded further distraction, and by the time they reached an old campground surrounded by piles of bear, sheep, goat and porcupine bones, they knew only that they were exactly where they wanted to be—in the heart of the wilderness.

The spot, which they had named Graveyard Camp on a previous journey, was to play an important role in the 1907 expedition. The trip was not so much a quest as it was an exploration, and Graveyard Camp, tucked away near where the Nashan (Alexandra) River branches off from the North Saskatchewan, was to be the launching point. There the men created a cache so that the foursome could spend the rest of the summer exploring the surrounding valleys, only returning to the cache between destinations to replenish their food supply.

The first of these side trips was a journey northwest to Fortress Lake. Mary had read about Dr. A.P. Coleman locating and naming the lake on his 1893 quest for Mounts Hooker and Brown, then believed to be the highest peaks in North America. She was keen to see it for herself. The first stretch of trail was delightfully easy; low waters facilitated navi-

Lake Nashan and Watchman Peak. Courtesy Whyte Museum, V527 PS-35.

gation of the riverbed. Mary revelled in the scenery that was becoming increasingly fine toward Wilcox Pass.

On the fourth of July conditions took a turn for the worse. The foursome awoke that celebratory summer morning to find themselves surrounded by snow. Undeterred, they pushed on into the blustery cold to initiate a reconnaissance of Wilcox Pass. The exploration was short-lived. Before long, the party conceded to the elements and took refuge in their cozy camp. By morning the fast-melting snow made Wilcox Pass "one of the longest, spongiest, most tiresome passes [Mary had] ever travelled."[13] A good night's sleep was followed by another exhausting day of trail finding. At one point they found themselves descending a dangerously steep slope on foot, leaving the horses to fend for themselves as they carefully picked a way around precipices. Several more days of difficult travel along the Sunwapta River led them to the long-awaited Athabasca Valley, which turned out to be "arid, fire-swept, and generally nondescript as well as hot and fly-ridden."[14] Mary, who had high expectations, was distinctly disappointed.

Nevertheless, she stuck with her plan to follow the Athabasca and the Chaba southeast toward Mount Quincy. At that point, the journey gained the additional excitement of uncertainty. Mary and her companions knew that Fortress Lake was nearby, but were not sure of its exact location. The best way to settle the issue was to scramble up the slopes of Mount Quincy. Although Mary had never been fond of climbing, her desire to catch the first glimpse of the lake was enough to make her suffer the combined burden of intense heat, plentiful mosquitoes and heavy brush. When the group arrived at a rock bluff where one guide had to toss her up to the other in an extremely "undignified, unceremonious fashion,"[15] she began to regret both her decision and the invention of climbing!

But upon first sight of the "long, pale, blue-green ribbon tossed in dainty abandon among the fir-clad hills,"[16] Mary's woes evaporated. She could hardly wait to see the lake up close. Unfortunately, when they did arrive on its shores, they found them too spongy and the forest too thick for a long stay. But the surrounding area beckoned. The party followed the Chaba to its source, investigated another stream coming from the southeast, and finally traced the Chaba back to its junction with the Athabasca. There, the great river was far more to Mary's liking. In fact, its "sense of loneliness, of freedom from all touch of human life"[17] tempted her to follow it farther.

For three days she and her party travelled through the valley of the Athabasca toward Mount Columbia. The last day of this leg was a traveller's dream. The ground was firm, the forest unburned, the river perfectly fordable. Wide shingle flats allowed the group to ride wherever they liked as they admired waterfalls tumbling down from surrounding mountains. Then came the view of Mount Columbia. Capped with snow, the mountain

Natives and horses on the Kootenay Plains. Courtesy Whyte Museum, V527 NA-98.

Brazeau Lake. Courtesy Whyte Museum, V527 PS-39.

stood tall and symmetrical, glaciers draping its slopes. It was truly a sight to behold.

The travellers made their way back to Graveyard Camp in anticipation of another view of Mount Columbia, this time from the south. By following the Nashan (Alexandra) River toward the southern face of the mountain, they were venturing into some of the little-travelled territory that made the expedition so exciting. Nobody had ever crossed Thompson Pass with pack horses. Breaking new trail was a rigorous task, particularly for the guides, who did all the chopping. It was with a sigh of relief that they arrived on the shores of Lake Nashan (Watchman). The picturesque lake, bordered by tall alpine flowers where it nestled at the foot of Watchman Peak, was a delight to both horses and riders. Awed by the beauty of her surroundings, Mary set out to climb to the top of the pass the following morning. She and her guide soaked in the beauty of the heavily treed valley below, then climbed a shoulder of Mount Bryce for the coveted view of the south face of Mount Columbia and the famous Columbia Icefield.

Stutfield and Collie had been awestruck by the Icefield in 1898; British climber Sir James Outram in 1902. Having read their accounts, Mary Schäffer was curious to see this plain of ice for herself. Yet when Mary finally saw it, she remained decidedly unimpressed. She found Mount Columbia less spectacular from the south than from the north, and, goaded by the cold, quickly pushed back to Lake Nashan. There she stayed for three sunny days—"an oasis in the desert of rain which had been [their] portion all summer"[18]—that the summer had turned out to be—before heading back to Graveyard Camp.

It was already the 8th of September, but hoping that the warm weather would last a little longer, Mary and friends set out for Brazeau Lake. They followed the North Saskatchewan to the previous summer's Camp Parker, then headed northeast over Nigel Pass. For two days they followed the main branch of the Brazeau River, searching for the lake. Nothing. Patience was running low, so Mary and Sid "struck off up the scrubby hill ... looked below and had [their] first glimpse of the lake."[19] The following morning, basking in the delight of a rare sunny day, they made their way to its shores. But that very same night, their hopes for an Indian summer were dashed when a sudden snowstorm blew in. After remaining at camp for several days, they resumed travelling up the valley to the north, hoping to find a pass leading to the mysterious lake mentioned by guide and trapper Jimmy Simpson. Imagine their disappointment on finding the way blocked by "glacier after glacier."[20]

Back on the Brazeau River, they decided to investigate Jonas Pass, which was reputed to be spectacular. Unfortunately, poor horse feed and high winds made the trip exhausting, and the riders resigned themselves to returning south.

The return journey soon became a hideous nightmare for Mary. Blinded by bright light reflecting off the snow, she was forced to let Nibs pick his own route over Cataract Pass. Branches and twigs snapping in her face, she truly felt the consequences of her decision to push on in wintry weather. The snowblind traveller was finally able to rest for a day when the group reached Pinto Lake, but this critical break forced the guides to cross the extremely challenging Pinto (Sunset) Pass to fetch the remainder of their food from Graveyard Camp.

When the men returned, Mary had recovered sufficiently to resume travelling. Gradually they made their way down the Cline River, following a popular Native trail to the now familiar Kootenay Plains. There they spent four delightful Indian summer days visiting with the residents of the area and would have loved to have stayed longer. But they knew the weather could not last long, and "the pleasure of stealing the first secrets of a primeval wilderness"[21] beckoned.

In 1902 Sir James Outram had caught a glimpse of the Valley of the Lakes from Mount Lyell, but as yet, no non-Native had explored the area. Mary, Mollie, Billy and Sid could not resist the temptation. After travelling to the forks of the North Saskatchewan, they turned north, then west up the unknown valley (Arctomys Creek). They "plodded on through closely grown and exasperating pines, so thick and so nearly impregnable that even [their] now depleted packs could not be forced through in many places, until the axe rang out and woke the silence which lay like a pall over everything."[22] They perhaps wished they had headed straight for Field.

Reluctant to continue with this drudgery, they climbed the slopes of a nearby mountain to gain a better perspective of the area. For once, their efforts were not rewarded with stunning beauty; quite the contrary. In place of the chain of lakes they had come to expect, all that lay in sight was a desolate valley filled with sloughs. Angry and disappointed, but "pretending not to mind at all,"[23] the four weary adventurers trudged back down the mountain and settled in for a good night's sleep.

They were finally convinced it was time to return home. But far be it for them to head back on the same trail upon which they had begun their expedition. That would have been far too dull. Instead, they ventured over historic Howse Pass, an important fur trade route crossed by such notables as David Thompson, Alexander Henry Jr. and Sir James Hector. The pass itself was easy, but on the far side they unaccountably diverted from the main trail up a side valley, struggling up steep faces through fields of boulders entirely lacking in horse feed. They were lost! On a ridge, the women and horses rested while the guides scouted out the terrain. Finally, Billy Warren returned with comforting news of a grassy area in a small valley beyond, and everyone breathed a sigh of relief. The following morning, all four set out to determine their whereabouts. Mary's and Sid's scramble revealed Mounts Collie and Habel to the south, marking the head of the Yoho Valley. It amused Mary to find herself, by pure coincidence, so close to Jean Habel's "Hidden Mountain." Having spotted the peak from the Kicking Horse hill under Mount Stephen, the German climber had spent days trying to locate it in order to accomplish its first ascent. And here Mary was, not even looking for it!

What she was really looking for revealed itself from the shoulder of the mountain she and Sid had been climbing: the familiar Beavertail Creek winding its way through the valley below from their camp. Only three days of easy travel separated them from Field, the terminal point of the grand adventure of 1907.

Mary Schäffer on Nibs on the Kootenay Plains. Courtesy Whyte Museum, V527 PS-2.

Above: Watercolour drawing by Mary Schäffer of Yellow Columbine (left) and Western Columbine from *Alpine Flora of the Canadian Rocky Mountains* by Stewardson Brown, 1907.
Page 50 top: Mollie Adams, Mary Schäffer, Billy Warren and guide Joe Barker in camp. Courtesy Whyte Museum, V439 PS-1.
Page 50 bottom: Mary Schäffer leading horse on trail. Courtesy Whyte Museum, V439 PS-5.

51

Above: Mount Athabasca and the Athabasca Glacier from the base of Wilcox Peak. Courtesy Whyte Museum, V527 PS-58.
Page 52 top: Mount Alexandra and Gable Peak from the Nashan Valley. Courtesy Whyte Museum, V527 PS-33.
Page 52 bottom: Horses in difficulty on Shovel Pass. Courtesy Whyte Museum, V527 PS-133.

Top: Crossing Nigel Pass with Nigel Peak in the background. Courtesy Whyte Museum, V439 PS-22.
Bottom: Mary Schäffer preparing dinner. Courtesy Whyte Museum, V527 PS-27.

54

The Indian Madonna, Kootenay Plains, ca. 1907. Courtesy Whyte Museum, V527 PS-51.

Top: The west fork of the Athabasca River. Pack train approaching Mount Columbia. Courtesy Whyte Museum, V439 PS-30.

Bottom: A hard bit in the bush. Courtesy Whyte Museum, V527 PS-17.

Life on the Trail

MARY SCHÄFFER HAD SET OUT ON her expedition filled with the excitement of venturing through valleys where no non-Native woman had ever been. She quickly discovered that, as she had been warned, there was "little in civilised life to prepare the nervous system for the shocks to be endured (with the best equanimity that can be mustered), on the trail behind untrained horses."[1] She often found trailing a challenge. Her health had never been good, and by 1907 her youth had long passed. But her spirit was indomitable. Even when the muskeg-covered terrain, abundance of fallen timber, swarms of mosquitoes and seemingly ever-present rain combined to make travelling excruciatingly difficult, Mary kept her head held high. There was nowhere else she would rather have been.

Helping to pull her through the most trying moments was her unshakeable sense of humour. During the early part of the trip, heavy muskeg slowed the travellers, wearing down their spirits. Mary's response? A joke that if she broke through the muskeg in her sleep, at least her air mattress (which she felt so dudish carrying) would float! Upon recovering from a near-miss incident involving a loose saddle and her embarrassing response to it, Mary was likewise able to laugh, mocking her own errors. Few traces of her earlier concerns about maintaining dignity remained; Mary had found her spiritual home and was able to relax there with true companions.

The great peace of the wilderness not only released Mary from concerns about her status and grief over the loss of her husband, but also allowed her to pursue her varied interests. She spent many quiet afternoons and evenings writing in her diary, sewing and knitting. She was eager to explore her surroundings, and would often go for a climb to gain a better perspective of the area.

These outings provided opportunities for the women to pursue their scientific interests. Mary and Mollie collected wildflowers and fossils and delighted in spotting wild animals. Mountain sheep, a panther, a fox,

Mary Schäffer in her buckskin at camp. Courtesy Whyte Museum, V527 PS-1.

a hawk, great owls, a black bear, a lynx and a mountain goat all passed before their eyes, far more fascinating than the stuffed specimens they were accustomed to.

Such delightful sights, along with the spectacular scenery in which Mary revelled, stimulated her interest in photography. Her enthusiasm grew to such proportions that at five o'clock one frosty morning she "bounded forth with camera and tripod, raced hither and yon in the frosty air, and returned breathless, successful, and half frozen to be asked if [she] had lost [her] senses. No, it was only a case of intoxication where the cold and beauty had gone to the brain."[2]

On another occasion, Mary's photographic eye led her to a spectacular shot. Three hewn trees serving as a makeshift bridge across a deep gorge formed the perfect viewpoint. The men assured her that it was perfectly safe, but Mary remained unconvinced. She got Mollie to grab a piece of her clothing as they crawled out just far enough to take the photo, then quickly retreated. Even her enthusiasm had its limits; she insisted that no scenery was spectacular enough to lure her onto "that old, disreputable log, on one end of which was scribbled: 'No toll.'"[3]

Nor did she feel the need to display machismo when it came to packing the horses. Knowing that she was small and not particularly strong, she unashamedly declared: "I have never insisted on my woman's rights when it came to laying the bacon and flour, the kitchen utensils and blankets slap up against the sides of the patient beast which is to bear the burden or to throw the tarpaulin over all, then adjust a tangle of rope that holds everything in shape till the next stopping place, with not a sore shoulder from a shifting saddle. At this point in camping I have always resigned my rights as a woman and what is more, when we travel hundreds of miles, I am willing to follow blindly the man who chooses the best horses, who knows at the beginning, how to make out his list of 'grub' for the months ahead, who knows how to find a ford in the deepest rivers (if there is one) and if not to abide by his decision if he says: 'Swim'!"[4]

Mary knew her strengths, and she knew her limits. She was not afraid to stretch those limits, especially after her years of confidence-building under Billy Warren's care, but she no longer felt a constant need to prove herself. She had no problems leaving the men to scout out ahead, do the trailblazing and pack the horses. When it came to camp chores, however, the class- and gender-based division of labour was less comfortable. Mary and Mollie preferred helping out with the cooking and other camp tasks to sitting around being waited on. But when they offered to help, they were usually shrugged off with the paternalistic injunction "You two go off and play now."[5] The normal camp routine was for them to be awakened to a fire and hot breakfast prepared by the guides, who also did the packing and the rest of the cooking.

Of course, when the guides went off alone for a day they lost all control over the women's camp activities. At these moments, Mary's childhood naughtiness resurfaced. Treated like a child, she rebelled like a child;

Mary Schäffer at makeshift bridge. Courtesy Whyte Museum, V527 PS-152.

the men's admonishments "not to meddle in the kitchen department, or to waste the laundry soap"[6] fell on deaf ears. Backcountry cooking and cleaning presented a whole new set of challenges to Mary, who had outgrown her incompetence in the home. She "often wondered what a real 'wash-lady' would say to a week's wash being accomplished in a collapsible rubber hand basin (which was always collapsing), with hot water which sometimes smelled of tea or showed signs of being heated in the mush-pot, with no boiling or bluing and not a flat-iron to finish the job."[7] Still, her love of cleanliness encouraged her to persist in her efforts. She even attempted to wash their musty rice. Sadly, the result was no more of a success than one of her puddings, which bore more resemblance to a cannonball than a tasty treat. She did redeem herself, though, by creating a few culinary delights—such as the pies she baked with freshly gathered berries.

She had also acquired, perhaps through practice of traditional Quaker needlepoint, skilfulness with a needle and thread. This ability proved invaluable one frosty morning near Fortress Lake when a fire lit too close to her sleeping quarters set the Egyptian sailcloth tent ablaze. The tent, highly touted for its light weight and small size, proved to be highly flammable, and in the few minutes it took to extinguish the fire, half of it was consumed.

Mary set to work abetting the disaster at first opportunity. With only a darning needle, coarse black thread and a pair of nail scissors at her disposal, the task was not an easy one. Aesthetically, the result left much to be desired. One guide likened the restored tent to a chicken coop; the other to a snow plow or bat. But seeing as they had traded their whole tent for the damaged one, both thoroughly appreciated Mary's accomplishment the next time it rained.

The friendly teasing Mary endured that day was typical of the jolly camaraderie that developed between her, Mollie, Billy and Sid. The four free spirits grew closer with every day on the trail, erasing any traces of Mary's former loneliness. Not only did they work together all day, they spent many delightful evenings around the campfire, known as the great equalizer of backcountry life. Distinctions between guides and clients blurred as they gathered around dancing flames, discussing subjects ranging from philosophy and politics to memories of the previous day's efforts.

Encounters with others were few and far between. The most startling was the appearance of a "strange, full-bearded, spectacled, and most respectably clad *man*"[8] in the doorway of the women's tent one lazy snowy morning. He had not expected to come across two women so far from the railroad, and they had not expected to have anyone at all peeking into their tent, let alone anyone so well dressed. All were startled, but quickly regained their composure and donned drawing-room manners. Much to Mary's delight, the stranger simply bowed politely and asked if there were any men in the camp.

Upon discussing the incident with Billy, Mary used her knowledge of alpine history to deduce that their visitor had accompanied geologist

Sid Unwin with burnt tent. Courtesy Whyte Museum, V527 PS-26.

A.P. Coleman on his search for Mounts Hooker and Brown in 1892 and 1893. Discovering a stray horse from the strangers' camp, she readily seized the opportunity to learn more about these historic journeys. She and Billy returned the horse to their morning visitor, casually asking about his trip to Fortress Lake. Mary was thrilled when he gave his name as L.Q. Coleman and proceeded to introduce them to his brother—Dr. A.P. Coleman himself!

Mary could not believe her luck in "literally falling over the man whose maps and notes [they] had been unable to obtain before leaving home, whose trails and camps were all [they] had to read in the long days on the Athabaska, whose name had been on [their] lips daily for weeks."[9] Coleman was also pleased by the experience. He later wrote: "It was a delightful surprise to have a charming woman ride in and out of the snow in the midst of the Rockies and join us in our lunch of bannock, bacon, and tea; and we got some very useful hints for the future from our guests, for Warren is an experienced and resourceful man who knows most of the mountain trails that can be reached from Laggan."[10]

Rare as non-Native women were that far from the CPR line, Mary and Mollie chanced to meet a fellow adventurer, Mrs. Mary de la Beach Nichol, at Graveyard Camp. The Welsh widow and her favourite guide, Jimmy Simpson, were out collecting butterflies for her impressive collection. At first, Mary found her presence rather disconcerting. The "butterfly lady," as she was known, still looked "every inch a lady,"[11] and Mary feared that "with no hat, clad in a boy's dark blue shirt, a scarlet kerchief at the neck, an old Indian beaded coat on, there was little of Philadelphia left clinging to [her own] shoulders."[12]

While both women were widows devoted to the study of natural history and drawn to travelling in ways forbidden to women, there was one significant difference. Once out of sight of society, Mary Schäffer defied cultural norms by dressing according to practical necessity, not proper feminine fashion. She shoved her hat, intended to keep her skin pale and ladylike, into the bottom of a bag and retrieved it only for incineration in their final campfire. She wore a skirt and rode sidesaddle only until "the village and critics were well left behind, [then] poked the old thing into [her] duffel bag and that was the end of anything but the modern breeches, till [they] hailed back to civilisation."[13]

Yet she still valued societal conventions enough to be somewhat embarrassed by her deviances. She found the presence of a woman who had been less ready to abandon the demands of feminine fashion a discomforting affront. And Mary's apparel was not her only faux pas. As she later explained, "the alacrity with which we accepted their invitation to supper that night was a positive disgrace, but we were so tired of mouldy tea, etc., and butter and jam would be such a delicious change that we quite forgot our manners."[14] Fortunately, she soon stopped worrying about propriety and simply enjoyed her first dinner party of the season.

Given the remote areas through which Mary's party was travelling, their next social event did not take place until much later in the trip, when Tom Wilson's neighbour and fellow outfitter Elliott Barnes invited them to dine with him on the Kootenay Plains. The dinner was highly enjoyable, but its significance pales in comparison with that of the ensuing bonfire, where they were joined by Stoneys Sampson Beaver (Frances Louise's father) and Silas Abraham. As they relaxed around the fire, talking and laughing, Mary's thoughts turned to the mysterious lake for which they had unsuccessfully searched north of the Brazeau. Conscious that the Stoneys were often loath to reveal information about their hunting grounds, she cautiously asked about the spot they knew as Chaba Imne, or Beaver Lake. She discovered that Sampson had been there as a youth, and boldly asked if he would draw her a map. When

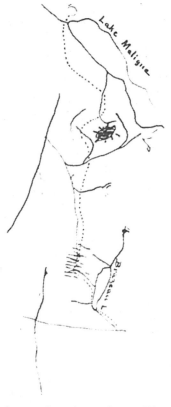

Sampson Beaver's map. Courtesy Whyte Museum, V527 PS-53.

he requested payment for his services, Mary indignantly reminded "him of the flour, tea, sugar, a dress for his little girl, a nice doll thrown in, that had come to his tepee and said very sharply: 'Now draw me the picture of how to get there.'"[15] He sheepishly obliged, adding fuel to the fire of Mary's wintertime dreams.

She realized these dreams were almost a year from fruition, and that she would soon have to return east. Her imminent "return to the beaten track, to four walls, and all the cares which know so well how to creep within them"[16] depressed her. Her only enthusiasm was "the thought of a fresh boiled egg and a cup of tea or coffee made from material which had not spent its summer bobbing around in sundry rivers and real bread and butter."[17]

Mary, Mollie, Billy and Sid marked their last night in camp with a small celebration, then cleaned themselves up as best they could in preparation for their return to society. But when a dog, forerunner of a carriage full of people, ran up to them the next day, Mary realized that her hankie, carefully folded to mask all evidence of its encounter with fire, no longer revealed its high-class eastern origin and that her moccasins, although spotless, were evidently acquired along the trail. Her tanned face further revealed her rebelliousness, making Mary feel distinctly embarrassed at the thought of meeting up with other travellers.

When those people turned out to be none other than Rudyard Kipling and his extremely well-dressed wife, Mary blushed all the more strongly. Kipling's account of the experience, published in his *Letters of Travel (1892-1913)* reads as follows: "As we drove along the narrow hill-road a piebald pack-pony with a china-blue eye came round a bend, followed by two women, black-haired, bare-headed, wearing beadwork squaw-jackets and riding straddle. A string of pack-ponies trotted through the pines behind them.

"'Indians on the move?' said I. 'How characteristic!'

"As the women jolted by, one of them very slightly turned her eyes, and they were, past any doubt, the comprehending equal eyes of the civilised white woman which moved in that berry-brown face."[18]

After Mary had bathed, wolfed down six boiled eggs and changed into an elegant evening gown, she again caught Kipling's eye. "That same evening, at an hotel of all the luxuries, a slight woman in a very pretty evening frock was turning over photographs, and the eyes beneath the strictly arranged hair were the eyes of the woman in the beadwork jacket who had quirted the piebald pack-pony past our buggy.

"Praised be Allah for the diversity of His creatures!"[19]

And it was in this transformed state that Mary remained until the summer sun melted the snow from Canada's Rocky Mountains the following June.

Unlocking the Treasure

CRUISING ACROSS MALIGNE LAKE, modern visitors are treated to the sight of increasingly massive mountains decked with waterfalls and glaciers, snow and verdure, barren ridges and rolling forests. Hidden bays and beaches reveal themselves as the journey progresses, culminating in the spectacular view from Sampson's Narrows. It is a feast for the senses. Yet until 1908 the lake's striking beauty was one of the best-kept secrets of the Canadian Rockies. Stoneys and Cree knew of its existence, but had given up visiting after depleting its beaver stock. In the mid-nineteenth century, Michael Klyne, the Hudson Bay Company factor at Jasper House, travelled along the Maligne River and past the lake on his way to trade with the Kootenays and Shuswaps on the Kootenay Plains. Henry MacLeod, a Canadian Pacific Railway surveyor, had come across the lake in 1875, but was so wearied from the journey that he named it Sorefoot Lake, noted that it was not a promising route for the railway, and continued his journey without giving it a second thought. Only in the early twentieth century were rumours of its existence beginning to arouse the excitement of Rocky Mountain adventurers—including Mary Schäffer.

In body, Mary spent the winter of 1907 in the east; in spirit, she had not left her beloved mountains. Not yet ready to brave a western winter, she kept her memories alive by dreaming of her next expedition and sharing stories and photographs of the past summer's delights. By bringing tales of her summer trips into Philadelphia drawing rooms and her slides into lecture halls, Mary was able to connect her two worlds. She struggled unsuccessfully to convince her peers she was not exceptional, that they too could find peace and joy in the wilderness of the Canadian Rockies.

Her old friend Mary Vaux did plan to join her 1908 expedition, along with a Mrs. Crandell of Philadelphia, but both ended up dropping out. The only new recruit for 1908 was Stewardson Brown. Keen to examine the flora of the remote regions Mary had been visiting, he and his guide Reggie Holmes

Mary Schäffer and Mollie Adams scrambling. Courtesy Whyte Museum, V439 PS-4.

joined the original foursome for their second major adventure. Sid Unwin's dog, Mr. Muggins, rounded out the party.

With an entire season on the trail behind them, Mary and Mollie were able to execute their 1907 winter preparations with far greater confidence than the previous year's. They knew that the food, clothing and gear they had packed for their first expedition had generally served them well. Only a few crucial changes were necessary. They replaced their highly flammable tents and purchased waterproof bags for the food. Prompted by memories of wet feet, Mary also scurried from store to store searching for the best pair of waterproof shoes that money could buy.

The two women also experimented with new types of lightweight, nutritious food. They purchased copious amounts of dried vegetables and spent hours roasting and grinding corn to prepare pinole, a corn flour touted as the camper's miracle food. They toiled over their concoction for hours, but in an unfortunate oversight neglected to subject it to the same rigorous taste tests they had applied the previous year. They were well into their journey before they discovered that the foul-smelling substance tasted so horrid even the horses refused to eat it! Thankfully, no event dire enough to force them to consume pinole transpired, and the wasted preparation time at least helped Mary and Mollie endure the winter's wait.

The excitement of the spring of 1908 was subtly different from the previous year's. In 1907 Mary and Mollie were filled with the slightly nervous anticipation of defying social norms and testing their mettle by setting out on an expedition many times longer than any of their previous wilderness excursions. A year later, there was no fear, just eagerness to recapture the delight of the previous summer's explorations. The only uncertainty was with regard to the object of their quest: Chaba Imne had eluded them once before, but with a map and an entire summer ahead of them, they were resolved not to quit before setting foot on its shores.

As soon as spring was well established in the east, they headed across the continent to the Canadian Rockies. Much to their dismay, they were greeted by a never-ending deluge of rain. They waited for it to let up in Banff, then at Mount Stephen House in Field. Before long, their patience expired. They resolved that, rain or shine, they would depart from Laggan on June 8. True to plan, they set out that morning over the same muskeg-covered terrain that marked the beginning of their 1907 expedition. They planned to follow the Bow, Mistaya and North Saskatchewan rivers to Nigel Creek, then cross Nigel Pass and follow the Brazeau River to Tepee Camp at the mouth of Brazeau Lake.

This time, Mary and Mollie felt like old pros. They set out on the trail ahead of their guides and spent days warning Stewardson Brown of the dangers involved in crossing the North Saskatchewan. Having endured the nerve-wracking crossing the previous summer, they did not want their companion to underestimate the strength of the great river. Imagine their

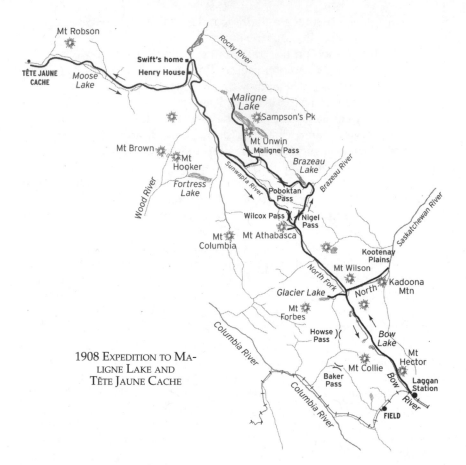

1908 Expedition to Maligne Lake and Tête Jaune Cache

embarrassment when the only difficulty turned out to be the horses' insistence upon rolling in the hot sand once they reached the far bank! They were vindicated several days later, though, when second and third crossings forced the botanist and Billy Warren to swim.

Familiar as this territory was, Mary and her friends did not hurry through it in a mad rush to attain their goal. Simply being in the beautiful backcountry was enough to subdue any haste that might have arisen from the thrilling prospect of finding a new lake. When they reached the North Saskatchewan River, they readily agreed to delay their northward journey so Brown could visit the Kootenay Plains. Riveted by her surroundings and loath to cross the North Saskatchewan unnecessarily, Mary chose not to revisit her Stoney friends. Instead, she spent one day in camp doing laundry with Mollie, then headed off to explore the Bear Creek canyon with Reggie and Sid while Mollie stayed and fished at the mouth of the creek.

The women's decision to spend the day apart is noteworthy. Because they were the only women on the trip, they spent most of their time together—

particularly their extra free time while the guides cooked, packed and set up camp. But Mollie was suffering from heart and eye trouble, so she could not always exert herself beyond the demands of their travel. The situation was similar to what Mary had experienced with Charles, but she no longer felt compelled to hold back. She went off on her own adventures while Mollie stayed in camp. At that distance from society's view, the two women did not worry about the potential impropriety of being alone with a man, particularly when it was only for a day.

On some occasions, such as their two-day stop at Camp Parker, Mary and Mollie may even have been quite eager to distance themselves. On the first day of rest, Mollie and Billy stayed in camp to do laundry, dry out the plant-press papers and make stew while the others climbed the lower slopes of Mount Athabasca looking for fossils. After placing some fifty pounds of rocks—and one dead gopher—in their bag, Mary and the men decided to return to camp. Large patches of snow on the mountainside complicated their descent. At first, the men dug steps in the snow with their heels and helped Mary follow them down. But before long, all three men had slid down the slope on the seats of their pants, leaving Mary frightened and alone at the top. She tried to descend slowly, digging in her heels as she had been taught. Then she looked down at the row of grinning men and was suddenly taken by the ridiculousness of her situation. Laughing, she abandoned her careful descent and quickly slid to her companions on her backside.

Poboktan Pass. Courtesy Whyte Museum, V527 PS-77.

A view of Maligne Lake from Mount Unwin. Courtesy Whyte Museum, V527 PS-61.

They arrived back in camp exhausted—so exhausted that Mary left skinning the gopher until the next day. The delay did not sit well with Mollie. Even the best of friendships is strained by continuous contact over an extended period of time, and theirs was no different. Mollie's diary entry captures the mood of the afternoon: "M. and I took a short walk, then M. started in to skin a gopher they caught yesterday. I objected a little to the smell thereof, and suggested that next time she should skin specimens the same day they were caught. But I was quickly squelched and told that was the nature of the beast."[1]

Fortunately, the conflict had blown over by morning, and in good spirits the group resumed travel toward Brazeau Lake. Contrary to a number of lurid descriptions that were published soon thereafter, Mary Schäffer insisted that the route to Brazeau Lake was "a very travelled one, very easy and very beautiful. Every mile of it, barring the fireswept district just north of Laggan (and that has been materially improved by leaving the old Indian route in the valley and following the eastern hill-slopes), a child could take."[2]

She was wise to enjoy the good trail while she could, because the same could not be said of the rest of the route to the mysterious lake. Coleman's 1892 trail to Poboktan Pass "was a little fierce [and involved] quick changes from burnt timber to rock-climbing, muskeg, quicksand, scree slopes, and mud slides."[3] The pass itself was no less taxing, still covered in deep snow although it was already July. Mary declared she "should never take the Pobokton Pass from start to finish for a pleasure trip; it is a miserable route, and one only to be used to accomplish an end."[4]

On the second day, the trail ended abruptly and the guides had no choice but to blaze their own until they found a camping spot with sufficient feed for the horses. The tents set up, all six travellers spread out to investigate possible routes. Normally, such scouting was reserved for the guides, but the heat was on. Most found nothing but lovely scenery; only Billy Warren discovered that their present route was leading them back toward the true Poboktan trail from which they had somehow strayed.

The following morning proved to be another snowy fourth of July, but by that point the explorers were too close to their goal to be deterred by foul weather. For two hours the guides chopped their way along a scarcely passable trail through a fire-swept valley. They then reached a junction, from which one trail led toward the Sunwapta River, the other toward a break in the hills to the north. Sampson's map was of little assistance. Some wanted to take the former route, others the latter. They could not achieve consensus. At last they came to a decision: northward it was. By the time they reached a stopping place that afternoon, all were exhausted with some—those who were convinced they were headed in the wrong direction—more miserable than the others.

The two head guides decided to spend the following morning scouting out the terrain. They returned with welcome news of a pass ahead, but still no sign of a lake. They decided to push on. What later came to be known as Maligne Pass "was a duplication of all other passes, soft and spongy,"[5] with lengthy snow patches making for a tiring journey. "A tiny frozen lake ... nestling among the snowbanks"[6] greeted the travellers at the top and soon the party was descending the most magnificent valley Mary had ever seen. Unlike the fire-swept terrain to which she had become accustomed, this flower-filled valley "swept away into an unbroken green carpet as far as the eye could see."[7]

Even this remarkable beauty did not keep the travellers from feeling "distinctly dismal"[8] the following day. They still had not seen a sign of the lake, and its elusiveness was beginning to wear down their spirits. As they were eating lunch among a great pile of forget-me-nots, conversation again turned to the lake. All of a sudden Sid, "who had grown more and more solemn for days, suddenly jumped up and shaking himself violently said: 'Well, it's two o'clock but I'm going off to climb something that's high enough to see if that lake's within twenty miles of here, and I'm not coming back till I know!'"[9] Mary was anxious to accompany him, but "knew he was in no mood to have a snail in tow, and then it was far more important to locate [their] quarry than that [she] should personally be in at the death."[10]

She and her companions were to wait eight-and-a-half hours. Much of the afternoon was spent hunting for flowers and fossils. Then, donning bug-nets and lighting a smudge of damp moss—the first real mosquitoes of the season were out with a vengeance—they sat down to wait for Sid's return. They waited. And waited. In spite of the heat, they lit a bonfire to help Sid locate their camp. Mary retired to bed. The others kept waiting. When they finally heard Sid trampling through the bushes, their tension skyrocketed. Were they almost there? Had they chosen the wrong path? With bated breath, they awaited his fateful announcement: "I've found the lake!"[11]

Relieved of their anxiety, all six members of the party passed the night in complete relaxation. They awoke the next morning in extremely high spirits, and after only two hours of easy trailing at last found themselves on the shores of the elusive Chaba Imne. Comparing it with the stunning Lake Louise, Mary declared: "Lake Louise is a pearl, Lake Maligne is a whole string of pearls."[12] She found that "the best part of it was its virgin soil, a sense that I was alone but for the dear ones who were with me."[13] Their search for signs of others revealed "not a tepee-pole, not a charred stick, not even tracks of game; just masses of flowers, the lap-lap of the waters on the shore, the occasional reverberating roar of an avalanche, and [their] own voices, stilled by a nameless Presence."[14] What peace.

Of course, whether it interested her or not, Mary Schäffer was bound to receive attention for being not only a member of the first party to visit the lake in over thirty years, but also one of only two non-Native women to reach its shores. Her name was evermore to be associated with Maligne Lake. Yet Mary refused to take credit for the success of the expedition. It was only her guides, she insisted, who had made the journey possible. She considered their perseverance even more important than Sampson Beaver's map and declared: "It was Mr. Warren's long outlook and Sid's determination, Mollie and I were like the tail to an active horse."[15]

The next step was to explore their find. Here, too, complications arose. It

Camp at Maligne Lake, 1908. Courtesy Whyte Museum, V527 PS-69.

Woman being carried to raft on Maligne Lake. Reggie Holmes on raft.
Courtesy Whyte Museum, NA66-1405.

soon became evident that the shoreline was too spongy for horse travel. The guides would have to build a raft. On this special occasion, Mary and Mollie were allowed to wash the breakfast dishes so their guides could get to work sooner. This small task accomplished, they headed to the lakeshore to watch the raft take shape. By 6:00 p.m. HMS *Chaba* was ready to sail.

When the time came to board the following morning, neither Mary nor Muggins was quite sure the raft was trustworthy. Faced with an unfamiliar challenge, some of Mary's earlier timidity resurfaced. Fearing the raft might sink, she sought to lighten the load by abandoning air mattresses and tents, but the men would have none of it; they were to travel the lake in style. In her insecurity, Mary fell into the role of a Philadelphia lady. The guides had to carry first the gear, then her and Mollie out to the raft.

It did not take long for Mary to realize that her fears were unfounded. She passed the comfortable journey wishing she could do something to ease the guides' exertion. But there being no question in anyone's mind as to the women taking hold of the sweeps, Mary was left to admire the remarkable scenery.

On their second day of travels, she became acutely aware of a blatant inaccuracy in Sampson's map. The narrows, which it indicated two-thirds of the way down the lake, was nowhere to be seen. She wondered how the map, which had served them so well, could be so alarmingly wrong. Then, she explained, "as we were rounding what we supposed to be our debarking point, there burst upon us that which, all in our little company agreed, was the finest view any of us had ever beheld in the Rockies."[16] Sampson's map was correct after all. They were not at the end of the lake, but only at the narrows, which they proceeded to name Sampson's Narrows.

Over the course of the trip they also named Mount Unwin, from which Sid Unwin had first seen the lake, Mount Mary Vaux, Mount Warren, the Thumb and Sampson's Peak. They left their mark in another way as well: Mary admitted to carving their initials and the date into a tree. Knowing how much they hated to visit inscription-covered campgrounds, the companions felt remorse for their deed, but their joy at visiting this hidden lake was such that they could not resist breaking their own rule.

It was time to consider the next leg of their journey. With two months of summer remaining, returning to civilization was unthinkable. The expedition of 1908 had begun as a quest, but realization of their goal was not just cause to end their trip early. Driven by Mary's interest in history, they headed west toward the Yellowhead Trail, a fur-trading route sporadically used since the 1820s and the path of the first Canadians to seek gold in the 1860 Cariboo Gold Rush. Not only was the trail of interest in itself, it would also lead them to Mount Robson, the highest peak in the Canadian Rockies.

This leg of the journey promised to be less daunting than the previous month of original exploration, but Mary and her friends would have been sorely mistaken to believe they had nothing left to fear. Their problems began with the near-fatal decision to shortcut to the Athabasca River by heading northwest down the Maligne River instead of returning the way they had come. When Sid Unwin attempted to cross the outlet of Maligne Lake, he quickly discovered why Sir James Hector had named the river Maligne—French for wicked. Its vicious undertow nearly killed both him and his horse. They managed to swim to shore; then Sid, not one to give up easily, attempted the crossing on a different horse. This time the two separated in midstream, the horse swimming to the far bank while Sid returned to his worried friends. It was a close call. The next day the explorers persuaded their unladen horses to swim the river and built a raft to safely convey themselves and their baggage across in five or six trips.

This difficult crossing was only the beginning of their troubles. They camped on the far bank while the two guides attempted to cut a trail through thick timber. The exertions this obstacle required of her guides led Mary to comment that "camping and exploration are great fun until you reach the point where you must see others suffer for your hobby, and then, if you possess even the smallest amount of conscience, you feel most mortally mean and uncomfortable."[17]

After five days, the men realized they had no choice but to take the other route, a detour of seventy miles. What a letdown! Five exhausting days of trailblazing, all for nought. Reaching Mount Robson was proving to be far more difficult than originally envisaged. The new route down the Poboktan Valley was not much of an improvement, and by the time they reached the Sunwapta, Brown and Holmes had decided to return to civilization, taking nine of the horses with them. Troubled as Mary was by a bout of neuralgia, she was not prepared to join them. She would not retire from the splendour of the Rockies until winter pushed her home.

The remaining four continued northeast along the Sunwapta until August 1, when they reached the Athabasca River. Delighted to immerse themselves in new territory, they eagerly explored its valley. They were tempted to venture along the Whirlpool River to Mounts Hooker and Brown and the historic Committee's Punch Bowl, but time was passing quickly. It was best to keep following the Athabasca toward the mouth of the Miette.

How to do so was becoming a problem. They had lost the trail, and no easy route was to be found. When the men scouted ahead, they found their path obstructed by a drop-off. What were they to do? Retrace their steps over a high rocky bluff to rejoin the trail several miles back? Warren pondered their dilemma overnight, then decided that tackling the wall was their best option. Chosen to attempt the feat first was the least useful horse. The bewildered creature "stepped forward and made a desperate plunge; his front feet, striking the rock about half way down, gave him just the impetus for the final leap which landed him safely below."[18] The precedent set, the others followed, accomplishing "one of the neatest horse-stunts"[19] Mary had ever seen.

Sid then headed down the valley to search for Lewis Swift's homestead. Swift was a man of the mountains who had settled near present-day

Suzette Swift and children in front of their home, 1908. Courtesy Whyte Museum, V527 PS-94.

Jasper in 1893. He and his family were resourceful individuals, helpful to travellers passing through and always glad of company. They also kept a boat, which Mary and her friends knew would carry them safely across the Athabasca. Unfortunately, Sid's initial scouting for the Swifts' home was a long and fruitless journey—except for the sight of several horses, a sure indicator of human presence. The entire party set out the following morning and had the good fortune to encounter the long-lost trail leading to the gorge of the Maligne River. There the men had to chop a path around the canyon so they could cross the river at a rare gentle point. On regaining the river flats, they had a view of the Swifts' farm. Separated from the settlement by the mighty Athabasca, the foursome reluctantly continued down the trail another mile and a half to the home of John Moberly (son of Hudson's Bay Company trader Henry John Moberly) and his family. A sign read, "Here's the crossing," but the canoes were on the far side of the river and no one was around to help. Discouraged, the travellers fired the rifle and began to prepare lunch, hoping the situation would somehow resolve itself.

Much to their surprise, Swift soon arrived and paddled across the river. The two women were impressed that he "conversed as politely as if [they] had not been dressed in breeches"[20] and delighted to hear that he had courteously exclaimed to Billy: "Women in your party? ... Well, well, whatever brought them here? Prospecting or timber cruising? No? Now, look here, I've been in this valley thirteen years and they're the first white women I've seen around these parts. Are you sure they aint prospecting?"[21]

Of course, the Swifts were neither conventional themselves nor accustomed to seeing conventional people. The remote location of their homestead meant their only visitors were prospectors, surveyors, timber cruisers and the odd tourist-explorer or two. They were always eager to welcome visitors to their home, and because Mary Schäffer's party had not seen anyone since June, they were equally delighted to camp for a couple of days on the homestead.

The Swifts treated their guests to fresh milk, eggs and new potatoes—a true delight after two months of dried food. Mary and Mollie visited with Lewis' wife, Suzette, a Métis from St. Albert. Like the two of them, she was a city woman drawn to the wilderness; her Métis heritage made her even more a bridge between two worlds than they. Mary and Mollie admired her tidy house and were even more impressed with Suzette's home-made clothing, including her bridalwear and silk-embroidered buckskin. They bought all the gloves, moccasins and coats she had for sale, and Mary even ordered a buckskin jacket to be picked up on her return journey. In the evening, Lewis shared tales of pioneering in the Rockies. Mary was delighted. Once again this western history buff came face to face with living history of which she, too, was now a part.

After two wonderful nights with the Swifts, Mary and her friends realized they would have to continue moving toward the Miette if they wished to reach Mount Robson before summer's end. Even with the help of a map produced by government surveyor James McEvoy, the going was tough. Mary later lamented that "from the day we struck the valley

Mount Robson. Courtesy Whyte Museum, V527 PS-104.

of the Miette, we realised what the trails were. We had never seen a really bad one before."[22] Although the route had long been used by trappers, prospectors and surveyors, no one seemed to have removed any obstacle they could possibly get around, which made heavy work for Billy and Sid. With steep, rocky hills and a soft, muddy valley to navigate, the party suffered; the eerily foreboding sight of numerous piles of horse bones along the trail dampened their already-sinking spirits.

Making the two women even more uncomfortable was the fact they had abandoned their breeches in favour of skirts. Comfortable as breeches were, it was considered entirely inappropriate for women to wear them in public. Even twelve years later, the *Banff Crag and Canyon* ran notices declaring: "The young women who strut about the street and dine in the hotels dressed in riding togs, should be soundly spanked and sent to bed"[23] and "Pants are made for men and not for women. Women are made for men and not for pants."[24] Having begun to encounter the numerous prospectors active along the Yellowhead Trail, Mary and Mollie felt they had little choice but to dress up.

Annoyances like skirts, a difficult trail and unimpressive scenery were quickly overshadowed by the splendid view of Mount Robson. This lofty peak was "a noble massive vision to the pilgrims who had come so far to see her."[25] Not content just to look, Mary and company decided to explore a lake rumoured to lie partway up the mountain's western slope. But when the lake remained hidden after several miles of climbing and bushwhacking, the four exhausted explorers opted to leave its discovery to someone else.

They themselves had decided to continue westward toward Tête Jaune Cache, where Tête Jaune—the fair-haired Iroquois first reported to have used the route—had stashed his furs. Although Mary and Mollie were concerned they might "be frightened to death or murdered"[26] by the prospectors and miners at the Cache, its attractions overpowered their fears. The trip would prolong their journey by a few days and the spot was historically significant, close to a Native village and home to Mr. Reading, a friend of Lewis Swift's. So off they went. When the first person they saw was "a terrible-looking man clad in rough khaki, his hands in his pockets and his eyes glued on the strangers with a stony stare,"[27] they began to regret their decision. Mary was terrified, until she realized her own party probably looked equally rough, and the man's apparent hostility was more likely simply astonishment at seeing women in the area. She was profoundly embarrassed to discover that the man who had so intimidated her was Mr. Reading, with whom she turned out to have many mutual friends in Philadelphia.

Thoroughly repentant of her earlier prejudice, Mary quickly invited Reading and his partner, Mr. Finch, to dine with her party. He gladly accepted, and reciprocated by proposing a gathering with all four residents of the Cache the following evening. This being the first and only dinner party of the season, Mary felt the occasion merited finer clothing than usual, but was not certain how to achieve the refined appearance she desired. Mollie was little help; she informed Mary that she simply intended to wash her hands and face and tie her hair with a new leather shoe string. In the end, Mary's only additional gesture was to don a new pair of moccasins and a fine purple handkerchief she had stowed away in her duffel bag.

She was not alone in her attempt to follow proper dining etiquette, but as the gourmet meal of fish, potatoes, bacon, beans, pickles, tea, coffee, cocoa, buttered sourdough bread and cheese progressed, everyone found formal dining-room manners increasingly difficult to maintain. The gentlemen had originally removed their hats, but were "very bald and the mosquitoes pitched in so unmercifully that they had to give up such frills pretty quickly."[28] Mary recalled bringing Mollie's "attention to the fact that when she was asked to have a second cup of tea she gazed into her cup and deliberately threw the cold remains on the floor behind her, and she retaliated by noting that when the dessert came round I forgot all my early training and peered into the pot saying, 'What's this stuff?'"[29]

By the time they had got through the stewed peaches, tapioca pudding and Klondike lemonade, they had abandoned all pretences of delicacy. Everyone was busy simply enjoying the delightful gathering. Surrounded by mountains, with good food on the table and kindred spirits around it, they could have stayed forever. But return they must, and Swift's warning that it was impossible to return south via the Columbia River left them little choice but to head back through the treacherous Fraser and Miette valleys.

En route, Mary had the opportunity to indulge in her passion for the human history of the Rockies by examining the ruins of what she presumed to be fur-trading posts Henry House and the Athabasca Depot. Then they all enjoyed another visit with the Swifts, including a fascinating tour of their flour mill. They left saying: "'Good-bye; will see you when the first Grand Trunk Pacific train comes through,' and passed on, knowing [they] were coming to the beginning of the end."[30] They realized that before long, trains and bridges would simplify the journey, "that the hideous march of progress, so awful to those who love the real wilderness, was sweeping rapidly over the land and would wipe out all trail troubles."[31]

Mary knew that the time for adventures such as hers would soon be past, that tourists would be flooding into these stretches of wilderness just as they had at Lake Louise, Emerald Lake and the Yoho Valley. Happy as she was that others would now enjoy the beauty of the Rockies north of Laggan, she was saddened by the knowledge that part of their charm would be removed. She returned to civilization after her second summer-long expedition with a strange combination of jubilation at having found Maligne Lake and regret over the rapidly changing wilderness.

To Asia and Back

MARY SCHÄFFER RETURNED FROM HER 1908 expedition as enamoured with the Canadian Rockies as ever. It was there she had honed her skills in photography, floral painting and botany; there she had learned to value the outdoor life. It was there, through her ever-increasing travels, that she discovered herself as an individual with her own particular talents and aspirations. She had been filled with both the ecstasy of splendid new sights and the great peace of the wilderness. The mountains had become her spiritual home.

Nevertheless, another fascination had begun to compete for her attention. With a knowledge of the Rockies greater than that of any other non-Native woman, Mary turned toward a new unknown: Asia. General interest in Japan was soaring, and, as with the Canadian Rockies some twenty years earlier, Mary Schäffer's curiosity was aroused. Enchanted by the stories emerging from this increasingly popular tourist destination, Mary began to read all she could about these oriental islands. By the fall of 1908 she had set the necessary wheels in motion, solidified preparations and made ready to set out on an Asian adventure. She, Mollie Adams and two other friends, Misses Bippinorth and McDonald, headed east as guests of the Japanese government.

Her trip to the far east was inspired by many of the same interests as were her Rocky Mountain explorations: history, flora and Aboriginal peoples. Whether in Asia or America, she was eager to take photos and collect botanical specimens wherever she went. She ventured into areas no white women had been before and endured the gawking that resulted. And in both countries she endeavoured to learn as much as possible about the indigenous people.

Upon arrival in Japan, Mary asked that along with the typical tourist attractions such as temples, lakes and Mount Fuji, she be taken north to see the Aboriginal Ainu. Most tourists stayed in central and southern Japan, where European hotels and other such conveniences had been introduced for their comfort. Mary enjoyed this part of the trip, just as she enjoyed staying in the CPR hotels in the Rockies, but it was not enough. She had not travelled half-way around the world just to see the glossy picture marketed to tourists. At first, her request to travel north into indigenous territory "was met with such a look of pity and tolerance as boded ill for its realization."[1]

Dissatisfied as she was with being an ordinary tourist, Mary was stalled until she could find a willing escort. In mid-November her wish was fulfilled with the discovery of a like-minded Japanese woman, Miss Kawai, a graduate of Pennsylvania's Bryn Mawr College. Off they set, and "neither the primitive Japanese inn with its rather scanty mats spread on the floor for sleeping, nor the one general trough in the public hall where all were expected to wash, nor even the boiled rice and raw fish for breakfast, failed to dampen [their] ardour to penetrate further to the haunts of the Ainu."[2] For four days the women travelled by boat, train and basha (a type of horse-drawn cart) to the remote village of Piratori.

Mary had wished to experience Japanese conditions of travel, and now she had her chance. She found them uncomfortable at times, but certainly not unbearable. More than the travelling conditions per se, it was her own obvious foreignness in these less-visited regions that caused some difficulty. She explained that "barring generally cramped conditions of the cars, eating cold lunches on the train, with insufficient heat in the daytime, and a thorough baking in the sleepers at night, our greatest trial was the frank curiosity of the populace who, accustomed only to an occasional passing missionary, peered into the low windows of the train till we were forced to draw down the blinds, or followed us in generous squads, making plenty of personal remarks which we fortunately could not understand."[3] It was something like the disconcerting stares she and Mollie had received at Tête Jaune Cache, only multiplied by hundreds.

Overshadowing the unease this unwanted attention provoked was the charge of excitement generated by the trip's purpose. At last Mary was to see the Ainu! Having studied their history and customs, she was eager to supplement her knowledge with firsthand observations. She readily embraced every opportunity to take photographs on the northern island of Yezo and expanded upon her documentation by noting as much about Ainu culture as she could. She was particularly interested in comparing the Ainu with other ethnic groups: her fellow Euro-Americans, the mainland Japanese, the Formosan headhunters whom she later visited and North American Aboriginals.

Indeed, Mary's ability to draw connections between what she was seeing in Asia and the condition of North America's Aboriginal peoples enhanced her understanding of the Ainu's situation. She could see that their freedom on Yezo was limited, just as the Aboriginal peoples of North America had lost their independence. Recognizing the similarities between her own country and theirs, she understood that the Japanese desire to exploit Yezo's rich natural resources would push the Ainu deeper and deeper into the hills until they could go no farther. It was a familiar story.

Nevertheless, Mary's sympathy and understanding were tainted by her imperialist perspective. She applauded the fact that the Ainu's intense contact with the Japanese had made them altogether "the most civilised savages [she] had ever seen,"[4] and when a young Ainu woman joined the Americans in their basha en route to Piratori, Mary responded just as she had to the lonely Alaskan woman nearly thirty years earlier. She found the girl attractive, was drawn to her "low and sweet and musical"[5] voice and pitied "the pathetic story of her life."[6] Again, a large part of the woman's charm stemmed from her assimilation into the dominant culture. Mary claimed that, "dressed in the garb of the Japanese, with a certain amount of education, minus the usual tattooing, she showed the good result of missionary work among these people."[7] It seemed that Mary could not shed the baggage of her cultural expectations.

The same held true during her travels in the Japanese colony of Formosa (Taiwan). Mary's curiosity had been piqued by what she had read of the island's history. Despite a reputation for cruelty dating back over a millennium, the indigenous people of the island had long been plagued by colonial interests. Japan's and China's use of the island as a pirate base was challenged by Portuguese, Dutch and Spanish imperialists from the late sixteenth century until 1661, when the Chinese gained control. The island remained a Chinese possession until 1895, when the territory was ceded to Japan.

Mary found Japan's response to the island's unassimilated Aborigines decidedly unique. A line of police stations had been established to divide colonized land from indigenous areas, with the option for bands to surrender to Japanese law and thus be more integrated into colonial society. It was largely in hopes of seeing some of these "surrendered savages" that Mary and her companions included Formosa on their Asian itinerary.

Once in Japan, however, the combined threats of severe storms, smallpox and the bubonic plague led Mary to question the wisdom of her travel plans. Nevertheless, she and her friends continued their journey, and even the deluge of rain that greeted their arrival in Kelung Harbour could not mask the inspiration behind Formosa's name—Portuguese for beautiful. Low hills bedecked with tropical palms, ferns and bamboo delighted foreign eyes. So little had been written about the island, the American visitors were utterly transfixed by the view as they sped by train through "the famous tea-growing country, the queer clusters of Chinese houses and their peaked roofs, the rank tropical growth, the garlands of purple flowers festooning the rail-road banks—ferns, ferns everywhere—the mouse-colored water-buffalo plunging and wallowing through the long rows of mud and water"[8] en route to Taihoku, the capital city.

Mr. Miyoshi, a Harvard graduate to whose care Mary and her friends had been entrusted, began by taking his charges to typical tourist attractions such as a government museum, historic Chinese forts, an opium factory, a camphor factory and a couple of schools. These places were interesting, but the biggest excitement for Mary was the unpleasant surprise of being asked to give a presentation at one of the schools. In spite of her experience with lantern slide shows, Mary was less than thrilled at the prospect of lecturing to a group of non-English-speaking children. She took advantage of her North American map as a visual distraction and gave what she termed "a lame duck sort of a talk"[9] on North American Aboriginals and her experience with them, her trip to see the Ainu and her intention to visit the Formosan headhunters.

As others had in Japan, Mr. Miyoshi tried to discourage Mary from venturing off the beaten track to visit indigenous peoples. Finally, he admitted that one surrendered band, a portion of the reputedly ferocious northern Atayal tribe, could be visited without threat to life. He did his best to dissuade his charges by describing the horrors of the route, claiming that "there was a *very steep* hill wh[ich] was all he could get up himself, so he could not assist [them], there was a swinging wire bridge that he had seen men turn back from, etc.,"[10] but to no avail. Mary did heed his warning that the Chinese chairs were infested with bedbugs by opting to walk rather than ride in one, but otherwise remained unconvinced. She found the terrifying hill laughingly easy after her summer's trek through the Canadian Rockies.

When they neared the suspension bridge, Mr. Miyoshi reiterated his warnings, assuring his guests "it was terrifying, as it swayed so, and for his part he was scared already."[11] Seeing that this approach was not working, he tried another. Perhaps if the women could not be frightened by talk of a shaky bridge, they would be deterred when he pointed out "a rock where 70 Chinese men, women and children had been killed by the savages"[12] two years earlier. No such luck. The women insisted they continue. And when they finally crossed the bridge they found that it "certainly did sway and bounce, but it had guard wires, and would have been hard for even a blind man to fall off."[13] Something told them Mr. Miyoshi was a bit of a tease.

For her part, Mary was thoroughly enjoying the journey. She noted that Formosan rural culture was markedly different from what she had seen in Japan. Most of the people were of Chinese origin, and their customs varied accordingly. As they neared their destination and met Aboriginals, Mary found that both the people's visages and their thatched huts bore much resemblance to Japan's Ainu, but their clothing and hair differed markedly.

Though she found her own curiosity reflected in their faces, she could not stay long enough to indulge it. Night was falling, pushing the travellers toward their lodging in the police station of Urai, the most remote destination to which foreigners were allowed to travel. Western calendars informed the travellers it was December 24, a Christmas Eve unlike any other. "Cold meat, jam, stale bread and tea formed that Christmas feast," Mary explained, "and as we ate it sitting round the floor before a low table, it tasted good enough for the gods, so tired were we from the wild, wonderful, exciting tramp of the day."[14] So exhausted was she after the day's journey that even a rat scampering through her hair did not rob her of sleep.

She knew she needed her rest if she was to set off on her habitual photographic quest the following morning. Her disappointment in learning that the men of both nearby villages were away on a deer hunt was allayed by Mr. Miyoshi's declaration that they might have refused permission to photograph. As it was, Mary's spirited hunt resulted in a most rewarding photography session—not unlike the time she and Mollie had spent with the Stoney women of the Kootenay Plains.

Throughout the Asian visit, Mary was kept busy observing, comparing and documenting. Although her frequent use of the words "queer" and "quaint" to describe her surroundings suggest a muted sense of superiority, she was extremely interested in the countries she visited. When she noticed such customs as Ainu tattooing, the painting of eyes on the hulls of boats and the binding of girls' feet, she was not satisfied simply to observe; she wanted to know the reasons behind these traditions. Thus, even though the suffering caused by foot-binding and the horrifying "pre-dilection for heads"[15] among the Formosan Natives disturbed her, discovering that small feet in Chinese women and the presentation of a human head were prerequisites for marriage somewhat reconciled her to these practices. She concluded that "where matrimony is so at stake, people must be pardoned much."[16]

Besides visiting standard tourist destinations and fulfilling her desire to travel into remote regions, Mary was also treated to such rare experiences as visiting with the governor general and the British consul of Formosa. But the highlight of the urban portion of her journey was bringing in the New Year with a twenty-two-course Chinese dinner.

This, too, was an exclusive opportunity, with invitations extended only to foreigners. Mr. Miyoshi was not on the guest list. Mary could not believe her ears. Unwilling to accept such discrimination, she went straight to the proprietor of the hotel and petitioned him to invite her obliging host. Quickly familiarized with her determination, he surrendered to her request.

The party was a great success. As much as they sometimes clung to the values and traditions of their own country, the four women astonished the other guests by tasting everything. Of the vast array of courses, Mary found that "some were good, some were queer,"[17] and that the "sharks fins and cuttle fish were a little trying, and the pigeon egg nearly finished me."[18] But good senses of humour all around pulled them through any awkward moments, and everyone laughed the night away.

Unfortunately, this delightful evening was soon overshadowed by tragedy. Mollie contracted pneumonia, and did not survive the boat trip from Formosa back to Japan. After years of increasingly arduous travel in the Rockies and now this Asian adventure, Mary had lost her dear friend. She returned home with yet another source of grief, leaving her friend "sleeping in Kobi [sic] on the beautiful heights overlooking the Pacific."[19]

Adventures With a Pen and Paper

MARY SCHÄFFER'S WORLD had shifted once again. No longer could she pass the winter hours preparing for the next expedition with her dear friend Mollie. She kept dreaming of new vistas she would have loved to explore, but her one compatible travelling companion was gone. Few women were in the position to joyfully take up travelling as Mary had done, and even she was finding long journeys increasingly difficult. Her neuralgia had troubled her over the summer of 1908, and a leg injury incurred on that trip was a continued source of pain.

The anchor that had sustained her since Charles' death was coming loose. But she had come too far to let herself be set adrift. Unable to dream of the future, she concentrated on keeping memories of the past alive. And what better way to do so than storytelling?

Sharing tales of her travels was nothing new for Mary. She simply could not resist communicating her knowledge that "there are some secrets you will never learn, there are some joys you will never feel, there are heart thrills you can never experience, till, with your horse you leave the world, your recognised world, and plunge into the vast unknown."[1] She knew her mountain experiences were a pivotal part of her happiness and firmly believed that if others could be enticed to explore the delights of Canada's wilderness, they, too, could achieve inner peace. So she dedicated numerous winter hours to composing accounts of her adventures, showing fearful would-be travellers that "with reasonable care, caution and good animals, one may travel almost anywhere in that great wilderness with perfect safety."[2]

Putting pen to paper was in tune with Mary's family and social traditions. Throughout her lifetime, writing had been seen as one of few appropriate careers for women, and although anti-intellectualism and anti-artistic sentiment had been common among Quakers until the mid-nineteenth century, several of Mary's relatives participated in the literary scene. Some ignored the Quaker concern that novels, romances, adventures and crime stories would promote unhealthy development in young minds, but most channelled their talents along more acceptable avenues.

In 1797 Nathan Sharpless, Mary's grandfather, co-founded Chester County's first periodical. Though *Literary Museum or Monthly Magazine* did not last long, the family interest in periodical literature did. Mary's father gained local celebrity as "John Plowshare," author of a series of articles on agriculture and current events for West Chester's *Daily Local News*. Mary's brothers Frederick and Herman carried on the family tradition by publishing narratives of their travels in the paper.

Mary took a slightly different route, directing her writings toward magazines and journals with a broader distribution. With her first published work, "The Burial of Cheronkee," she ventured into fictional writing. By 1904, when *Rod and Gun in Canada* published the story, the Quakers had relaxed their strict doctrine of simplicity that forbade such writing. Indeed, the previous year fellow Philadelphian Owen Wister had captivated the city with his western novel *The Virginian*, the most widely read book ever authored by a Philadelphian.

Neither Owen Wister nor Mary Schäffer lasted long writing fiction. The bulk of Mary's subsequent works were travel narratives and botanical articles whose educational value would have pleased her fellow Quakers. More important, they reflected her personal mission to convert others to a love for the Rockies. Mary was particularly determined to convince other women that mountain adventures were not the male preserve she had once believed them to be.

Her article about the trip she and Mary Vaux took to the Nakimu Caves begins with the customary "hope [that] this little description will reach those who would venture, if they but knew the delights and pleasures of the expedition."[3] She geared her description of the trip toward easing tenderfoot fears and took particular care to advise women new to alpine activity to "wear something that water, mud, stones and briars will not spoil or tear, an easy mind helps one over many hard places. Wear a good stout pair of boots well greased, with a few hob nails to avoid slipping. Either boots to the knees, or puttees to protect the leg are most advisable. Last of all leave skirts behind and use a pair of stout bloomers. A skirt in the cave is an impossibility and the walk through the valley and up the steep slopes loses one-half the fatigue with the freedom thus obtained."[4]

Likewise, an article in *Rod and Gun* describing Mary's first trip through Ptarmigan Valley was addressed to women who might be tempted to make such a journey but were intimidated by potential hardship. She promised they had nothing to fear from the wilderness so long as they dressed appropriately, carried as little luggage as possible, trusted their horses and brought "along an abundance of good nature,"[5] which she rightly believed "helps to turn snow and water better than an umbrella, and makes the camp-fire burn brighter."[6] Mary's enthusiastic account of her week-long trip assures readers that wilderness travel involves "no lasting hardships, only life, great broad, inspiriting life."[7] All one need fear, she insists, is catching "the spirit, the love of the solitudes"[8]—a most delightful predicament indeed.

When Mary wrote for publications with more experienced readers she altered her style accordingly. Her 1907 article for *The Bulletin of the Geographical Society of Philadelphia* is much more formal than most. "The Valleys of the Saskatchewan with Horse and Camera" begins with a brief history of travel in the Canadian Rockies and an equally brief annotated bibliography of explorers' publications. It then gives a detailed account of Mary's 1906 trip, complete with geographical data, a map and several scenic photographs. Readers evidently appreciated the style, because the *Bulletin* published similar pieces in 1908 and 1909 describing her two major expeditions.

The tone of Mary's articles in the *Canadian Alpine Journal* is slightly different again, demonstrating how she adapted to various publishing niches. In describing her 1907 expedition, she incorporated more sentiment and literary devices. Even the scientific articles she wrote for the *Journal* have a storytelling tone, clearly reflecting her intent to lure visitors—this time botanists—to the Canadian Rockies. Mary certainly knew how to target her writing to draw various audiences to her summer playground!

Most often this talent was used only for her own satisfaction. But on at least one occasion, commercial interests were also at stake. In the early twentieth century, railways made extensive use of advertising pamphlets filled with stories and photographs of exciting destinations along their lines. Because the Canadian Rockies were ideal for this purpose, alpine enthusiasts with visual material at their disposal were in high demand. Always resourceful, Mary Schäffer put her talents to work for the Minneapolis St. Paul and Sault Ste. Marie Railway Company, writing *Untrodden Paths in the Canadian Rockies*, a 23-page promotional brochure describing her 1906 trip through the Saskatchewan Valley to the Kootenay Plains.

Although the brochure was commercial propaganda, the spirit behind it was genuine. Mary Schäffer did not promote tourism in the Rockies just to make money. Her pamphlet offers cheery advice on what weather to expect, what clothing to bring and where to find the best guides. Of course, she also included a number of kind words about the railway and tempted hunters with wildlife photographs taken by Jimmy Simpson, the well-reputed mountain guide and marksman. But most of the brochure is devoted to sharing verbal and visual descriptions of the magnificent peaks, beautiful flowers and fascinating Stoney Indians of the North Saskatchewan River valley. Mary assures readers that "ere long the camper, the trailer, and the hunter will learn that if he follows in our footsteps, he may have from two to five weeks as happy and restful a vacation as can be found the world over."[9]

This sense of peace was the highlight of Mary's own travels; it was this all-encompassing calm for which she hungered upon her return from Asia.

Not yet ready to return physically to the west, she decided to nurse her memories of Mollie and the delightful times they had spent together by composing a book-length account of their 1907 and 1908 expeditions.

Mary's decision to write a travel narrative was far from unprecedented. Such books had become extremely popular in the United States during her adolescence, and as soon as the Canadian Pacific Railway opened the Rockies and nearby Selkirks to tourism, the mountains became a favourite subject. William Spotswood Green's *Among the Selkirk Glaciers*, the first narrative describing an area off the main line of the CPR, was published in 1890. Later adventurers followed suit: *Camping in the Canadian Rockies* by Walter Wilcox appeared in 1897, *Climbs and Explorations in the Canadian Rockies* by Hugh Stutfield and Norman J. Collie in 1903, *The Selkirk Range* by A. O. Wheeler in 1905 and *In the Heart of the Canadian Rockies* by James Outram in 1906.

Mary's familiarity with the travel genre and her own writing experience gave her a strong sense of what appealed to readers of travel narratives. Herself a fan of such works, she had little trouble meeting readers' expectations. Expressing a sense of kinship with nature, interpreting wilderness as evidence of God's strength and goodness and associating Aboriginal people with nature all corresponded with her own world view. She also found it relatively easy to present the action and adventure that her readers would anticipate.

In other ways, contributing a text to this typically male genre was more challenging. Mary knew that if she presented herself as a serious writer and explorer, she would be subject to criticism from those who did not believe women could or should be participating in such activities. But disproving such beliefs was one of her primary aims. Moreover, Mary's years of travel and lecturing had taught her just how intrigued the general public was by women's unconventional activity.

Many women travel writers of the time responded to this quandary by adopting a self-effacing pose to defuse potential attacks. Accordingly, Mary coloured her work with such pleas as, "Alas! that my pigments are so crude and my brushes coarse, the scenes are so fair and the artist so unequal to her task!"[10] Even so, she points out it was not so much her own inadequacy that troubled her as the fact that no human being is capable of describing the beauties of God's creation. Her lamentful "Alas! it takes what I have not, a skilled pen"[11] continues: "Perhaps the subject is too great, and the picture too vast for one small steel pen and one human brain to depict,—at least it is a satisfaction to think the fault is not my own."[12]

Just as Mary carried a hat on her expeditions but refused to wear it, her writing both complies with the demands of femininity and slyly subverts them. She presents herself as helpless and fearful—as expected—but does so mockingly, and side by side with subtle indications of her strength and capability. Since these were attributes expected of male travel writers, Mary could slip them in reasonably unobtrusively, but she had to be careful. If she violated too many of the demands of either femininity or the male-dominated travel genre, her book would be rejected.

Mary managed this balancing act well enough that G. P. Putnam's Sons, a prominent American publisher, agreed to publish the 380-page manuscript, along with one hundred of Mary's and Mollie's photographs. In the spring of 1911, *Old Indian Trails of the Canadian Rockies* became available to both armchair adventurers and those who would be inspired to follow the trails described therein. Disappointed that "those who needed 'enthusing,' they with aches and pains, with sorrows and troubles ... looked upon [her] mountain world as but a place of privation and petty annoyances,"[13] Mary hoped her book would "bring to them the fresh air and sunshine, the snowy mountains, the softly flowing rivers,—the healers for every ill."[14]

In order to meet the various needs of her readers, Mary provided advice pertaining to equipment, the route, campgrounds and scenic points of interest, and included humorous anecdotes about her own experience on the trail. Conscious of the scandal that might arise if she disclosed details about the personal relations between members of her party, Mary instead focused on the personalities of her horses. "Living with them, trailing with them, watching over their interests," she explained, "they soon ceased to be beasts of burden alone, and became our friends with characteristics almost as marked as though they were human."[15] She was aware that "there may be those who read these pages who will think that [she had] infused too much human personality into [her] four-footed companions of the trail,"[16] but defused such criticisms with the simple statement: "I, too, might have thought so once, but that time has gone by."[17]

Mary's attempts to dodge potential attacks against her work were extremely successful; critics loved the book. One reviewer declared that "even a cripple would be tempted into mountaineering by this vivid and vivacious volume."[18] Others concurred, although some in a manner less flattering than most. One tactless soul commented that, "judging from the pictures one of the adventurers was by no means young, so that what they accomplished others can do pretty easily!"[19]

Fortunately, the high praise lavished upon Mary in other columns overshadowed the cutting edge of this one ill-conceived remark. The reviewer for the *Banff Crag and Canyon*, who would have had considerable contact with avid mountaineers, asserted that "those who know Mrs Schäffer will readily understand why this book has an individuality all its own. For twenty years Mrs Schäffer has been coming to the Canadian mountains and she has got closer to them in every sense of the word than any author, newspaper editor, descriptive writer or the special man ever will if he lives a thousand years."[20] High praise indeed.

Rudyard Kipling and the Alpine Club of Canada were delighted with the copies Mary sent, and even the prestigious *New York Times* offered a glowing review. Its critics found it "difficult to decide just what impresses us most: the excellence of the writing, the picturesqueness of the country described, or the personality of the author herself"[21] and concluded:

"Although there was much picturesque scenery along the various trails, there are no verbal flights of sentimental ecstasy to be endured, nor is there any attempt on the part of the author to prove to the reader what a rarely sympathetic soul she has. She is sincere, as all good travellers should be. One sees it all and longs to go there too. A genuine, quiet love of beauty, considerable descriptive ability, and an active sense of humor join to make the book worth reading."[22] Mary's foray into a full-length travel narrative was, to all appearances, an unmitigated success.

But she herself was not sure what to make of the work. She had carefully researched the region's European and Aboriginal history and corresponded with Tom Wilson to ensure the accuracy of a number of details. Nevertheless, she considered it a "rather silly book."[23] Her publishing experience convinced her that "you cant put the SPIRIT of the trail in a book without tearing your heart out"[24] as "the best part of anything written must always be left out. Our small disappointments, our fun which lasted as long as our days, some terribly funny things which happened just because they could not help happen, the perfect understanding with all our cultured men."[25] In fact, she confided, "no one may know I went among those hills with a broken heart and only on the high places could I learn that I and mine were very close together. We dare not tell those beautiful thoughts, they like to say 'explorer' of me, no, only a hunter of peace. I found it."[26]

Plagued by these doubts, Mary let the book go out of print when she felt its price was becoming exorbitant—a decision she later regretted. By the 1920s and '30s she was desperately searching for copies. Prominent Banff tour operator Jack Brewster pressured her to reissue the book, and so many people personally asked Mary for copies that she was tempted. She got Putnam's to bind the 260 copies being stored in their warehouse and put them on the market, and in the 1930s attempted to get the Canadian National Railway to reissue the work. Unfortunately, they did not have the money to properly undertake the project. It was not until 1980 that Mary's dream was realized with the Whyte Museum of the Canadian Rockies' publication of a new edition titled *A Hunter of Peace*.

After sending *Old Indian Trails* off to the publisher, Mary Schäffer had another burst of creative energy. She penned an article describing her trip to see the Ainu, a greatly condensed version of *Old Indian Trails* for *Travel* magazine, an overview of the scenic attractions of the Banff area for the *Banff Crag and Canyon* and a botanical guide, "Haunts of the Wild Flowers of the Canadian Rockies," for the *Canadian Alpine Journal*. When this outpouring subsided, Mary temporarily retired her pen. Her grieving heart had been soothed, her stories were circulating, new visitors were pouring into the Rockies, and the next stage in her life's great adventure beckoned.

Maligne Lake Revisited

A STARTLING REQUEST JOLTED MARY SCHÄFFER from her period of retirement. Although she was neither trained nor experienced as a surveyor, and government policy discouraged women from even accompanying survey parties, Dr. D.B. Dowling of the Geological Survey and Geographical Board of Canada asked her to survey Maligne Lake.[1] Mary was astounded. At first she scoffed, insisting she could not survey a pond, let alone a lake. But Dowling persisted, assuring her he could easily teach her the necessary technical skills. He promised to lend her surveying instruments and ensure that she was comfortable using them. He got Parks Commissioner Howard Douglas to approve the plan, and even secured the funding to cut a trail from the Athabasca River, near the present-day Jasper townsite, to Maligne Lake. How could Mary resist? Although she still had grave doubts "that anything seriously worth while could possibly result"[2] from her efforts, the project was too enticing to pass up. Mary agreed to try her best.

Still, she could not help wondering why Dowling had selected her for the task. Even more puzzling was why higher up officials had agreed to an arrangement that violated their policies so flagrantly. But Dowling knew what he was doing. Mary Schäffer was a prominent Philadelphian, the most experienced female explorer in the Canadian Rockies, a well-respected member of the Alpine Club of Canada and several geographical societies and an individual keen to encourage others to follow in her footsteps. The notoriety she had earned for her rediscovery of Maligne Lake, coupled with the fact that her account of the expedition would soon hit the shelves, put her in a prime position to attract public attention to Maligne Lake—and the merits of protecting it within Jasper Park. Once again, Mary's reputation as a mountain enthusiast had led to a precious—though somewhat intimidating—opportunity.

The Rockies had seen tremendous change during recent years. While Mary's adventurous travels were put on hold, others were quick to pick

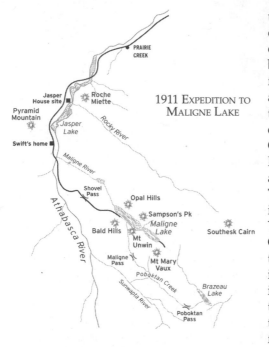

1911 EXPEDITION TO
MALIGNE LAKE

up where she had left off. Her desire to see increasing numbers of people discovering the joys of backcountry travel was being fulfilled; the period of hidden lakes and valleys was rapidly drawing to a close. The region was also experiencing the pressures of Canada's westward expansion. Immigrants were flooding in, and a new railway, the Grand Trunk Pacific, was slowly making its way westward toward the Yellowhead Pass and Tête Jaune Cache. Like it or not, Mary had the rare opportunity of experiencing "the difference between entering a country locked away from the world and the same one when the door was swinging wide open for the first time."[3]

But before Mary could set out on this new adventure, she had one more wrinkle to iron out. She needed to recruit another woman to accompany her. She knew this trip to Maligne Lake would not be as challenging as her first, when her party had had to break through rough terrain guided only by Sampson Beaver's crudely sketched map. This time, a professional trail gang would be preceding her, significantly reducing the potential for hardship. Mary did not need an intrepid explorer, just someone who would enjoy a long train trip and a week's trail ride, followed by an indefinite period of relaxation on the shores of what she considered the finest lake in the Rockies.

Scouring her mind for someone this holiday would appeal to, Mary soon dreamed up the ideal scheme. Her nephew Paul was suffering from whooping cough, and Mary was convinced a trip to "a land where they have no coughs, where it is just ponies and fishing, bears and swimming, fresh air and fried bacon"[4] would bring back "a stock of health and rosy cheeks"[5] to last the winter.

Paul's mother, Caroline Sharpless, was not overly enthusiastic about the idea. She had heard tales of the Wild West and was not convinced that either she or her son ought to experience it. It was troubling enough that her husband, Mary's brother Fred, had been travelling the globe for the past decade in his work as a mineralogist. She did not need the additional stress of removing herself and Paul from their urban setting. But Mary persisted, insisting that a summer in the mountains would be just the cure for Paul. Finally, Caroline decided "she preferred *seeing* him killed in that wild country to having it telegraphed her,"[6] and agreed to accompany her son to the Rockies.

May of 1911 saw first Mary, then Caroline and Paul Sharpless, board the Grand Trunk Pacific for the cross-continental journey to Edmonton. This was a new experience for Mary. She had always ridden the CPR along its southerly route, stopping over at familiar haunts. Instead she found herself searching for a place to stay in a booming provincial capital that lacked sufficient accommodation to meet the growing demand.

At last, staff at the King Edward Hotel offered her space with the harsh reminder that a man in her position might be left to walk the streets. Mary thanked her lucky stars for being a woman, but could not help remarking that the "water pitcher suggested a mud bath"[7] and the bed was merely "an inch-thick mattress reposing on a bunch of tight wire springs."[8] Philadelphia was a long way away.

Edmonton's social scene was much more to Mary's liking. She, Caroline and Paul spent several days running errands, attending teas and luncheons and visiting with friends and acquaintances as they waited for the Sharplesses' trunk to arrive. Away from the intensity of her home city, Mary was able to relax and enjoy such gatherings. Still, when three days had passed without any sign of the trunk, she and Caroline simply begged, borrowed and bought what replacement clothing they could and resumed their westward travels. The problem of the missing trunk was far less significant on this shorter, less demanding expedition.

As Mary prepared to leave the city, she was again reminded of the difference between this trip and those of 1907 and 1908. Rather than setting off from Laggan by pack train after enjoying a delightful breakfast cooked up by her guides, she spent the early hours of June 7, 1911, scouring her hotel for a porter. None was found so the three "draggled and spiritless"[9] adventurers ended up filing "solemnly and silently to the station, each lugging his and her quota of camp outfit, and all breakfastless."[10]

The GTP train was also quite a shock to one accustomed to travelling on Canadian Pacific cars that catered to wealthy tourists. Immigration to western Canada had been booming since Sir Wilfrid Laurier's government instituted policies favouring farming over ranching, and Mary Schäffer's train was packed with pioneers eager to reach the fringes of settlement. These new settlers looked nothing like the people Mary normally shared her trains with.

In spite of her rebellion against upper-class standards, Mary could not shake the status-conscious remnants of her upbringing. She instinctively judged her fellow passengers by their appearance, and was disturbed to note they did the same. She could scarce believe that "even in that jumping-off part of the world, where one would naturally suppose that slouch hats, short skirts, and buckskin coats had their original being, [her dress] caused heads to turn and eyes to open."[11]

This unfortunate concern with status and appearance, from which Mary had so often tried to escape, prevented her from appreciating a crucial stage in the development of the west. Even her fascination with western history

Restaurant on GTP line, ca. 1911. Courtesy Whyte Museum, V439 PS-58.

was not strong enough to make her mingle with the immigrants on her train. Except to be specially escorted to the dining car, where the brakeman ordered all of the occupants to stop smoking until the ladies had departed, Mary and her family kept to their own first-class car, hoping the disinfectant "had been as copiously applied as it smelled."[12]

By the time they reached the Grand Trunk's divisional point at Edson, they were eager to broaden their horizons. Not even a deluge of rain could keep them from tramping the boardwalks to the simple restaurant reputed to be the best in town. Mary was delighted with the food—and even more taken with the proprietor. Recovering some of the pluck and sociability of her youthful travels, she conversed with the woman, gaining ever more respect for her initiative and capability.

She was sorry to leave, especially when she realized the train from Edson to Hinton was a single colonist car crammed with immigrants hoping to find work completing the line. Mary could not even bring herself to board. Gone was any trace of Quaker respect for the humanity of all people. Mary knew that tourists were rare in the new country and was not keen to be confined in a car with people no more excited to be with her than she with them. Were it not for a resourceful mining engineer who started a rumour that she and Caroline were on friendly terms with the president of the Grand Trunk Pacific, Mary's snobbery and timidity would have left her stranded on the platform. As luck would have it, she enjoyed the ride from the privacy of the caboose.

Not unlike her father's 1833 trip to Philadelphia, it was a rough, slow ride along recently laid rails. At the end of the line Mary, Caroline and Paul had to join their fellow passengers in an old farm wagon being used to bus people to the nearby construction camp of Prairie Creek. Only the fact that it was a short ride with few other people made it tolerable. The women breathed a sigh of relief when they saw the tipi their guides, Sid Unwin and Jack Otto, had set up slightly beyond the town limits. The rest of the journey to Maligne Lake was to be completed on horseback—a much more appealing mode of travel.

Three years after first setting eyes on Maligne Lake, Mary Schäffer was returning to her mountain paradise. But even this leg of the journey was a far cry from Mary's previous experience. She and her companions did not struggle alone through the mud and green timber, but were surrounded by pioneers burdened with outfits even more heavily loaded than their own. "All Hinton was going west"[13] and now that she was in safe and familiar company, Mary was fascinated by this "sight of which most of us have only read."[14]

On her early travels through the western States, Mary had seen various stages of European colonization, but never before had she experienced it at first hand. Before leaving Prairie Creek, she and Caroline took advantage of the opportunity to do a little last-minute shopping and take in the sights and sounds of a temporary frontier town. Then they set out on the trail, eyes peeled for such sights as a Cree village and an abandoned construction camp. Even when the trail grew almost impassable, signs of human presence in no way abated. Groups of men, women and children made their way along the trail in both directions, those retracing their steps having lost even the dreams that had sustained them. These were people who had staked their livelihood on their westward journeys; their toil was for survival, not pleasure. The sight of their struggle filled Mary with pity and admiration, particularly for the women whom she considered the true pioneers, the true sufferers.

Her own journey was difficult at first, but was soon eased by a few luxuries. The Yellowhead Trail was beginning its transformation from the fur trading route it had been for hundreds of years into the highway we know today. Though there were not yet restaurants that far from the railway, Mary got a break from camp food when her friend Mr. Morris and the miners of the Jasper Park Collieries invited her to dinner. After the meal there was no need for her guides to spend days scouting out a safe crossing of the Athabasca River as they had three years earlier; a new ferry shuttled them across.

Saddened as Mary Schäffer was by the advances of civilization into her summer playground, the new developments strengthened her awareness of how precious her previous adventures had been—and how much she had learned from them. Now, with a clear trail and signs of human presence all around, she basked in the confidence of an experienced mountain

Ferry crossing on the Athabasca, ca. 1911. Courtesy Whyte Museum, V527 PS-122.

traveller. Just as she and Mollie had been proud to share their expertise with Stewardson Brown in 1908, she was now able to guide her sister-in-law and nephew through the Rockies. When warned that the going would be rough, she willingly stayed behind her skilful guides. But whenever possible she eagerly ventured on ahead, revelling in the glory of transferring her guiding role from paper to reality. The woman who confronted a pesky marten by threatening, "You impertinent little rascal, clear out yourself, I am big enough to choke you!"[15] was a far cry from the timid tenderfoot assigned to Billy Warren's care less than a decade earlier.

Following a brief visit with the Swifts, she, Caroline and Paul even decided to help Jack Otto drive the horses across the Athabasca. The task turned out to be more challenging than they had anticipated. The horses simply did not want to cross. Paul accused the women of being too slow; they retorted that he was getting in their way. The horses, sensing the tension, grew less cooperative than ever. Before long, Mary, Caroline and Paul were all hot, bothered and coated with dust. Two well-dressed women had descended from a nearby village to watch, further aggravating Mary's inflamed temper. Extremely conscious of her party's dusty clothing, sunburned faces and hot tempers, Mary wished the women would leave them to their task in peace. No such luck. The women continued to observe the easterners' struggle until, angry with themselves, the horses and their audience, Mary and Caroline abandoned the task declaring that "the old horses weren't ours anyhow, and it was up to Jack to get them over."[16]

Paul was shocked. He had believed his aunt to be infallible, "the very essence of trail life."[17] How could the horses refuse to obey her commands? And how, the following day, could she miss the grouse she tried to nab with a stick? Paul was thoroughly disappointed. Never again could he look at Aunt Mary in the same way. But at least he was better prepared for her next slip!

On June 17 Jack noticed two specks on the skyline. Mary examined them through a pair of binoculars, then confidently declared them to be sheep. All afternoon, the hungry travellers pushed toward the pass through snow eight feet high, conjuring up images of the delightful feast they could pre-pare that evening. But when they reached the long-anticipated summit, Mary's "sheep" turned out to be shovels abandoned by the trail gang. How disappointing!

Reminded of the humiliation she had sometimes endured during her early years of trailing—and of how she had learned to deal with it—Mary did her best to laugh off the incident and good-naturedly agreed to name the spot Shovel Pass. Less than a day later they met the workers themselves. Apologizing for having been slowed by wet and spongy terrain, the trail gang "rushed frantically ahead of [the] outfit, slashing a tree here, tossing a fallen log there, anything to get Jonas [the unlucky horse selected to carry the boards for the survey boat] and his load to the end of the journey."[18]

Getting those boards to Maligne Lake was no easy task. They were sixteen feet long, eighteen inches wide and over an inch thick. Strapped on either

Jonas and the boat on Shovel Pass. Courtesy Whyte Museum, V527 PS-131.

side of Jonas, they extended the length of his body in front and behind. Any stumble, especially on an incline, was dangerous. During one stream crossing Jonas turned his foot on a loose rock, lurched forward and imbedded his boards in the far bank. He was thrown to his knees, his head pinned under the water until Jack managed to release him. It was truly a relief to see him reach the shores of Maligne Lake, boards intact.

The next step was to assemble the boat. The men hammered away for several days while the women cooked, washed dishes, kept the fire going and did laundry. Pouring rain slowed their progress, but just as people were beginning to wonder if the assembly would ever be finished, the men returned from the shore triumphant. The boat was ready. Breaking an old vinegar bottle (formerly Caroline Sharpless's rolling pin) over its prow, the travellers christened it HMS *Chaba II*.

Mary set out on her survey the following morning, filled with trepidation. The boat moved very slowly, and it troubled her "to sit hour by hour, with nothing to distract the mind from the rower's weary task but to guide the rudder with a piece of frazzled twine taken from a side of bacon."[19] Moreover, she knew the eye of the media would be upon her as soon as she emerged from the wilderness. Any mistake that could not be corrected by then would be thoroughly humiliating. The early signs were not auspicious: within her first two days of work Mary had made one false start, then lost the spool overboard. Fearing she would lose the respect of the entire alpine community, she wondered why she had ever agreed to try her hand at surveying.

While Sid Unwin returned to Edmonton to fetch another spool, everyone else was left to amuse themselves at the lake. Discouraged as Mary was by both the delay and her difficulties, she was thrilled by the opportunity to indulge her old passions. She mixed exploring, botany and photography with healthy doses of reading, writing, cooking and card playing. But she could not forget that Paul was still a young boy in need of constant stimulation. At first it was enough to promise him that if he obeyed certain conditions, such as fetching wood and eating his bread crusts, she would name a mountain after him. Then Paul grew bored, and a bored child is a troublesome child.

Keeping him entertained became a full-time job. He loved listening to stories, but even as avid a storyteller as Mary was quickly worn out by his insatiable appetite for her tales. He was also fascinated by hunting, but his skill developed far too quickly for Mary's liking. When he accidentally shot a mother duck warming her nest, all agreed upon the need to curb his activity. Mary tried to divert his attention by interesting him in photography, the two embarking on a variety of expeditions to photograph young birds. Paul also attempted to share his interests, but without much success. Aunt Mary was not the least bit interested in being dragged out clamming!

When Sid Unwin returned with the news that the missing spool could not be replaced in Edmonton and would have to be shipped from Toronto,

Paul Sharpless assisting Wheeler on Maligne Lake. Courtesy Whyte Museum, V439 PS-70.

Mary seized the opportunity to share yet another of her interests with the boy: exploration. They steered the HMS *Chaba II* toward the narrows to search a valley they named Sandpiper for the trail the Stoneys had followed from Brazeau Lake. Unsuccessful, they continued to the newly named Pixie Valley at the upper end of the lake, but to no avail. One of the guides then tried the only other apparent valley, Bear Valley, but found it to be blocked by glaciers.

This fun-filled exploration lasted a week before the long-awaited spool arrived in the hands of a man referred to only as Wheeler—likely Oliver, son of former government surveyor and Alpine Club of Canada co-founder and president A.O. Wheeler. Having had her diversion, Mary was eager to get to work. She and Jack set out first thing in the morning for a full day's effort. They continued the following day with Wheeler's assistance. All appeared to be going well, until Mary sat down to sketch a map from several days' notes. The image she traced looked nothing like the outline of the lake before her. She "pored for hours over the result—drawing, re-drawing, going over and over each measurement"[20]—but could not locate the source of her mistake.

Worried that her first attempt at surveying would prove to be an irredeem-able failure, Mary got Wheeler to take her out for more measurements. But her bad luck only took a turn for the worse. No sooner had they set out than the spool fell overboard and got caught among some rocks! Mary simply

Mary Schäffer with Paul and Caroline Sharpless, ca. 1911. Courtesy Whyte Museum, V527 NA-78.

could not bear to wait for another spool to be sent from Toronto. Anxious to preserve her pride, she convinced Wheeler that the price of a new spool was worth diving into the freezing water to retrieve the old one!

Having the spool back eased one headache, but did not alter the fact that something was dreadfully wrong with Mary's measurements. She and Wheeler suspected the trouble was linked to the metal in the tripod they had been using. Jack assessed the situation and determined that their hunch was correct. They promptly replaced the tripod with a piece of wood.

Mary did not waste a minute in getting back to work. She resumed her survey immediately, returning to camp only to sleep before setting off at seven o'clock the following morning. She was bound and determined to complete an accurate survey as soon as possible. On July 24, a little over a month after arriving at Maligne Lake, she achieved her goal.

Mary was proud to discover she was more competent than she had dared hope and glad the ordeal was over. On the other hand, the peace and beauty of the wilderness had always meant more to her than any other accomplishment, and with the survey finished, she knew she would have to leave her delightful summer home.

All too soon, she and her party were headed back to the outside world. Mary did not even make it to Edmonton before being forced to proceed with the next phase of her project. Dr. Dowling, eager to hear how she had fared, crawled into her tent at Buffalo Prairie to discuss the survey. This was not the first time a gentleman had peeked into the premises. Dowling's visit reminded Mary of her encounter with L.Q. Coleman four years earlier. How much had changed during those few years. Now, rather than

Pixie Valley. Courtesy Whyte Museum, V439 PS-75.

stumbling surprisedly across women in the backcountry, a man entered Mary's tent to hear a report on work he had commissioned. He examined her work, assuring her that the quarter-mile deviation she suspected in her measurements near the mouth of the Maligne was perfectly acceptable. In fact, he encouraged her to send both the measurements and her map, marked with the names she had given various features, to the Geographical Board in Ottawa.

This utilitarian approach to wilderness was a new departure for Mary. Accustomed as she was to studying the flowers and fossils she discovered on her travels, she had never before approached her mountain surroundings as an entity to be measured and documented—except through landscape photography. In previous years the names she had given to various features were simply personal references; now her names were to be registered with the Geographical Board of Canada. The Rocky Mountain wilderness Mary had loved from first sight was rapidly being appropriated, and to a certain extent urbanized, by Euro-Canadian society—herself included.

Much as Mary regretted these changes, they did not detract much from her pleasure. She had been balancing urban and wilderness life for decades, and 1911 saw her make the shift between the two even more frequently than usual. After leaving Maligne Lake, Mary spent several days enjoying Edmonton's urban lifestyle—running errands, going to the movies, visiting with friends and acquaintances (including Billy Warren) and even taking a tourist excursion on the river. She then bid farewell to Caroline and Paul and headed to the town of Banff, where she remained until the new year. She was beginning to think of Banff as a year-round possibility.

An Activist Emerges

MARY SCHÄFFER'S 1911 SURVEY expedition opened her eyes to just how near Euro-Canadian civilization was drawing to her precious lake. In 1908 it had taken her weeks of trailing to reach its shores; in 1911 a mere eight days were sufficient. With good reason, she feared what the future had in store, not only for Maligne Lake, but for all the wilderness she loved so dearly. She knew that change was bound to occur, and that even she had contributed by having a trail cut to Maligne Lake. But she also knew that so-called progress could not continue unchecked. Mary's passion for the Rockies would not allow her to sit by and watch them be developed and exploited like any other piece of North America. She would have to act; Canada's fledgling preservation movement needed her energy.

Like Mary herself, this movement had drifted north from the United States. Over fifty years before the completion of the Canadian Pacific Railway, Americans had begun to realize that their wilderness was rapidly disappearing. From its former status as a detested obstacle to be surmounted at any cost, wilderness had become an intriguing novelty, then the perfect symbol for the young American nation. The more disenchanted nineteenth-century Americans became with materialistic urban life, the greater their appreciation for untouched wilderness.

Nevertheless, those in power maintained economic growth as their top priority. The main reason for the 1872 establishment of Yellowstone, America's first national park, was to prevent private ownership of its geysers, hot springs and waterfalls. It was merely a coincidence that wilderness had been set aside. At mid-century, when Henry David Thoreau began insisting that the success of civilization and the fulfilment of human potential depended upon the preservation of wilderness, his message fell largely on deaf ears. But by the 1880s and '90s, his compatriots were becoming highly receptive to similar messages from wilderness publicist John Muir. In 1890, the American government set aside Yosemite Park specifically for the purpose of protecting wilderness.

At that time, Canadian parks were still in their infancy. On November 25, 1885, an order-in-council had set aside 10 square miles as the Banff Hot Springs Reserve. As with Yellowstone Park, the original purpose of the reserve had been to prevent private ownership and exploitation of the hot springs. But when George Stewart of the Dominion Lands Branch began to survey the new reserve, he was captivated by the area's superlative natural beauty and urged the government to protect a larger area. In 1887 Parliament complied, giving birth to Canada's first national park: 250 square miles of wilderness that was named Rocky Mountains Park. Still, the park was intended to be more of a resort than a wilderness preserve, as were the parks and forest reserves established at Glacier and Yoho in 1886, Waterton Lakes in 1895 and Jasper in 1907. Their primary purpose was to generate tourism revenue. Mining and other development were encouraged as further sources of income.

Another two decades passed before the Canadian government paid much attention to conserving natural resources. Again, the initiative came from the United States, where the emphasis was on efficient forestry practices. In 1881 the American Congress created a Division of Forestry within the Department of Agriculture. Ten years later, the Forest Reserve Act allowed the president to give reserve status to certain forested areas, but did not clearly define the purpose of such forest reserves. Some conservationists, including Gifford Pinchot (later chief forester), believed the act ought to have insisted on scientific forestry practices. Others, like Muir, were convinced the new forest reserves were essentially national parks. The 1897 Forest Management Act proved Muir wrong. When he broke with Pinchot later that year, he and others who wished to keep wilderness untouched became known as preservationists, distinct from Pinchot's "wise use" conservationists.

This split did not occur in Canada. After attending President Theodore Roosevelt's North American Conservation Conference in 1909, Canadian government officials established their own Commission of Conservation. Clifford Sifton, a strong advocate of development and rational planning, chaired the commission. Working under him were a number of businessmen and professionals who, while opposed to Canada's inefficient resource exploitation, had no desire to preserve wilderness either for its own sake or for its aesthetic and spiritual value. Planned resource exploitation was the order of the day.

Even so, some preservationist ideas were filtering into parks management. In 1911 Parliament passed the Dominion Forest Reserve and Parks Act to separate the administration of national parks from that of forest reserves. Its first commissioner, James B. Harkin, combined a great love for the aesthetic value of wilderness with the understanding he would have to provide other more pragmatic reasons for its preservation. The changes in parks management that he oversaw implied that the government intended to restrict commercial development and resource exploitation in order to emphasize wildlife preservation. The great disappointment of the act was that in order to better patrol the parks, the government drastically reduced their size. In June of 1911, just as Mary Schäffer was setting out on her survey expedition, Jasper Park was reduced from 5,000 square miles to a narrow 1,000 square-mile strip bordering the Grand Trunk Pacific.

Mary Schäffer's correspondence with Howard Douglas, superintendent of Rocky Mountains Park between 1897 and 1908, indicates that she kept abreast of these policy developments. As soon as she reached Edmonton in August, 1911, she began employing judiciously targeted comments to lobby for the reinclusion of Maligne Lake within Jasper Park. She responded to Canada's growing concern for social reform by emphasizing the benefits of outdoor recreation for physical and spiritual health. She catered to the legislators' need for a practical reason to set aside parks by pointing out the opportunities they offered for scientific research. She demonstrated her awareness of current park priorities by insisting "there is no finer tourist ground in America."[1] And she contributed to a sensitive parks debate by commenting that "even close to the railway we saw one flock of 28 mountain sheep. I made careful inquiries and could find no indications of the game laws having been broken. This, coupled with the plentifulness and tameness of the game, speaks well for the strictness of the regulations within the park. Now that these areas have been cut off, however, one cannot say what will happen."[2]

Had Mary Schäffer been alone in her concern about the reduction in park size, even these pointed remarks would have had little effect. Fortunately, both the Canadian National Railway and the Grand Trunk Pacific were also lobbying for park expansion, as were the Alpine Club of Canada and the Campfire Club of America. All of these groups, along with members of the general public whose concern Mary Schäffer had helped arouse, combined to exert significant pressure on the government. With the parks commissioner and several other civil servants behind the cause, few were surprised when a June 14, 1914, order-in-council enlarged Jasper Park to 4,400 square miles including Maligne Lake.

This victory did not stop Mary Schäffer from insisting upon the value of wilderness. It saddened her that what were once great journeys on unmarked trails could be made by rail or automobile, that "'Progress' [was] steadily marching on and the day [was] coming when there [would] be no secret wilderness left."[3] She loathed railway expansion into territory that she considered her own; she referred to railroads as pythons wriggling their way into the spectacular scenery and bitterly complained that the GTP would bring swarms of timber cruisers and hunters to kill all the game and force Natives onto their reserves.

Mary was also disgusted by the destructive behaviour she witnessed on the trail. She resented the careless travellers who left debris lying around popular campsites and wished that everyone who entered the wilderness had the respect to leave it unsullied for future visitors. Even more upsetting than garbage were the traces of forest fires, dark scars disfiguring the landscape. Natural fires were one thing, but these "fire-demon[s] eating [their] way up the mountainside"[4] were the despicable result of human carelessness.

Of course, Mary's own wilderness etiquette was hardly up to modern standards. Her idea of the proper disposal of tin cans was to throw them in the river or bury them. She believed bighorn sheep to be an "emblem of the vanishing wilderness,"[5] but nevertheless referred to them as "mutton-chops." She complained of the "thousands who gather [flowers] only to throw away, those who in gathering, ruthlessly destroy the roots, and those who are collecting, who pluck till the last rare specimen is in their vasculum,"[6] but admitted cutting off at least one branch of rare blossoms to photograph them. Like it or not, Mary's presence in the backcountry—along with all those she encouraged to join her—put at risk the very wilderness she was there to experience. No wonder the Métis she, Caroline and Paul passed in 1911 "stared at the two women and small boy as though they meant the beginning of the end."[7]

Just as American society struggled to resolve its tension between wilderness and civilization values, so too did Mary. Much as she deplored development in her beloved wilderness, she was so intent on reincorporating Maligne Lake into Jasper Park that she advocated building a steam launch on its shores to increase its tourism potential. Such were the ironic twists in a period when the Canadian government's willingness to protect wilderness depended on revenue generated by tourists.

Mary's desire to share the peace of the wilderness with those less adventurous than she only heightened the tension. She assured her lantern slide show audiences that "every convenience under the sun may be found in the heart of the wilderness. Ponies carry people to the higher lakes, Mirror and Agnes, small tea houses have sprung up, [and] at least 100 miles of trail ramify every interesting point."[8] She knew that accessibility depended on a certain level of development, but much as she wanted the accessibility, she could not help resenting the development. Hence her equivocal declaration that "the march of progress has wiped out the poetry of living in these vast hills. It has also wiped out much hardship."[9]

Even changes in alpine nomenclature were upsetting. On her expeditions, Mary Schäffer and her trailmates had named their camps and various other geographical features for the sake of easy reference. She had no expectation these names would be formally adopted. But once Dr. Dowling assured her that her names for features around Maligne Lake were perfectly valid, she was loath to have them replaced. After all, she had brought the lake to public attention, and it was she who had first surveyed it. The names of Mounts Unwin, Warren, Mary Vaux and Paul were dear to her heart. Sampson's Peak, Leah Peak, Sampson's Narrows and Mount Charlton (H.R. Charlton, publicity agent of the Grand Trunk Pacific, had helped sponsor the surveying expedition) were all infused with gratitude to those who had helped her along her journey. Sunshine Falls, Veil-of-Tears, Pixie Valley, Sandpiper Creek, the Thumb, Little Lysyfran, The Ramparts and Opal Hills all brought back warm memories of her 1911 sojourn at the lake.

As per Dowling's request, Mary had sent her measurements and her map, with the names of the various features inscribed on it, to the Geographical Board in Ottawa. But even the complete support of Dr. Dowling did not ensure ready acceptance of her names. Arthur O. Wheeler, director of the Alpine Club of Canada, had also measured Maligne Lake in 1911 and was infuriated that Mary had arrived ahead of him. She later declared: "When I met him (accidentally I assure you) the next spring, he asked me what length I had made the lake and on replying '18 miles,' he said 'All wrong, its only 17 miles.' I smiled like the cat at the cream and replied: 'You perhaps did not go far enough to see the FOOT at the end of the lake and where my lovely Pixey Valley is.'"[10]

Unable to further question the accuracy of Schäffer's survey, Wheeler mounted opposition to her nomenclature. He complained to A.H. Whitcher that Unwin and Warren were "not illustrious men, even as packers,"[11] and that it would therefore "be a mistake to place their names upon the most prominent mountains bordering the lake."[12]

Upon learning the names had been accepted, Wheeler again wrote Whitcher: "I think the Board should formulate some rule with regard to the application of personal names. It is the generous impulse of all mountain parties, whether foreign or otherwise, to confer the names of their packers, to whom they are indebted for quick, satisfying meals when hungry and soft brush beds when tired, upon our prominent peaks. It is a generosity that costs them nothing, but has the ill effect of drawing severe criticism upon us from the real geographers of other countries. This tendency has frequently been brought to my notice by members of the Royal Geographic Society."[13]

Similar concerns were expressed in the 1912 *Canadian Alpine Journal* article that seems to have been written by Wheeler. The author includes numerous references to spots he named after their physical properties, only to discover that other names, proposed by Mrs. Schäffer, had already been accepted. He graciously concedes that Mary's frequent visits to the Rockies made her "altogether Canadian in her love for them"[14] and praises her success in sharing their delights with others. He also acknowledges her as an original explorer and claims that "she first visited and brought to notice this beautiful lake, which had previously been known only to the Indian and the hunter. She has ... undoubtedly the right to name its features."[15] Nevertheless, he cannot resist expressing his wish "that personal names had not been so prominent, for the surrounding peaks have many striking characteristic features that seem naturally to supply the names."[16]

Ironically, it seems to have been the name "Maligne" that came under greatest criticism, if not from Wheeler then from others. This was by no means one of Mary Schäffer's personal names, but was selected in accordance with the principle that as many features as possible should go by the same name. Mary named the lake after the river that flows out of it, her compliance with this practice being endorsed by the Royal Geographical Society. With Dowling's assistance, this and all of Mary's names around the lake were upheld and continue to be used today.

Mary was also disturbed by what she perceived to be a constant changing of names set by earlier explorers. She lobbied particularly hard for the restoration of names applied by Samuel Allen, a Yale student who had been heavily involved in early mountain climbing around Lake Louise. In 1924 Mary remembered her old friend and sent copies of his manuscripts and map to Dr. Dowling, who in turn forwarded them to J. Monroe Thorington, a Philadelphia mountaineer and mountain historian. She felt there had been instances where Allen's "thunder had been utterly stolen"[17] and demanded that it was "time to call a halt, return the names to those who placed them there and at least recover some old data and then cling to it."[18]

With the same determination that enabled her to become the first non-Native woman to explore vast areas of the Canadian Rockies, she wrote numerous letters to both Thorington and Dowling insisting her "mission [was] not to have things 'filed.' You might as well put them direct in the cemetery."[19] She argued "the men who calmly took Allen's names when he was forever a sick man, changed them, shoved them off, turned them round (and mind you Allen is not the only person who has got such a rotten deal) need to get a good shove themselves."[20] How disappointing when this spirited offensive was rebuffed by Thorington's suggestion that rather than changing the names of all the features Allen had named, his name might be given to an unnamed range.

This was one battle Mary simply could not win. While government officials shared her concern for protecting alpine nomenclature, they acted upon it by refusing to change already accepted names. Understandably, they felt this was preferable to restoring the first given name for a feature, which might involve an endless series of name changes as new documentation of earlier travels surfaced. Moreover, most of the earliest names were Aboriginal, a fact Mary never acknowledged, in spite of her efforts to mention that Natives had preceded her most everywhere she had gone.

But it would be a mistake to let this one failure overshadow Mary Schäffer's string of successes. After surmounting the hurdles blocking women from making major expeditions in the Canadian Rockies, Mary was ready to exert her influence. Her survey expedition and subsequent lobbying helped re-extend the boundaries of Jasper Park to include Maligne Lake. Her names for features around the lake were accepted and approved. Her book *Old Indian Trails in the Canadian Rockies* was an inspiration to many. The unfortunate fact that her deteriorating health had halted her major expeditions by no means curtailed her love for the Rockies; she simply found other ways of expressing her enthusiasm.

A New Beginning

MARY'S WANDERING HEART HAD FOUND ITS true home in the Canadian Rockies. How then could she continue to live in the eastern United States? Her parents and husband had died; her brothers were both world travellers. Her Philadelphia home was no longer even her own; she had turned it over to the Academy of Natural Sciences after Charles' death. The relationships that did continue to draw her eastward were outweighed by an increasing reluctance to go back to homes that had been "crushed by death."[1] At fifty, Mary began to ponder the practicalities of a move west.

Her first step was to spend the fall of 1911 in Banff. In the past, the region's early winter had always pushed her reluctantly homeward. But something was changing. Perhaps it was a burst of courage after realizing she was capable of surveying Maligne Lake. Perhaps the depressing blandness of solitary Philadelphia life was finally getting to her. Or perhaps a certain "chiefly" guide beckoned.

Whatever the reason, Mary rented a cottage in Banff from which to investigate off-season mountain life. She spent October working on slides with botanist Julia Henshaw and the next two months going over her treasured Samuel Allen manuscripts with outfitter Tom Wilson. Sitting snug by the fire with her bulldog, Beau, for company and protection, she lost all fear of Canadian winters. She declined invitations east for Christmas, preferring to host "a half dozen who were as driftless as [she had] been in the past."[2] And after years of curiosity, she was able to attend the New Year's celebration on the Morley Reserve.

In fact, Mary had practically made up her mind about Banff before winter even began. Having been "restive for three years for a home in the west, where [she] could go out, saddle [her] pony and ride among the hills [she loved] better than smoke-stacks,"[3] she had asked Billy Warren to help estimate the cost of having one built even before moving into her rented cottage. He responded with an offer she could not resist: a bad debt had

Tarry-a-While. Courtesy Whyte Museum, ALR V488, Block 27, Lots 23-24-25.

left him with two Banff lots he had to build on by spring or lose entirely. If she put up a house, the lots would be hers.

Mary was thrilled—until she learned of their location: directly opposite the town cemetery! But she could not allow Warren to see her disappointment. As she later explained, "He had done his best which is what all men do and when their best looks like a mistake, we women are always making the best of it and then go on hoping for better."[4] Cemetery or none, she took the lots. In fact, she was so keen to have a home in Banff that she neglected to inform George Vaux Jr.—her lawyer, financial advisor and friend—that the bad debt which had brought her the lots was not her own. Moreover, she was so confident he could arrange the financing that she told Warren to go ahead and begin superintending construction before obtaining his approval.

Mary soon found herself caught between an awareness of her limited finances and a strong desire to have a comfortable, well-built house. Though her confidence that Vaux could "scare up the cash somewhere to pay for a home"[5] was not misplaced, obtaining money from her eastern investments was sometimes a frustratingly slow process. On more than one occasion she resorted to borrowing from Warren—and having him borrow on her behalf—until Vaux could call in her investments and transfer the funds. In order to avoid the "foreigners' surcharge" on construction, she and Warren also conspired to pretend that the house was his and she would merely be renting it. Uncomfortable as Mary was with telling fibs, she felt she could not "afford to be truthful."[6]

The strain on her conscience was compounded by her internal struggles about how best to assist her brother Herman, who had amassed considerable debt following a nervous breakdown. When things were going well and Herman's future looked promising, Mary assisted with a generous and willing heart. But when she found her own economies being mocked, she resolved that "there was no use in economising to give to others—I might as well begin to have a few things myself."[7]

In spite of these tensions, Mary was confident that her house, Tarry-a-While, was a good investment with strong resale potential. Even before construction was complete, potential purchasers were making enquiries. With views of Mount Rundle, Sulphur Mountain, Cascade Mountain, the Spray Valley and a panorama of named and unnamed mountains and valleys she termed "the Valley of Everywhere," the location was excellent. Mary was also proud to report that local workers had declared it the best-built house in town.

Still, she was not sure how long she would stay in it. "My idea is," she explained, "that if I like this kind of way of spending the fall and spring months, then I can look round and find an ideal spot, sell this place and build exactly what I want. The *log* shack is only in abeyance. There is a lovely slope across the R.R. track, on the Stony Squaw, where a Swiss chalet would catch all the sunshine going, where this whole splendid valley would lay stretched before you, and if it is feasible, that is the spot I am working for. I am cultivating Bennett, the new Rep, I am on best of terms with Dr. Brett, so will probably have no trouble with the incoming Govt. to get what I want from The Park."[8]

In the meantime, she was busy having her own house and stable built—which kept her and Warren in close contact. When the two first met, she had sensed that he was "a man who wanted a little heartening up."[9] Even as she struggled to recover from her own deep losses, Mary did what she could—and found her kindness repaid many times over. By the fall of 1911, her concern for this young man was such that she advised Vaux to will both the house and the lots to Warren, explaining that "if anything happened to me all of a sudden, I don't him to suffer for it. He is just getting on his feet."[10]

Vaux would not have been remiss in wondering about the close bond developing between Mary and her former guide. Wishing to ease any concerns, Mary assured him that Warren "is the sole person save thyself who has worked for my interests without one thought of what he was to get out of me. All of our expeditions have been worked out on the plan that I was to have the best for the least amount of money ... Mr. Warren has stood between me and the greedy element many and many a time."[11]

But even the language of finance could not mask the couple's relationship forever. The months they spent together on the trail were a testament to their compatibility, and their attachment had only been strengthening during the seven years since they had first met. Though Mary was careful to hide it, she and her guide had succumbed to Rocky Mountain romance. Amidst the warmest congratulations of their neighbours—and the chuckles of Warren's fellow guides, who noted that Mary had married a man 23 years her senior only to be widowed and marry one almost as many years her junior—a Vancouver wedding united the two in holy matrimony on June 24, 1915.

Unlike Charles Schäffer, William Warren was not an established gentleman leading a life of privilege. He was a young entrepreneur looking to make it in the world. He began by moving from Tom Wilson's employ to his own outfitting business out of Lake Louise and Field. When the increasing popularity of automobiles began cutting into the demand for guides and outfitters, he diversified. In 1919 he and Clarence Sibbald founded the Cascade Garage and the Banff Motor Company. In 1920 he purchased the Alberta Hotel and converted its lower floor into four shops. The following year he built Cascade Hall. In partnership with James McLeod, he also purchased the King Edward livery business and modernized it into the popular Rocky Mountain Tours and Transport Company.

Mary's personal savings were likely crucial in getting her new husband started. Nevertheless, his success cut into her sense of self-worth. Although she had managed alone very well for twelve years after her first husband's death, she declared: "If this husband of mine had not turned up with his strong practical character, I often wonder where I would have landed."[12] She grew to consider herself incapable of earning a cent to support herself and insisted the only reason she was considered clever was because she had "the wits to think of something out of the common run."[13]

This sense of dependence affected Mary's leisure activities. Just as Charles Schäffer's scientific snobbery had provoked Mary to abandon stamp collecting, William Warren's keen eye for business discouraged her from pursuing interests that he did not consider sufficiently profitable. On one of their vacations, Mary "noticed the orchids were bestirring themselves and odd plants putting their noses out among the ferns."[14] Ever the flower-lover, she was intrigued by the sight, but felt "it was no use [a]sking to be allowed to gather them for Will thought I would only wear my poor [amount] of strength out."[15] Moreover, "there is not a cent in wild plants, not the way I would go after them. And Wm. looks for cash production. One must be a dreamer to work among plants."[16]

Mary knew where impractical dreaming led. Her parents had been dreamers. Charles Schäffer had been a dreamer. William Warren, on the other hand, was a successful entrepreneur. Mary was confident he would never leave her in the dreadful predicament she had suffered after her first husband's death. But this security came with a price. She would have to subdue her own fanciful side.

Even if Mary had been able to generate income from her botany, William would not likely have supported her pursuit of it. He would not be dishonoured by having his wife earn money. He could not even stand her writing professionally. Mary sent one of her articles to a friend with the following note defiantly scribbled in the margin: "It annoyed Will but he can't stop my pen except with teeth and tonsils!"[17]

Mary's writing did slow around the time of her move to Banff. In 1912, she submitted "The Finding of Lake Maligne" to the *Canadian Alpine Journal*. Then, the combination of her move, her marriage and her lack of new backcountry expeditions to write about led to a five-year hiatus. William Warren got his way.

Mary's writing rarely appeared in print after their marriage. Her only major published articles in the decade after her second marriage were a 1917 *Canadian Alpine Journal* obituary for Sid Unwin, who had been killed in the First World War, and "The Byways of Banff." This 1919 *CAJ* article was a criticism of Banff tourists who followed her former pattern of arriving at the end of June and remaining "till exactly the middle of September, when they all depart as they came—smug and self-satisfied over their meagre achievements."[18] Chastising those who escaped the rigours of a prairie winter by fleeing to the west coast, Mary—always eager to give advice—presented the itinerary of her ideal winter vacation in the Banff area. It included such pleasures as skating, ice boating on Lake Minnewanka, sleighing, tobogganing, bathing in the hot springs, skiing and snowshoeing.

Mary Schäffer Warren's next published work did not appear until the summer of 1926, when she reminisced about an early trip to the Ptarmigan Valley for the *Trail Riders of the Canadian Rockies Bulletin*. The following year she composed several articles about the Palliser Expedition and her own encounter with Sir James Hector, then virtually nothing. Mary's years of being published were over. Most of the pieces she wrote after her second marriage remained private. They have become available to the public only since being housed in the archives of the Whyte Museum of the Canadian Rockies.

Some of these unpublished manuscripts are very much like Mary's published articles describing her travels through the Rockies. "The Story of Revelstoke" relates Mary's various adventures around the town between 1898 and 1913; "A Glimpse of the Head-hunters of Formosa" describes her adventures in Taiwan. Likewise, "Jonas" and "An American Boy in the Canadian Rockies" describe her 1911 survey expedition, "Trail Life at Lake Louise" is a tourist guide, and "My Garden" is the text of a lecture on Mary's early botanical activity.

Her other unpublished manuscripts reflect her diverse interests and incorporate a variety of styles and themes. "A New Year in the Wilds" describes the New Year's celebration of food and dance that she attended at the Morley reserve. "The Heart of a Child" relates her growing fascination with Natives and her earliest experiences with those of the western United States. "Tepee Life in the Northern Hills" responds to a series of *Saturday Evening Post* articles on western life by recounting Mary's own evolution as a mountain woman. Mary's interest in history is revealed by narratives about early exploration in the Rockies and the "Story of Famous Ride of Doctor Red Deer Valley." She also delved into fiction with a couple of children's stories and two fictional accounts of pack trips. The latter are fascinating in that they almost seem to be autobiographical, but are narrated from a masculine perspective. Perhaps Mary was exploring what her life might have been like had she been a man.

The differences in style and theme between these works and Mary's published articles suggest she may not have found a market for them even if William had not objected. She was branching out in new genres less appropriate to her favourite journals.

Her income-generating photographic work also slowed after her second marriage. The high point of her photographic career had been in 1907, when *Alpine Flora of the Canadian Rocky Mountains* was published. This book was the culmination of her and Stewardson Brown's efforts to complete Charles Schäffer's botanical study. Combining Brown's scientific expertise and Mary's illustrative skill, the work promised to be a great success. Delighted reviewers praised Mary's skill; their only major complaint was that "the artistic effect of Mrs. Schäffer's work [was] considerably impaired"[19] by the book's pocket-sized format.

But favourable reviews did not guarantee commercial success. Julia Henshaw, another botanically minded lover of the Rockies, had recently published *Mountain Wild Flowers of Canada*, a much-praised guide that cut into the market for *Alpine Flora*. Mary was disappointed her work did not sell as well as anticipated, but even more bothered by a feeling of having been cheated. Julia Henshaw had observed her and Charles at work, asked Mary to share her techniques for painting and photographing the flowers, then seemed to have virtually duplicated their work. Mary's first response was to write "her as kindly a letter as I could, [telling] her I was glad hers had come first for mine was only meant in memory of a great botanist and I trusted it would not interfere with her work."[20]

This humility was typical. In her personal correspondence, Mary maintained she "was a dumb-bell about botany"[21] who wished to avoid the folly of getting caught up pretending to be more clever than she was. She often declared the key to her success was simply that she could "sketch botanically correctly, press just right and photo all right and had the wits to get a good botanist to attend to the real work."[22]

Even so, Mary believed *Alpine Flora* to be her only weighty publication. Beneath her modesty lay a strong reservoir of pride. When Julia Henshaw failed to respond to her letter, Mary grew increasingly bitter. Asked to colour Julia's slides the next summer, Mary smugly refused. Though her feelings of resentment persisted to the end of her life, by 1911 she was again working side by side with Julia at Glacier House.

Her pride in *Alpine Flora of the Canadian Rocky Mountains* came out even more strongly when requests for copies exceeded the number available. Mary feared Putnam's had destroyed the colour and photo plates for the book, making reprinting impossible. She was so desperate that all interested parties have a copy that she became angry with one "friend who care[d] no more for a plant than a toadstool"[23] yet refused to give up her copy for someone Mary considered a real botanist. She was not the only hoarder; Mary's old friend Tom Wilson took great pride in his collection of four copies, one of which was autographed.

Mary's reputation for photographic skill had begun to spread even before the publication of *Alpine Flora*. In 1900, Frances Benjamin Johnston had selected several of her floral photographs for a Paris salon exhibition, "American Woman Photographer." Five years later, A.O. Wheeler decided to include several Mary Schäffer photographs, including a panorama of Mount Sir Donald, in *The Selkirk Range*. Then came *Alpine Flora of the Canadian Rocky Mountains*, *Old Indian Trails* and Mary's collection of articles, all enhanced by her photos. In 1920, having recovered from his 1911 tussle with Mary over alpine nomenclature around Maligne Lake, Wheeler and famed mountain photographer Byron Harmon selected a variety of her photographs for the Canadian exhibit at the Congress of Alpinism in Monaco.

For the most part, Mary's artistic work after her second marriage focused on drawing tourists to the Rockies. Where Charles Schäffer's botanical work had been furthered by flower paintings, William Warren's enterprises depended on advertising. Mary gladly obliged when the Canadian Pacific Railway asked her to paint a series of photographs advertising Banff and its Indian Days Celebration for eastern CP hotels. Likewise, she coloured several scenic views taken along Banff-Windermere roads as publicity for the Rocky Mountain Tours and Transport Company.

Mary also used lantern slide shows to draw tourists to the Rockies. Having spent much of her life around Philadelphia, "the lantern slide capital of America,"[24] it was only natural she should participate in the phenomenon. The shows offered her the opportunity to educate her audiences about the flora, fauna, aboriginal peoples and history of the Rockies. They also fostered recognition of her adventurous nature and talents for photography, painting and storytelling.

The earliest record of a slide show is a 1907 clipping from an eastern American newspaper: "The lecture by Mrs. Charles Sh[äf]fer, on her experiences of life among the Canadian Rockies, filled Library Hall last evening with an interested audience, and one which must have assured a very neat sum for the benefit of the sanatorium at Mont Alto. Many of those who composed the assemblage were relatives or early friends of Mrs. Sch[äf]fer, who as Miss Mary Sharples[s], spent her girlhood here, but there were many others who came out of interest in the subject, and all went away much pleased with the evening's discourse."[25]

Even after moving to Banff Mary continued to make frequent trips to her former home, always accompanied by her slides. She delighted a wide variety of audiences with her stories and photographs, lecturing for geographical and natural history societies from Philadelphia to Calgary, Banff and beyond. Though she admitted to exaggerating certain stories for the tenderfoot traveller, she loved to laugh, even at her own expense, and was not afraid to admit to disappointment and bad moods. Banffites enjoyed her shows as much as her former neighbours in the east, and with all of her efforts being voluntary, William Warren could not have been happier.

Mary Schäffer Warren at home in Banff, ca. 1920. Courtesy Whyte Museum, NA66-527.

A True Banffite

EARLY TWENTIETH-CENTURY BANFF, with its combination of cosmopolitanism and rugged outdoor life, was the ideal home for Mary and William Warren. The town's sophistication arose from its status as a posh tourist resort and the fact that many Banffites, including William Warren, were transplanted Victorian Britons who had carried much of their former lifestyle with them. Formal balls were common and the town had its own amateur theatre. But Banff was also a town on the frontier of a newly opened wilderness, full of eccentric characters eager to escape to it: guides, packers, cooks, cowboys, entrepreneurs—all those who wished to "live without thought of high rents, expensive clothes, electric light bills, so long as a Ford will carry a few pounds of bacon for them and include a tent and the dog."[1] Asked what the town was like when he first arrived, Jimmy Simpson replied, "Well, we used to play poker in the police barracks, and we used to play polo where the Mount Royal is; we didn't have a decent Main Street until R.B. Bennett lost one of his rubbers in the mud and said, 'I'll have this damned street paved.' What was Banff like? It was a real place then."[2]

Yet rough and rugged as these guides and outfitters liked their town, their homes, like Mary's, were filled with art and literature. She described her home as "a mountain bungalow, a spot which so many come on unexpectedly and in looking round almost invariably say: 'Here is a home.' Its not rustic, but it has a great hearth and great hearts."[3]

Though unassuming from the outside, Tarry-a-While boasted an elegant interior, finely decorated with heirloom furniture. Mary had brought various treasures with her from Philadelphia, including an early nineteenth-century carved bed (now in the Moore home at the Whyte Museum of the Canadian Rockies), two chandeliers, one of the first wooden reclining chairs, an eighteenth-century grandfather clock and an elegant triptych mirror. She decorated the stained fir panelling walls with the handiwork of her ancestors and rounded out the décor with photographs, candlesticks, carved wooden animals and her extensive collection of Native artifacts (now held by the Whyte Museum of the Canadian Rockies).

To maintain this lovely home in the tradition to which she was accustomed, Mary decided to hire a couple of servants. The task was more challenging than anticipated. As Mary explained to an eastern cousin, "It is not hard to have a home in this new country, but it is very hard to find servants to run it. They are without any exception the most difficult creatures of their kind I ever came in contact with. They all seem to have been living for years on the great western ranches, where they are 'one of the family.' There is only one mistake in that phrase: they *are* the family, you are an outsider and only tolerated so long as you conduct yourself to their liking."[4]

Mary had not waited this long to move to Banff only to feel like an outsider in her own home. She fired her first servants, preferring to do the work herself until she could find the right people. Her efforts paid off; in later years Mary was adamant that neither she nor William "ever has trouble with those who serve us."[5] "They treat me as a sort of old baby," she explained, "and I treat them as something that is human."[6] She even took their side against her friends, complaining "Its the people who range in my own set whom I do not understand. I never go to a tea without giving the maid a smile and get such a nice one in return. No one ever nods to my maids no matter what they do for them and I could slaughter such."[7]

This tension reflected a deeper unease with Banff society that was not unsimilar to Mary's Philadelphia experience. She knew the bulk of the women to be kind, but not much interested in her company. Nevertheless, instead of mixing with the middle class, she kept to an elite group of women, struggling all the while not to be identified with their renowned snobbery.

Her greatest comfort lay among the young people of Banff. Indifferent as their parents may have been, the children were fascinated by Mary and her home. Most were ignorant of her literary, photographic and exploratory credentials, but they had heard she kept both a monkey and a parrot as pets. Intrigued, they longed to be sent to Tarry-a-While on errands, hoping to catch a glimpse of the monkey before it was put away. And when they did drop by, Mary was as pleased as they. She regretted her own childlessness, wondering why "nice boys [are] given to women who know nothing about them and those who could love a doz[en] are left starving for what would be a wealth to them."[8]

Even more delightful to Mary than the children were Banff's young adults. She filled her empty home with the local youth and treated them like her own children. Sunday evening was bridge night at Tarry-a-While, complete with prizes. Etiquette demanded that Mary, as hostess, not play herself, but that did not keep her from delighting in the company. Her spirit was rejuvenated, though her aging body often protested against her efforts to keep up with the younger generation. Mary, who "simply [could not] feel aged,"[9] never wanted to miss a thing her young friends were involved in—including staying out dancing until 3:00 a.m.!

Mary's ties with young adults intimately connected her with the unfolding of the First World War. Local enlistment rates were high; Sid Unwin and Mary's nephew Eric were both among the recruits. Though her husband was not well, he was prepared for the possibility that older men might be called to fight. Mary's personal attachment to many of Banff's soldiers, her fondness for the British Empire and her belief that victory would bring a just and democratic world prevailed over Quaker pacifism.

Her strong support for the British war effort provoked tension with some of her peers. Tom Wilson, with characteristic contrariness, offended her by siding with the Germans. Dr. Nolan of the Philadelphia Academy of Natural Sciences drew her ire by stating that England might benefit from a few centuries of German rule. More significantly, her nephew Paul's lack of sympathy for the war effort intensified the rift that had developed between Mary and his father (her brother Fred) over their differing approaches to Herman's financial woes.

Herman's son Eric, on the other hand, was keen to devote himself to the cause. Mary and Eric were extremely close. When he was two weeks old his mother had told Mary, "He is half yours as you have none."[10] The family stayed with Mary during the summer of 1912 until Mary arranged work for Herman in Calgary. After the move, Eric took advantage of his family's proximity to Banff to visit often. When he declared his intention to enlist, his parents begged Mary to thwart his intentions by sending him to a private school in Pennsylvania. But she could not bring herself to deny the wishes of her favourite nephew—or to come up with the tuition money.

Eric was well respected as a soldier, rising quickly through the ranks. Mary, who sometimes worried she had spoiled him by playing the role of the wealthy aunt, found that in a few short months the war had completely transformed him "into a loving, thoughtful man."[11] He was the only officer in his company not wounded at Ypres, but his luck ran out at the Battle of the Somme. On September 15, 1916, he fell. Sid Unwin searched three days for his body, but to no avail. A mere three months later, he too was fatally injured.

Both of these losses deeply affected Mary. Eric had meant so much to her that a fellow lieutenant with whom she had been corresponding regularly could not bear to write her after Eric's untimely death. And Sid Unwin had been far more than a guide; he was a dear, dear friend. Mary's determination to commemorate and validate their immense sacrifice intensified her own war efforts.

From the war's outset, she had been sending letters, North American reading material and three pairs of socks a week to the men overseas. As time went on, she turned her attention to comforting wounded soldiers. She sent books to start a library at the Frank Sanatorium for returned soldiers and developed a lantern slide show, "In the Heart of the Canadian Rockies with Horse and Camera," for presentation in British hospitals. The emotive power of Mary's slides was such that one young man wrote: "I had a splendid night last night. Was wheeled into the assembly hall of the hospital and there were the photos of Banff; it was dark enough that the other fellows did not see the tears. It made me pretty homesick, but I am getting along alright and will soon be back."[12]

The American attitude towards the war also goaded Mary to resume her role as an activist. Though initially pleased with American neutrality, she later declared: "I have seen too many of my friends here go off to be slaughtered by those beasts to care to call myself neutral."[13] In April and October of 1916 she wrote to the editor of the *New York Times*, encouraging American involvement. In 1918 she devoted four months to travelling across North America presenting fundraising lectures in Canadian Clubs and cheering returned soldiers with her stories and slides.

Mary also continued her war work in Banff, both independently and through the Imperial Order of the Daughters of the Empire. Her involvement with the IODE had begun on February 5, 1915, when she opened their meeting with a description of Reverend Rundle's missionary work among the Stoneys. In October 1918, her name was suggested as a potential member. Five months passed before she was elected and another before she was enrolled as a member. But once admitted, Mary contributed to the organization with the same determination and resolve that characterized her alpine activity.

Her priority, given her losses, was the creation of a memorial for Banff's war dead. When opposition to the project mounted, Mary summoned forth the ruse she and Mollie had used in 1906 to keep their trailmates from shortening their last trip of the season. She slyly proposed a motion that would keep the current president, who supported the monument, in power until it was complete. The 10-foot-high Rundlestone and marble monument still stands in front of the Legion on Banff Avenue, just as the stained glass window she and Caroline Sharpless donated in Sid Unwin's memory continues to adorn St. George's-in-the-Pines Anglican Church.

Memorial window. Courtesy Whyte Museum, V25 PA-14.

The bleakness of the war years had a profound impact on Mary's faith. "Death is before us, behind us, above us," she explained. "Not a day but it stalks into some home here, word from the front, and such cruel deaths."[14] The shock of Eric's death led her to chastise her friend George Vaux for continuing to adhere to Quaker pacifism. "There is no such thing as neutrality any more," she wrote; "there is

Mary Schäffer Warren in Quaker costume. Courtesy Whyte Museum, NA 66-1240.

no religion that warrants sitting down and saying they do not believe in war."[15] She found her "whole religious attitude ... changed"[16] by the war's end. "Heaven is nearer, our dear boys closer," she wrote. "It's unexplainable. I hate the Hun and I've no desire to 'love my enemy.'"[17] Even at war's end, she could not bring herself to celebrate New Year's. Saddened by the losses caused by war and influenza, she simply stayed home that night and reflected on the kindness of old friends.

Mary was also affected by the poor investment climate during the war. She and William were careful to economize, putting any extra money into Victory bonds. Her garden, which had been her pride and joy since 1913, consisted entirely of vegetables by 1919. Their caution paid off, and the Warrens found themselves in a solid financial position at war's end. The Cascade Garage surpassed all expectations over the summer of 1919; the following winter Ford officials asked William to build another west of Banff.

Meanwhile, Mary was becoming increasingly involved in the many volunteer organizations around which life in small Alberta towns revolved. She had supported the St. George's Anglican Church building fund in 1913 by describing her discovery of Maligne Lake to "a keenly appreciative audience"[18] at the Banff Springs Hotel. After the war she participated in more conventional fundraising activities, such as organizing the souvenir booth at one of St. George's annual bazaars. There being no Quaker meeting in town, Mary seems to have aligned herself with the Anglicans, Banff's social equivalent to the Quakers in Philadelphia.

Mostly, however, she continued to dedicate her efforts to the Imperial Order of the Daughters of the Empire. She frequently hosted meetings in her home and served on various committees, from cemetery maintenance to liaison with the Great War Veterans Association to coordinating refreshments and decorations at fundraising events. She was also thrilled to acquire the Reverend Dr. Robert Rundle's diary for the chapter which bore his name. In 1924 she was elected first vice-regent; the following year she was acclaimed second vice-regent. In 1926 she was elected regent but, perhaps owing to failing health, did not accept the office.

The IODE also offered Mary the opportunity to resume her role as Rocky Mountain publicist. When a group of British women visited western Canada in 1927 under the auspices of the IODE, Mary was selected as guide. She escorted the group to the mining village of Canmore, then treated them to tea at Tarry-a-While. Her hospitality and enthusiasm for history did not pass unnoticed. Her guests, particularly impressed by her tales of the old west and collection of Native artifacts, found her a "charming and versatile hostess."[19]

They were not alone in their esteem for Mary Schäffer Warren, whose celebrity followed her into her "retirement." Strangers continued to arrive on her doorstep eager "to 'see the woman who writes.'"[20] Others wrote her praising the beauty of Maligne Lake and expressing their pleasure that it was a woman who had discovered it and named its features. Avid mountaineers like Mary Jobe and fellow Philadelphian Lillian Gest visited her home, as did suffragist and writer Nellie McClung. Mary's unconventional travels were an inspiration to others eager to challenge the boundaries of conventional femininity.

Various organizations also acknowledged Mary's remarkable achievements. The Alpine Club of Canada deemed the combination of her exploratory activities at the headwaters of the Saskatchewan River and her botanical studies as grounds for acceptance as an original member. The National Geographical Society, the Royal Geographical Society, the Philadelphia Academy of Natural Sciences, the Association for the Advancement of Science and the Calgary Natural History Society all appreciated her involvement. When the Trail Riders of the Canadian Rockies were established in 1924, they selected Mary as a charter member. Her years of riding experience, dedication to sharing the glories of the Rockies, and keen interest in the area's history made her an obvious choice.

It seems the Trail Riders did not realize just how obvious their choice was. At their inaugural meeting they presented Mary with a button recognizing only 200 miles of horse travel in the Rockies. Shocked, Mary informed them of the true extent of her travels; her button was duly replaced with one for over 2500 miles, and the potential rift repaired. How embarrassed the committee must have been to have slighted one of Banff's prominent "old timers"!

Both Mary and William were included in this category; whenever a tribute was organized, they were in some way involved. Mary was among those who poured tea at the Golden Wedding Anniversary of Dr. Harry Brett of the famous Brett Sanatorium. Later, she and William presented flowers at his funeral. They were involved in birthday celebrations for Tom Wilson and pioneer rancher Andrew Sibbald, and when the Trail Riders of the Canadian Rockies unveiled a monument to Tom Wilson in 1937, Mary was chosen to open the ceremonies. Unfortunately, illness kept her from the ceremony, and she had to perform her role through a letter read by her friend Lt. Col. Phil Moore.

The Warrens were also on virtually every list of donors published in the *Banff Crag and Canyon*. The recipients of their benevolence include the IODE's monument fund, Banff's Amateur Athletic Association, the Great War Veterans, the Banff Curling Club, the Canadian Patriotic Fund, the Banff Winter Carnival, the Banff school, the Ski Club, the Fire Brigade, the Wolf Cubs, Banff's Indian Days and the community Christmas tree. Mary's generosity was such that when she won a handmade lace yoke in a Red Cross draw, she simply turned it over to be raffled off again, this time for the Prisoners of War Fund.

Like Mary, William was extremely active in Banff life. In what free time managing his various businesses left him, he played in community sporting events, was a member of both the Banff Lodge of the Protective and Benevolent Order of Elks and the Banff Chapter of the Royal Arch Masons, and for a time was president of the local Conservative organization. The organizations were different from the ones to which Charles Schäffer had belonged, but Mary once again found herself the wife of a local elite.

This position kept her busy with numerous social engagements. Besides her card parties with the local youth, Mary hosted and attended a great number of teas and balls. Banff visitors, including Prime Minister R. B. Bennett and his sister, could frequently be found lodged in her home. But as Mary grew older, she tired of all but a few visitors. Bennett, of course, was always welcome, as were her brothers' families and mountaineer Lillian Gest, who remained a kindred spirit, but Mary stopped answering calls from others. She found Banff tourists expected too much in the way of hospitality and announced, "I simply refuse to be bored at this stage of the game by people who want to tell me all their woes."[20] After decades of promoting tourism in the Rockies through her writing, lectures and hospitality, Mary Warren was ready to enjoy her home in peace.

Ever the Traveller

AS HAPPILY AS MARY SCHÄFFER SETTLED into Banff life, her wander-lust continued to push her beyond the town. She had high hopes of spending the summer of 1912 travelling down the Mackenzie River, but her inability to find a companion who could pay her own way kept her closer to home. The days of her major expeditions were over. Nevertheless, she continued to visit the alpine country that had been charming her for two and a half decades. She was as determined as ever to take full advantage of her new home's glorious setting and to share its beauty with others.

Her gift for drawing visitors to her alpine playground was recognized by officials in the town of Revelstoke, who invited her to the sod breaking of a new aerial road (part of today's Meadows in the Sky Parkway) on August 21, 1912. The promise of a little extra money combined with her curiosity "to see for myself a rapidly growing city, a city which I had known so well in its babyhood"[1] to draw her westward. Mary found the town markedly changed. Automobiles and a sternwheeler sped her to places previously only accessible by canoe, foot and horse. But Mary remained unimpressed: she preferred travelling the old-fashioned trails, seeing "it all as nearly as Nature had made it."[2]

Even the allegedly crude trails were much better kept than any Mary had ever been over. But the area was not so tame as to preclude any possibility for adventure. Mary awoke on the second morning of a two-day trip to Eva Lake to discover that all but one horse had strayed away overnight. Her memory flashed back to her and Charles Schäffer's first visit to the Big Bend, when a practical joker had set their horses free. Then she remembered the strain she and Mollie Adams had repeatedly suffered chasing stray horses on their wilderness expeditions.

Prepared as she was to help track down the missing horses, Mary was reluctant to miss seeing Eva Lake. One of her trailmates suggested she carry on alone, but Mary's longstanding fear of bears flared up. It seemed she was not to see the lake after all, until the master of the one remaining pony offered to accompany her by foot as she rode his Dolly. Mary was well aware that Dolly had bucked a woman off the previous week, but her fear of bears now far exceeded her timidity with horses. She much preferred to ride Dolly than to walk the five miles alone.

For three miles, Mary, Dolly and her former rider peacefully travelled along the trail. Then a flurry of movement caught their attention. The missing horses! The search party had headed out in the wrong direction; Mary and her companion had unwittingly located the strays. The gentleman had little choice but to drive the horses back to camp. If Mary still wanted to see the lake she would have to walk the trail alone.

Her solitude proved to be a mixed blessing. Never having travelled alone in all her years of Rocky Mountain adventures, Mary was preoccupied by the danger of her situation. She could not help dwelling on the possibility of encountering a bear without any sort of gun for protection. At the same time, nothing could be quite so glorious as gazing, completely alone, into the depths of a picturesque mountain lake. In hindsight, Mary realized "that of all the lovely mental pictures [she had] stored away of Revelstoke and her surroundings, that mile and a half alone, hand in hand with Nature and her little folk, [was] the prettiest one."[3]

Much to Mary's chagrin, she found the line-up of people eager to visit her in Banff kept her confined to the house more often than she would have liked. During the summer of 1912 she was so tired from doing her own housework she even declined Mary Vaux's invitation to camp. Still, Mary was able to do some riding, and was thrilled to be able to introduce a young cousin to trail life during the summer of 1913.

After her 1915 marriage, Mary continued to tour the Banff area. Sometimes William joined her. Sometimes, when he was busy, she went with friends. Occasionally these trips involved forays into the backcountry but mostly, particularly as Mary grew older, they consisted of short car trips to Calgary, Canmore and various parts of Banff and Glacier national parks.

She and William also began to travel farther afield. After their extended honeymoon along the Pacific coast, they regularly travelled to central Canada and the northeastern United States. They visited El Salvador, where, as had long been Mary's custom, they befriended some Natives. In 1924, they began a series of annual winter trips down the Pacific coast; in 1936 they extended the voyage with a cruise to the West Indies. The following year they ventured into Mexico.

Most of these tropical vacations were primarily for William's pleasure. Mary made little reference in her letters to photography or to indigenous peoples, and her only mention of botany was the comment that she dared not ask William to allow her to traipse up a Jamaican hill to collect some rare flowers. Moreover, Mary found the tropical climate particularly hard on her health. She complained: "I am far from in love with any hot climate whatever and being forced, owing to a boat connection, we were planted in Kingston, Jamaica, for five intolerably long weeks."[4] Although she did enjoy the boat and the fine

Nibs and his mistress. Courtesy Whyte Museum, V14 AC55-PD18.

food its staff served, she threatened to "walk out with a divorce and demand alimony"[5] if her husband ever dragged her to the tropics again.

The ambience of their destinations was often no more pleasing to Mary than their climate. Hollywood reminded her of a delightful-looking apple with a fat worm eating away at its core. She got the impression it was "a *rotten* place, no home life, no real love, nothing but disgusting living in the main."[6] She found its richness oppressive and felt the place lacked refinement and respectability. When she and William arrived in Beverly Hills, Mary simply could not bring herself to locate her friends and attempt to incorporate herself into Californian high society.

While she enjoyed some parts of the vacations, the negative tended to overshadow the positive. The old Spanish architecture of San Antonio was pleasant, but "both Los A[ngeles] and San Diego seemed to be largely made up of mediocre bungalows, all flattened against each other and if anyone popped out of the many doors, he would look 90 and ready for the grave."[7] William enjoyed El Paso, but Mary despised it. She complained, "The hotels are grubby, to put it mildly. Mexican maids are anything but agreeable, our room was small and sordid, food excellent, the lounge big and comfortable but a raucous radio going night and day."[8]

In Jamaica she was impressed with the beautiful cathedral in the centre of Spanish Town, but complained that the town itself had "gone completely native and that is saying the worst one can think of."[9] The thatched houses seemed altogether too dirty for her, as did the abundance of animals in the road. She warned others not to "expect a thing of Montego Bay. As a friend described the beach, 'it can be covered by a postage stamp.'"[10] She also felt intimidated by some of the locals. She recommended that "no lady go alone to Dr.s cave or C[a]sa Blanca"[11] and commented, "You have to watch the native or he will have your eye teeth before you are in that island a day."[12]

At times, Mary's fellow travellers only added to her discomfort. On the ship to Jamaica, she found one had to be a bridge player or a drinker to fit in, neither of which she was. But she did take a fancy to one young doctor, and found the antics of an eccentric Danish baroness entertaining. She explained that the woman "marched to an 8 o'clock breakfast without even combing her hair, her panties all awry and her slippers all down at heel. At night she regaled us with astonishing evening clothes, new ones each evening, and not another soul responded. She was really a mess all morning and an apology all afternoon. At night she was a veritable fright."[13]

The homeward journey aboard the M/S *Canada* was even less pleasant. Finding their boat "alive with a bunch of yelling, shouting gutter[a]l Danes male, female and infantile,"[14] the Warrens spent the first leg of the journey hoping some English speakers would board in Los Angeles.

But more disturbing than the Danes were the snobbish Britons they encountered: "English folk who impress any American, Canadian, or any sort of nationality that they are a superior race, the only folk who speak PURE English."[15] Snobbery was one attitude for which Mary had very little tolerance.

She had struggled so long to escape its trappings that she grew to loathe those whose lives revolved around social status. She took to duping people by dressing in outmoded clothing, then—if they deigned to speak to her—revealing that they travelled in the same circles. Many a time had she been humbled by such a revelation on her western travels, and it was now time to turn the tables. But even the satisfaction thus gained did not make up for the misery Mary suffered on most of these trips.

Mary Warren's accounts of her winter travels suggest she would have been better off staying home in Banff. Victoria, the one place she longed to visit, was out of bounds. The climate was not hot enough for William, and Mary knew visiting her friends there would bore him. Even if she were to attend the social gatherings alone, she would have to listen to William's complaints about how burdensome it had been to stay in the hotel alone in her absence. Unable to untangle this dilemma, she resisted pressing the issue. She gave up suggesting they stop on Vancouver Island and never followed through on her plans to make the trip alone.

Even travelling through the Rockies was becoming a strain. Mary became quite particular about her accommodation, advising her friends to stay away from Canadian Pacific hotels as the company's employees were mistreating loyal customers and catering "to nothing but exaggerated MONEY."[16] She was offended enough to proclaim, "The C.P.R. is no longer an old friend of mine, they do such silly things, work against themselves, employ some abominable people and are generally slipping down hill."[17]

She was also becoming exasperated that the women she travelled with all had "different times, hotels and ideas and what is more, never a one of them has ever asked me to share their cars. The one who is most insistent, has two cars which she can use almost any time and tho I have known her a[t] least 15 years, she never offers to take me on any of her jaunts. She does not hesitate to ask for a trip to Columbia valley, even to the coast and tho she has so many nice qualities, she always hangs back when it comes to paying the hotel bills."[18]

Such inconsideration was becoming insupportable. For a time, Mary suffered in silence, realizing the alternatives were not much brighter. Travelling with only a chauffeur was dull, and her maids always got carsick or bored if she brought them along. But she could only keep this up for just so long. Mary was too old to let other people keep her from enjoying the mountain scenery so soothing to her soul. In the end she decided to travel alone with her chauffeur.

Mary's age and ill health were taking their toll on her spirit. After decades of pushing herself to try new things, to broaden her horizons and to push aside the class prejudices she had grown up with, Mary was hardening. In her seventies, she was more inclined to settle down with the familiar than to stretch the bounds of her comfort. She would travel the Rockies as she wished. And though she grudgingly continued to accompany William on his annual southward journeys, she was almost relieved when ever-worsening health forced them to abandon travel altogether in the spring of 1938.

Opinions, Opinions!

A WOMAN BOLD ENOUGH to venture into Aboriginal villages searching for a sympathetic soul, determined enough to travel through the mountains like a man, brave enough to conduct a highly publicized survey of Maligne Lake without any previous experience and zealous enough to wholeheartedly devote herself to drawing others to her cherished mountains was bound to be opinionated. And opinionated Mary Schäffer Warren was. Some of her views changed over time; others were resolute. Most were complex and even apparently contradictory. All provide invaluable insight into her character.

Mary's various responses to Native people are a strong case in point. Her sympathy and admiration for them are well documented. Her early trips to the American west taught her that "there is great affection in the hearts of the Indians if one finds the key."[1] This fascination with Natives persisted well into adulthood, nurtured by Mary's love for the Canadian Rockies, home to the Stoney people.

Mary considered the Stoneys almost a part of the wilderness she so loved, free from the societal constraints against which she struggled. She considered their chant "as wild as the race from which it sprung. There is the cry of the wild animal in it, the roar of the rivers, a song written by Nature herself for her people and none other could sing it."[2] She admired the Stoneys as experts on how to survive—and pleasurably at that—without all the encumbrances of urban life. She found they kept themselves "a part of the whole [whereas] the white man, with his tin-cans and forest-fires, desecrates as he goes."[3] The Stoneys, she believed, could teach her own people much about ecologically sensitive wilderness travel.

Perhaps if this teaching had taken place, colonialism would not have damaged North American indigenous peoples to the extent it did. Mary knew the Natives she saw were living but a shadow of their peoples' former existence. She was disgusted and saddened by how cruelly Euro-American settlers continued to erode the dignity of the indigenous people she saw on her travels through the southwestern United States. Though the Stoneys' plight was less dramatic, Mary knew that they, too, had lost much. In one of her lantern slide shows, she explained they "still return year by year to their old hunting grounds, but under vastly different conditions. Today their costumes are still brilliant with imported beads, the buckskin of former years is almost gone. There are no buffalo hide tepees, few soft skin garments, just gay prints, cheap ribbons, and until recently a very poor type of blanket. The glamour of the Aborigene is departing. He feels it. Where he once stepped a proud, free man, the wild creatures of the hills his for the hunting, he comes now as a ward of the government. The old men of the tribes pass on to the younger generation the stories of the glory of the past. It is tragedy at our door."[4]

Images of pre-contact life fired up Mary's imagination. She described an abandoned campsite as "a little theatre whose walls were of spruces"[5] where "the stage had at one time been set for an Indian hunting-party. There stood the tepee-poles as the actors had used them last—five lodges. But the grass waved there untrod, moss covered the long-deserted fireplaces, and probably many of those who had last played their part there had gone to the Great Theatre of all. Goat and sheep bones, bleached by many summers' suns, lay strewn about, a little circle of symmetrical pebbles (a favourite plaything of the forest child) told of the sometime presence of children, and a crudely fashioned horse lay on a crumbling log. It was all such a pathetic story, such a bit of the savage life before the days of reservations, when whole families took to the trail for the fall hunt, the bucks to bring down the game, the squaws to skin the animals and smoke the meat; the children to play at the life which for their elders held such little joy. Yes, a deserted stage, the actors gone and for many of them 'lights out.'"[6]

Evidently, Mary's ideas of Natives strayed into romanticism and stereotyping. She passed from extreme to extreme, sometimes idealizing pre-contact Native life, sometimes uncritically reflecting her society's condescension toward indigenous cultures. In spite of her insistence that Natives "were just human like herself with warm affections if only her own people would take the trouble to study them,"[7] she declared: "After all, Indians are only tall children."[8] She was scornful of their fear of nighttime spirits and made such remarks as "it looked too much like work to be of Indian manufacture"[9] and one would "almost aspire to be a ward of the government—a Stoney Indian—and idle away his life among the hill flowers and beside the Bow river."[10] In *Old Indian Trails* she mused, "I often wonder when passing an Indian camp-ground, be it ancient or modern, if ever for an instant the natural beauty of a location consciously appeals to them."[11] Later, referring to mountain goats and other game, she "could not help wondering a little if it had been given these children of the hills to feel some of this great beauty about them."[12]

It is not surprising Mary Schäffer should have held such contradictory views. Cousin Jim's horrible story of the orphaned Native baby clinging to its dead mother certainly contributed to her sympathy for indigenous peoples, as did the Quaker sensitivity to their plight. But most Canadians and Americans looked down upon Natives, and even Quakers tried to force their values upon them. They encouraged Aboriginals to adopt a sedentary agrarian lifestyle and urged them to bring their gender-based division of labour more in line with the American standard.

The idea that the dominant way was best was so pervasive that in 1907 even Mary set out to "convert" Silas Abraham on the Kootenay Plains. The attempt did not proceed quite as hoped. As Mary explained: "The time seemed ripe for some missionary work which was perceptibly needed along more lines than one, and every one else had stopped to listen. 'Now, Silas,' I said impressively, 'you should be like the white men, you should do the work for your squaw. We do not put up our tepees or pack our horses or cut the wood, our men do that.' Taking his pipe from his mouth and inspecting me from head to foot leisurely, he said, 'You lazy!'"[13] Whether or not Mary accepted Silas's cultural criticism, her attempt to impose her values on him was cut very short!

Mary Schäffer was caught in a difficult position. She was aware that the indigenous peoples of North America had been wronged, but knew history could not be undone. She was disturbed that mass immigration from the east had destroyed the traditional Aboriginal lifestyle, but could also see the practical advantages of teaching Natives to communicate with their new neighbours and to survive in the culture that had been imposed upon them. She sympathized with the Natives' plight, but the closest she appears to have come to lobbying for their rights was to connect the secretary of the American Indian Commission with a member of the McDougall family of missionaries—who gave them details "that the [Indian] Agents either did not know or were too lazy to give."[14]

She also defended Aboriginal peoples in her writing. She frequently emphasized that they, too, were human, that their babies cry "just like white folks'"[15] and that their New Year's celebration was "a very good lesson in politeness and self-restraint to their higher cultured brothers and sisters who pretty universally are under the impression they are made from more superior clay."[16] She criticized those who called Natives sullen and stupid and declared that so far as she could tell, their alleged "superstitious dread of photography"[17] was "simply a matter of fair trade."[18] She collected and preserved a wide variety of Native artifacts, pointed out that pemmican was originally a Native dish—not an invention of Arctic explorers—and adamantly defended the value of their ponies.

Although she could not completely escape stereotyping, she tried not to judge from afar, but entered right into villages and even personal homes. Presumptuous and rude as her intrusions may have been, they reveal a strong desire to learn about the people and their culture firsthand. Mary and Mollie Adams even went so far in their identification with Native women as to refer to themselves as "white squaws."[19] They communicated with the

Stoney women "with smiles and signs"[20] and spent at least one delightful afternoon taking photos while, "with musical laughter and little giggles, [the Native women] allowed themselves to be hauled about and pushed and posed in a fashion to turn an artist green with envy."[21] Mary Schäffer's personal relationships with Natives distinguish her photographs from the standard portraits taken by white photographers.

Still, Mary's experience of Native culture was not all rosy. She found the Stoneys dirty and complained that the Native hunter "cleans out as he goes, and is consequently a most destructive hunter."[22] Sometimes, she felt taken advantage of, claiming: "There is a too great friendliness about [them] which breeds a love of distance"[23] and labelling their dogs a bunch of "consummate thieves."[24] Though these judgments may not have been entirely fair, it is important to note they arose from Mary's personal experiences, and did not merely echo popular prejudice.

In fact, Mary's criticism of the European immigrants she encountered in 1911 was far more prejudiced. Her upbringing in a literate, highly refined Anglo society led her to complain that the train between Edson and Hinton was only "for carrying the flotsam and jetsam which pour always into a newly opening country."[25] The immigrants' dirty appearance upset Mary even more than the Natives', perhaps because she was confined in a small car with them and did not know where they had been or what diseases they might have come into contact with. Even in the wilderness, she was quick to censure those who did not appear to conform to the standards of her class.

This judgment was somewhat ironic. Mary was condemning others for violating the standards of a society from which she herself had deviated. In her heart she knew her judgments were often unfair, a feeling that was confirmed when she delved beneath the surface. In 1911, for example, she quickly realized that voices in frontier towns "are lower and actions more respectful than one may expect in the streets of our culture-proud cities."[26] She and her companions were even more impressed to discover that some of the residents of Hinton "could almost have given [them their] family history for two generations back."[27] Humbled by her mistakes, Mary advised others to think twice before jumping to conclusions about western pioneers. When her cousin, Struthers Burt, published an article reinforcing stereotypes about life in the Wild West, she spewed out an angry rebuttal insisting that "solitude breeds refinement"[28] and that articles like his were responsible for creating the false expectations and prejudice that had initially blinded her to the reality of the west.

Her instinctual prejudice subdued, Mary developed deep respect for people who had given up everything to carve a new home for themselves out of the wilderness. Having herself suffered the loss of her husband, parents and best friend, Mary knew how traumatic starting anew could be. She was also well aware of the difficulties that could arise when travelling through the mountains for fun—let alone when venturing to a homestead with all one's possessions. Faced with the pathetic sight of weary pioneers trudging along her 1911 route to Maligne Lake, she "longed to call after them to 'stop and have a cup of tea,' but knew if [she] gave tea to every deserving way-farer that passed [them, her] family would go thirsty in a week."[29] Passing a "weary, discouraged and hopeless"[30]-looking woman, she "longed to say something which would raise the cloud from a face that was once pretty, but there seemed nothing adequate to the occasion. Nodding to her, I called out, 'I wish I could take you with me on my fresh little pony over this stony hill.' The driven face lit into one of almost beauty, and she shyly said, 'O thank you for that kind thought.' Then closing the window of brightness as quickly as she had opened it, her head went down. We rode on by, wishing, wishing it might have been in our power to do more than toss her a word."[31]

Material assistance seemed out of the question, but Mary's concern and admiration for pioneer women led her to do what she could to encourage them. She realized these women were often following their husbands into an unfamiliar land against their will, and that their new lives would involve a great deal of "hardship, poverty, loyalty [and] wordless misery."[32] She hated the way "the world goes on singing the praises of the pioneer, the 'man who opens the door'"[33] without acknowledging his wife's enormous contributions. Her own view was that "since our ancestors first touched this continent ... it has been the women who were the true pioneers, the women who suffered. One of the vastest continents of the world has been meekly and silently conquered by women and, even at this late date, few men know it."[34]

In response to "The Man in the Shack," a poem printed in Canada West Monthly praising the virtues of male pioneers, Mary composed the follow-ing elegy to their female companions:

She is brave, she is true, as the day it is long,
Her work is as endless as that of the song
The tried heart repeats to keep courage alight,
Till she lays down her task with the coming of night,
For she stands by the man who has builded the shack—
His comrade, the woman who never looks back.

At the coming of dawn she is there by his side—
A smile, a good word, whatever betide,
Though her toils are all humble, obscure or unseen,
She yet is his guiding star—quiet, serene.
In courage and patience she never shows lack—
His comrade, the woman who never looks back.

We speak of the *man* who has opened the door
Of the great teeming West, who has brought to the fore
The wealth of the prairies—so vast and so wide,
But how many think of the one at his side,
The one who has made him a *home* in the shack—
His comrade, the woman who never looks back?[35]

Strong as Mary's admiration for these hard-working settlers was, she was not pleased when they began to unite to improve their lot in life. A devoted adherent to the Protestant work ethic, she believed the key to success was individual hard work and determination. She advised her young friends to stay out of debt and to "emerge from a very poetic, idealistic mind and become a very hard boiled egg."[36]

But woe to those who sought to achieve such ends through collective action. Mary's individualism, reinforced by the Quakers' traditional disapproval of labour disputes, led her to describe striking workers as "a spoiled lot, mostly down-trodden foreigners with 'liberty' gone to their heads. Very ignorant and easily led."[37] Convinced as she was that "life is really a poor thing if one does not have to fight for it,"[38] striking was evidently not the type of fight she had in mind.

This contempt extended just as quickly to status-hungry mountain lovers as to militant labour unions. Thirty years after coming head to head with Julia Henshaw over the publication of their botanies, Mary still had not forgiven her for apparently copying Charles Schäffer's work without giving him credit. Even more disturbing was seeing someone earn a fellowship in the Royal Geographical Society by showing Mary's slides as her own. Incensed, Mary withdrew her own membership.

She simply could not understand why other people would go to so much trouble to glorify themselves when her own "explorations were just a matter of having a glorious time wherever [she and her friends] felt the way was new and untrod."[39] She had not racked up first ascents, nor had she chased glory; she had simply wanted to soothe an aching heart, to restore peace and beauty to her life. It pained her to see something so important to her devalued by people undertaking "for personal glory the work of the true enthusiast."[40]

She was particularly upset when others publicized error-laden work. She claimed that though Dan McCowan called himself "the naturalist of the Rockies"[41] and "had slides made as like [hers] as he could ... he [did] not know the meaning of the phrase."[42] Likewise, the apparently false information Lewis Freeman presented in his 1925 National Geographic article describing his travels to the Columbia Icefield disgusted her. She declared him "either a mighty poor trailer or a very imaginative one."[43]

Mary Schäffer Warren had substantial personal knowledge of the Rockies. She kept an extensive library of works pertaining to the history of the area and frequently drew on the knowledge of old timer Tom Wilson. She was also connected with a number of highly respected scientists. Consequently, she was extremely sensitive to sloppiness. Her views may also have been tainted by traces of envy. By the 1930s, age and illness made it impossible for her to travel through the mountains as she once had. In her seventies she was forced to sit back and watch others publish work she would have loved to have undertaken, becoming frustrated when the work did not live up to her own standards of accuracy.

Ironically, one of Mary's strongest grievances was against old-timer Dr. Charles Walcott, secretary of the Smithsonian Institute. Mary's ill feelings toward him were rooted early in the century. She had gathered numerous fossils for Dr. Walcott, only to be told they were useless. Humbly accepting his verdict, she carried on her way until, much to her disgust, Walcott visited the area himself and concluded her specimens had indeed been rare and valuable! Modest as Mary strove to remain, this blatant disrespect for her efforts angered her. In 1937 an unidentified article Mary received aggravated the wound, leading her to proclaim: "I have come to the conclusion that the Institute in Washington is one of the weakest societies in the U.S. It was run pell-mell by Dr. C. Walcott whose blunders were always condoned or not seen by those who provided him the funds to run the place ... When Walcott used to come out here and scatter himself all over the mts. it was astonishing the terrible mistakes he made and how he got the Canadians to pay all his expenses."[44]

Even Walcott's wife, her old friend Mary Vaux, failed to escape Mary's scathing tongue. She insisted Vaux's botany could "be a guide to no one"[45] and exclaimed: "She once said I was her inspiration and I gently said I trusted not as she had made so many mistakes."[46] Evidently some deep hurt—likely related to Mary's impression that the work she and Charles Schäffer had done was not being adequately appreciated, nor their standards maintained—was finding its release in Mary's old age.

Even so, there were numerous people who had secured her unshakeable respect. Among them were British professor and climber Norman J. Collie and his cohort Hugh Stutfield, eminent Scottish geologist Sir Archibald Geikie, and many of Banff's veteran guides and climbers. Mary's attachment to her own guides—particularly Billy Warren and Sid Unwin, who had shown her the "heavenly hills under circumstances such as no one else ever did or could"[47]—did not preclude respect for the competition. Mary conceded their chief rival, Jack Brewster, was "a nice fellow."[48] She referred to Jimmy Simpson as "one of the REAL men of our hills ... clever, a splendid marksman and a marvelous guide"[49] and even called his wife Billie "a wonderful mother"[50]—quite the compliment from one whose unfulfilled maternal desire made her highly critical of others' mothering styles.

Mary also had great loyalty to a frequent Banff visitor who had helped make her own adventures possible: Canadian Prime Minister R.B. Bennett. When Nellie McClung came to visit saying she "was calling on literary people,"[51] Mary Warren humbly replied she "did not know there were any clever people in Banff and very few anywhere."[52] In spite of her concern for pioneer women, her own remarkable achievements and her delight that clothing standards were gradually changing to facilitate women's activity in the mountains, Mary Schäffer was not a suffragist. Her politics proved to be radically different from McClung's; Nellie's scornful enquiry as to why Mary "kept Mr. R.B. Bennett's picture beside a very beautiful mirror"[53] shattered any hope for agreement. Relating the incident to a friend, Mary commented, "Politics or no politics, Mr. B. and I are life-long friends and he is equally fond of my husband. I have great cause to worship him for his goodness to me in the year[s] gone by and his goodness to many more. We all have likes and dislikes and Nellie did not endear herself to me by speaking her own thoughts."[54]

Not only was Bennett a financial advisor and friend, he was also a political hero. William Warren was heavily involved in campaigning for Bennett and his party through the local Conservative organization, and although some Banffites initially feared Bennett would not be enough of a booster, they most heartily supported him during his years in power. When rumours first arose that he was leaving politics, the Banff Crag and Canyon published an editorial praising his successful efforts to bring federal money to Banff and thanking him for his strong representation. A decade later he still had the paper's support. Huge headlines in the 1920s openly encouraged voters to "Vote Early Thursday for R.B. Bennett Vote Early."

Even when the editor of the Banff Crag and Canyon complained Bennett had neglected his constituency in favour of national and Empire affairs in his final term in office, Mary Warren refused to waver in her support. Of course, it was not only Bennett's boosterism she admired. His support for the Empire and desire to escape economic and political domination by the United States were fully in line with her own sentimental attachment to Britain. Likewise, his initial emphasis on hard work and optimism during the Depression reflected her own work ethic. She insisted it was because of his policies that the economy picked up in the late 1930s. When he retired from politics altogether she lamented, "We are losing one of our greatest men. He will come among us as a friend, but never again as a politician. He was so clean and true and honest. I no longer take any interest in politics. They smell to high heaven of graft, etc. Mr. B. has his finger on what has gone on here and elsewhere, but will never use his strength again."[55]

Although Mary did not abandon her interest in politics, she had a hard time finding anything positive to say about Bennett's successor. She despised Mackenzie King—partly out of personal loyalty to Bennett and partly because her values were better represented by Bennett's policies than by King's. She complained that the King government was "turning people out of their homes, poor people who have no money to go anywhere else"[56] and considered his reluctance to declare Canada's support for Britain in the upcoming European war traitorous.

King's close relations with the American president furthered Mary's distrust. She referred to Franklin Delano Roosevelt as a "Mad Hatter ... demanding taxes to assist a large percentage of grouchers who have no desire to work."[57] His methods of alleviating poverty were an affront to her strong work ethic; she felt it was "the lame and the lazy who went for him like an avalanche"[58] and was convinced that many poor Americans were "heartily sick of being watched and cherished, they want[ed] to get back to honest toil and decent cash."[59]

Her criticism of the American people was equally harsh. She had devoted considerable effort to encouraging both Canadians and Americans to enlist in the First World War and reported that, despite their late start, the Americans were wholeheartedly committed. But their boast that the Allies would have lost the war without their contribution profoundly offended her.

Like those of certain alpine travellers, the collective American ego seemed overblown. Mary could hardly believe that "just to have a Canadian car caused [her] to have a sound snubbing"[60] when she travelled through the States in the mid-twenties. After one trip, she wrote a Banff friend, "I hate it, just think theyre fast and smart. After paying taxes on everything we've bought, a man asked me where I came from and I said 'The land of liberty.' That is a strong phrase among the conceited, blatant Americans. They almost tax your purse empty. After *our* calm and respectable bringing-up, the people do not compare favorably."[61]

Whenever anyone referred to Mary as an American—which her accent encouraged them to do—she was highly offended. Her response to an American radio announcer's declaration that the rest of the world was jealous of the United States was, "Funny. I've been thankful I was under the British flag."[62] Even as an American citizen, Mary had always felt more attached to the Crown than to Washington. Her ancestors had emigrated from England in 1644 and ever since had only married other British immigrants. The Sharplesses imitated the British as much as possible, even going so far as to import from England the materials with which to construct their homes. It was only because Quakers frowned upon migration that the family did not move to Canada as United Empire Loyalists. For her part, Mary delighted in hearing the British radio message at Christmas and was involved in the patriotic and imperialistic efforts of the IODE.

Mary Warren's scorn also extended to more local levels of government, most particularly to the premier of Alberta. She completely distrusted William Aberhart, first leader of the province's Social Credit party, whom she declared "as slippery a scoundrel as ever lived"[63] and "one of the worst characters [she] ever saw."[64] She considered his promise "of $25 to those who cannot or do not want to work"[65] an insult to British justice and argued that even Roosevelt was more honourable because "he at least [did] not pretend to put himself in the gosp[e]l class while old Abe holds the bible in one hand and calls anyone who does not favor him all the cuss words he knows."[66]

"So far as I can make out," she declared, "he takes credit for there even being a Heaven on earth or anywhere else. So far as some of us are concerned, he has made our province far more like hell than a haven of rest. Anyone who owns any sense of decency or preservation of private pride, would enjoy seeing him get a good cas[e] of flu or anything that would remove him from the public eye."[67]

Most of the province's bankers and businessmen shared Mary's displeasure with Aberhart's economic policies. The *Banff Crag and Canyon* reported that all anyone could understand of his election promises was that each adult in the province would receive a dividend of $25 a month and that "he has admitted that he has no plan, but if his party is returned to power he promises to engage social credit experts to work it out. Does it not seem foolish to elect a party to power which has made such lavish promises, yet freely admits it does not have a plan?"[68] Mary firmly supported the paper's editor in his assertion that "Alberta needs a man of business ability at the head of the government if we are to again get sound footing."[69]

She would, however, have had to live several more decades to see Alberta's Social Credit party voted out of power. This was hardly possible. When Aberhart was elected premier in 1935, Mary was already 73 years old. As far as her physical condition was concerned, she was well past her prime. Though still keenly interested in the environment, politics and society around her, she was no longer able to be actively involved. The increasing frequency of her complaints suggests she was feeling decidedly out of her element. In many ways, she was a remnant of an old world feeling pushed out by the new.

Legacy of a Mountain Lover

IN HER PRIME, Mary Schäffer Warren was one of the square pegs of a round-holed society, who through unswaying devotion to their unconventional dreams open the door for others to follow. In particular, her dedication helped make accessible many activities once forbidden to women.

The first signs that Mary was to be an influential figure appeared around the time of her major expeditions. A woman who dared venture into the wilderness for months on end could not escape media attention. Confident of public interest in Mary's eccentric exploits, Canadian and eastern American journalists seized the opportunity to make news. Their reports of her travels were complemented by Mary's own storytelling in numerous articles and lantern slide shows encouraging others to follow in her footsteps. Esther Fraser, author of *Wheeler*, claimed that A.O. Wheeler's interest in recreational mountaineering grew in part out of discussions with Mary Schäffer. Other less prominent mountain enthusiasts wrote or visited in hopes of gleaming some fragment of her expertise. For one novelist, the impact of a brief encounter was so profound that she used Mary as a model for her next heroine!

The novel was *Canadian Born*—published in Canada as *Lady Merton, Colonist*. In many respects, Elizabeth, its heroine, does resemble the Mary Schäffer Mary Augusta Ward met in 1908. Elizabeth is a wealthy widow enraptured by the wilderness of the Canadian Rockies. She shares Mary's love of flowers, her "sudden intuitive sympathy"[1] with Native people, her need to be liked by her servants, and her compassion for the immigrants piling into the country. And, like Mary, she feels "there is at the very root of me a kind of savage—a creature that hates fish-knives and finger-glasses and dressing for dinner—the things I have done all my life."[2]

But Mary was not the least bit flattered by the comparison. "Ye gods and little fishes," she exclaimed upon learning that Elizabeth was modelled after her. "I could have died under such an idea. All I could think was that no one would ever think such a thing and I don't believe they did."[3] The sentimental romance did not appeal to her in the least; Elizabeth was not a writer, a painter, a photographer or an explorer; she was simply a beautiful woman who falls in love, gets married and prepares to bear children.

Still, the publication of *Canadian Born* is one indication of the level of interest Mary Schäffer's story generated—at least between her first major expedition in 1907 and the publication of *Old Indian Trails* in 1911. By the time of her second marriage in 1915, Mary Schäffer was falling into the shadows. Not coincidentally, her health began to deteriorate around the same time, preventing her from participating in the type of mountain activity that had brought her into the limelight.

Mary had never been a terribly healthy woman. Letters from Charles Schäffer to Tom Wilson around the turn of the century suggest Mary was frequently ill. She had suffered her first case of neuralgia when she was only four years old, and by age 50 this painful disease of the nerves was the limiting factor for long days on the trail.

During the war years, Mary's nerves were in bad shape. Poor health led her to cancel many of her travel plans the summer of her second marriage. A new treatment back east the following year brought some reprieve, but by 1917 her nerves were so inflamed she travelled to the west coast to see a famous doctor there. Despite her high hopes for the massage therapy she received, she suffered a nervous collapse less than three years later.

Mary's health problems seem only to have intensified as she grew older. Late in March 1924, at the age of 62, she fainted, striking her left eye during the fall. It turned black and blue, and a large blood clot formed on the top of her head. A year and a half later she dislocated her shoulder in another fall and required an operation. During Christmas 1926 she was again admitted to Banff's Brett Hospital, and in the spring of 1930 she was hospitalized in Calgary.

The numerous letters Mary wrote during the final six years of her life reveal she was suffering from some form of illness more often than not. She never completely recovered from a 1933 car accident. A year later she declared: "My broken nerves … are yet the most touchy things I ever came across. I had repeated set-backs and Dr. finally put me in bed for 3 wks, all curtains down, my meals brought in, no talking, not a friend and my husband excluded."[4] This treatment was akin to purgatory. Not only was Mary isolated, but she could only sleep with the help of sedatives and lost thirty-two pounds. Even two years after the accident she was complaining she had "never shaken off the atrocious nerves. They linger on and leave me feeling 'queer.' No way to explain the nasty symptoms."[5] But because she looked well, "Everyone yelp[ed] attitude at [her]"[6] when she complained.

During the summer of 1936, Mary's attention was redirected to severe pains in her foot. None of the doctors she saw were able to make a clear diagnosis or prescribe an effective treatment. At last, the sixth sent her to a dentist who relieved the pain by extracting several teeth. It was a welcome relief, but Mary's improved health did not last long. Soon after the dental work, she suffered three terrible falls. She described the situation as follows: "The old nerves were in fine shape till I walked into my bed-room in the dark, had a maid who was going to clean it and she had every weapon known stacked catterbiased in the doorway. I fell over all she had and to save my skull I threw myself back and nearly broke my spine. (That is No. 1) An osteopath worked on me for three weeks and its still fairly painful. One morning I wanted to speak to our gardener and not knowing the workings of the back step I had a awful fall, including about 15 slivers in my left arm. Well, the pain seemed to ease the right side and I thought it was all right. No. 3 was trying to shut the windows in the morning, when my foot slipped on a rug, down I crashed tumbling over a heavy mahogany chair and crashing into a clothes rack of solid mahogany. I waked the entire house as you can imagine … as my husband is anything but strong he came in and I said it was the furniture. I can assure you my whole body looked like a map of Russia, as well as Germany and other places which are not speaking to each other."[7] Her suspicion that poor eyesight was causing her trouble proved correct. She later found, much to her dismay, that her "left eye [was] practically out of use."[8]

Compounding Mary's troubles was the fact William was extremely ill. Not wishing to worry one another, both kept quiet about the true extent of their illnesses. "My husband is so far from well," Mary revealed to mountaineer Lillian Gest, "that I lie like a perfect invalid till he is well out of the bath-room before I attempt to take my bath with its inumerable bruises on legs, back and anywhere that I can have struck myself."[9] But she also complained that he was "English to the core—all sympathy to anyone else suffering but keeping his own groans to himself."[10]

During the winter of 1937, William finally followed R.B. Bennett's advice and travelled to a heart specialist in Portland, Oregon. Mary was desperately lonely in his absence. The days seemed "long and dreary"[11] to one who felt "life is worth so little without one's husband."[12] But because he refused to discuss his suffering, she resolved to do the same, and when she wrote to him it was "all about teas, etc. and not a moon over the long, lonely nights."[13] In actual fact, she was so unnerved during his absence she ended up sending three Christmas cards to her friend Humphrey Toms! By way of explanation, she confided that her worry had kept her from sleeping, making her "just about crazy."[14] She had "tried to get interested in [her] cards, to have guests, anything to keep a shaky mind from going off, [but still she] never knew four more terrible weeks."[15]

Mary doubted she had the strength to survive another loss. As fate would have it, she never had to find out. Mary passed away of pneumonia in her Banff home on the evening of January 23, 1939. Two days later, Banff's Anglican priest, the Reverend Canon H.T. Montgomery, held a private home service. Six prominent members of the Banff community—Jimmy Simpson, Norman K. Luxton (known as "Mr. Banff"), Banff surveyor and engineer

Claude M. Walker, J. English, Charlie Reid and Charlie McAuley—then carried her coffin for burial in the once-despised Banff cemetery.

Shortly after Mary's passing William moved to Vancouver, where he remained until his death on July 13, 1943. As per his desire, he was cremated and his ashes brought back to Banff to be buried next to Mary. The execution of his will revealed he had left an estate of $165,507 to his sister, Mrs. Rose Warren, of London, England.

During her lifetime, Mary had steadfastly resisted any suggestion of her importance. She informed one correspondent that "the importance you put on my name ... leaves me quite cold except that you have passed on kind words."[16] She insisted she had neither discovered Maligne Lake nor ever claimed to. Neglecting to mention that nearby Mary Lake was named in her honour, she informed people that Mt. Schäffer (near the famous Lake O'Hara) was named only for her husband.

For a time this humble denial of fame seemed accurate. A few laudatory obituaries were published, including the *Banff Crag and Canyon*'s declaration that "in the death of Mrs. Warren Banff loses its greatest friend."[17] Then Mary Schäffer Warren passed into temporary obscurity. The preoccupations of the Second World War overshadowed any interest in the story of a dead explorer.

After peace was declared, Mary's accomplishments resurfaced. In 1948 Dan McCowan mentioned her botanical contributions in his *Hill-Top Tales*. The following year, Mabel B. Williams described her exploratory activity in *Jasper National Park*, with numerous historians following suit throughout the 1950s and '60s.

But it was Elsie Park Gowan, a prominent Alberta playwright, who best succeeded in bringing Mary to the public eye. Gowan was commissioned to write a play celebrating Alberta's history for the province's fiftieth anniversary celebrations in 1955. As the narrator of the resulting musical, *Jasper Story*, explains, large audiences gathered "to remember the men and women who once travelled this valley. Their eyes first saw the beauty of its mountains. Their footsteps made the trails that are the highways of the modern world. The romance and adventure of their lives are part of the building of Canada. This adventure is enacted now by the people of the Jasper community; to-night we tell our pioneer story ... to the travellers of today."[18]

Gowan selected the Jasper area, with its relatively lengthy European history, as the focus of her play. The Overlanders of 1862 set the stage in their quest for gold and were followed by the early tourists and settlers, among whom Mary Schäffer was so prominent. After a song emphasizing the shortage of women on the frontier, Gowan has Mary Schäffer dramatically appear at the Swift homestead. With the help of details from Mary Schäffer's travel writing, Gowan recreates their first encounter. Some of the dialogue, such as Mary's explanation that it was the beauty of the mountains, "the peace and silence of the wilderness,"[19] that brought her so far from the railway, are almost direct quotations. Other aspects of Mary's character, including her interest in the Swift children and her gentle explanation that she had "plenty of dresses, in Philadelphia. But on the trail I like to ride free, without a skirt,"[20] are extrapolated.

The story is also embellished to make it more attractive to audiences of a historical musical. An encounter with a railway developer is worked in, allowing Mary to exclaim: "I know what you'll bring. The hideous march of progress. Crowds of tourists. Empty bottles ... tin cans. I don't want the country spoiled. I love it the way it is now ... the way God made it."[21] Certain statements, like Mary's "Don't let him do it! I hate railways,"[22] become melodramatic.

Like Mary Augusta Ward, Elsie Park Gowan portrays Mary Schäffer as a romantic heroine. She gives Suzette Swift the prophetic power to inform Mary she and Billy Warren would be married in seven years, and when the railway developer complains Mary is simply representing the interests of wealthy tourists, she suggestively replies: "I would live there, like Mrs. Swift ... [THE WOMEN EXCHANGE A LOOK] if anyone asked me to stay."[23] But, unlike Ward, Gowan recognizes Mary as an important part of Alberta's heritage, a daring explorer, a woman ahead of her time.

Since then, Mary Schäffer's contributions to Rocky Mountain history have gained increasing recognition. No longer is there the shortage of reliable information on Mary's life that in 1970 thwarted a would-be biographer. That same year, Parks Canada recognized Mary Schäffer Warren's important contribution to Jasper Park by constructing an interpretive walk describing her exploration of Maligne Lake. A few years later, the Hunt Institute for Botanical Documentation, a research division of Carnegie Mellon University in Pittsburgh, Pennsylvania, honoured her work by incorporating it into their permanent collection. In 1980 the Whyte Museum of the Canadian Rockies reprinted her major writings in a volume entitled *A Hunter of Peace*. Parks Canada began presenting interpretive programs about her and museum curators assembled exhibits. In a time when women participate in all walks of life, one who was bold enough to challenge restrictions formerly placed on women's activities inspires awe. Yahe-Weha, Mountain Woman, Hunter of Peace—all of these names are becoming increasingly well known as mountain lovers learn and share the story of Mary Schäffer Warren.

This new phase of interest has resulted in a second theatrical representation of Mary Schäffer: Sharon Stearns' *Hunter of Peace*. Stearns takes considerable creative licence with Mary's story. She replaces Sid Unwin with fellow guide Bill Peyto, adds Mrs. de la Beach Nichol to the crew and makes Mollie the trip planner who had to convince the others to join her. She portrays the 1907 expedition to the headwaters of the Saskatchewan and the Athabasca as Mary's first trip to the mountains, includes romantic scenes between her and Billy, and has Mollie die on the trip. Nevertheless, Mary's character rings truer than in either of her previous literary incarnations.

Unlike her predecessors, Stearns does not emphasize romance or even history, but rather the development and strengthening of Mary Schäffer's character through her mountain experiences. She captures Mary's early insecurity by having her dead husband haunt her with criticisms of her flower drawings. She depicts Mary's fear of bears, her problems mounting horses and her disastrous first attempts at cooking. But far from making Mary an incompetent fool, she skilfully demonstrates how she regained strength—and then some—after her first husband's death. Her Mary has enough gumption to stand up to Peyto and tell him she is just as capable of a trek through the wilderness as he and to insist they finish the journey after Mollie's death.

Just as important, Stearns conveys in a convincing manner how several spirited women were able to push changing notions of femininity to the limit. She gives a sense of the strong support network that must have existed among these women, enabling them to confront the obstacles that stood between them and their dreams.

Mary Schäffer Warren's dreams bound her inextricably to the Canadian Rockies. She revelled in their splendour while assisting her husband with his botanical work. When his death shattered their happy world, she could think of no better place to ease her sorrows. Free of domestic obligations, she travelled Canada's Rocky Mountains more and more extensively until she, Mollie Adams and their guides were exploring places few non-Natives had ever been before. She explored, she photographed, she surveyed, she wrote, she lobbied for wilderness protection. She moved to Banff and married a mountain guide.

As disgruntled by change as she may have been, as sick and crotchety as she may have become, as far as she may have travelled, Mary Schäffer Warren always remained loyal to her one true love—Canada's Rocky Mountains. Though she left no biological descendants, the number of her spiritual kin is great. All those who are fascinated by the natural beauty of the mountains, whether they delve into the backcountry or just read about it in books, are in some way connected with this great lover of the Rockies.

Mary Schäffer Warren's Previously Unpublished Manuscripts

Author's Note

I wish to thank the Whyte Museum of the Canadian Rockies for allowing readers greater insight into Mary Schäffer Warren's life and character
by granting permission to publish these manuscripts. In selecting which
of Mary's numerous writings to include, I have attempted to reflect the
diversity of her interests and writing styles without duplicating material
that has been published elsewhere. A number of delightful manuscripts
had to be passed over owing to incompletion (at least as preserved in
the archives of the Whyte Museum of the Canadian Rockies). Partly for
this reason, none of her historical writing is included, but my hope is
that the following samples of fiction, botanical/tourism literature and
autobiographical tales will provide intimate knowledge of this remarkable woman's character and style. In transcribing the texts, I have tried
to remain as true to the original manuscripts as possible without straining
readers. I have standardized some punctuation and corrected some errors,
but have left intact most idiosyncrasies of style and spelling.

A Chapter of Accidents

Bill called it the "jack-pot." Looking back over the lapse of years, every detail stands out as prominently as tho. it were but yesterday, but also years have flown and the principal actor has long passed from most men's minds.

Bill said it was pure cussedness, maybe it was, but I have always laid the blame on some outlandish garments that he insisted on carrying on that trip. It was a suit of pink silk underclothes—pale rose pink. If there is any thing I detest it is pink silk in any form or shape, and when I told this to Bill, and said I expected disaster, he pooh-poohed scornfully, told me I was getting old, wished he had two suits, and hoped to die in one like it.

We were starting on a little trip to look out some new trapping-ground for the coming winter, and were sorting over the grub, and putting it into package shape. Bill had made out the list, and, being a connesseur of a good grub-stake, I knew it was unnecessary for me to ask if he had every-thing; but when he spread this suit on a clean pack-mantle and asked my opinion of it, I—well—

"You don't know good things when you see 'em!" he flared back, as he folded the garments carefully and placed them in his dunnage-bag. "Them'll be mighty nice when the weather gets real hot."

Trouble started with us. Bill walked four miles for the horses the morn-ing we started and told them several things they didn't know. Then his best pack-horse "Four-bits" snagged itself; and on the third morning I was bucked off and sprained my wrist. This threw double the work on Bill, but of course he did not mind that, but when his saddle-horse "Billy," in at-tempting to rub off a troublesome horse-fly, caught Bill an upward sweep on the nose with a concha of his bridle, he began to take a worried look. The blow was a hard one, judging from the amount of blood that flowed, and Bill afterward declared that he could see down his nostrils and inspect his back teeth.

Next a porcupine ran into the tent and filled the blankets with quills. Bill's well-trained dog had given us warning that one of these pests was at the saddlery pile, and we had run out with sticks to drive it away. I went back to the tent for the 22, and the porcupine, rushing for the shelter of the trees, had run into the tent, where he lashed right and left with his tail, filling the blankets (specially on Bill's side) like a pincushion full of pins. This kept us up most of the night, and Bill talked repeatedly.

Then followed a complete drenching. A sudden thunderstorm caught us in burnt timber and we simply had to ride it out, during which, a piece of a fallen tree caught in a lash-rope, and the pack-horse, in endeavoring to wrench itself free, tore off the pack.

The next was a day of perfect peace. It was one of those days pleasant to look back upon, and at the time we enjoyed it immensely. We had made a short day, and had camped on the south shore of the Saskatchewan, with the prospects of having to swim it on the morrow. Supper over, we loafed and smoked. Bill sat with his back to the saddlery pile lazily blowing rings of smoke; in the slough below camp, the music of the horse-bells floated up to us, and the splendour of the waning sun lit up the rocky slopes of Mt. Murchison in a glorious light.

Bill's eyes roved occasionally over the grassy slopes of the mountain, then drowsily half closed; he yawned, stretched himself, struck at a mosquito, and rose to his feet; he walked over to the edge of the bank and stood gazing at the muddy torrent below,—crooning melodiously "Bingen on the Rhine." The tune ceased, and he swore softly at a passing goose that his roving eye had discovered flying high down the river. As I joined him, he observed, "I see where we get our fifth ribs wet to-morrow," and later when we sat by the camp-fire, he grew reminiscent, and spoke of various crossings of this river, some of them hazardous, and most painfully unpleasant. Morning dawned clear and hot. Bill arranged the sugar and other perishables so that they would be kept dry, saw that cinches were properly adjusted to allow easy swimming, for the horses, and when all was to his liking, he mounted Billy, gave me final instructions, gazed critically at the far shore, lit his pipe, and urged his saddle-horse in. He had mounted me on his best swimmer, and as the pack-horses followed him, I watched his progress.

He rose and fell like a boat in rough water as Billy felt for bottom with his hind legs—then I had other things to interest me.

The motion of a horse swimming is not unpleasant, and after the first minute I looked around me. I had passed some of the pack-animals and was just above and behind Bill when I noticed him go lower in the water as his horse felt for bottom. He took off his hat and struck Billy over the ears. Billy disappeared. Bill ditto. Suddenly the water parted, and they appeared. At the same time, I noticed some of the pack-horses wading ashore, felt my own horse strike bottom, and realized we were across.

"Ugh! Suffering Pete, aint she cold!" said a voice behind me; then—"A last year's bird's-nest is full of wisdom compared to me. No sir, the horse aint to blame, I should have let him alone."

Bill certainly looked wet, but he had retained his hat and pipe. We rounded up the pack-horses which were endeavoring to roll in the warm sand, and made for the camp-ground a short distance away. Here he spread blankets and everything that had suffered, in the hot sun, while I got a light meal going. This partaken, the disadvantages of the day took on a lesser magnitude.

In a few hours every thing was dry and Bill's good nature much in evidence. After supper he again grew reminiscent, and while in the midst of an entertaining experience, suddenly stopped, and pointing, said,—"What's that!" "A wasp's nest," said I. "Yellow-jacket's nest, hey? Let me show you something."

He picked up his axe, drove it into a standing dry pine, wringing it in

147

such a manner that a large chip flew clear. He split a piece from it, whittled it with his sheath knife leaving the shavings adhearing to the end. Next he picked up a long pole and deftly splitting the thin end he stuck the piece of dry pine in the split and observed "Watch the fun." He lighted the shavings, seized the pole, walked over to the wasps' nest, which was hanging to a dead limb, and held the flame under the hole or opening of the nest, smiling sweetly as he did so. Suddenly he dropped the pole, his head jerked back, bringing his right hand smartly to his face, doubled over backwards. He leaped to his feet and dashed thro. the brush flinging his arms like a wind-mill. "Hell," he roared, "what's happened?" "Don't know, do you?" I replied. "Wisdom's coming mighty quick," said he as he fingered a fast growing lump on the bridge of his nose. "Did one get you?" I asked. "One did more than that," he replied. "Yes, laugh if you want to." I laughed most of the evening while Bill fingered his nose carefully and muttered incessantly and tried to see his reflection in a new tin cup.

Then came a few days of peace. Bill placed me on the lead as he said he could not see over his nose and go straight. It was a glorious day when we climbed to the higher level of the valley, climbed the 10,000 foot of zigzagging trail with never a slip of a pack, and gazed across the mighty canyon to the glacier-clad peaks to the south of us. Once Bill stopped and picked up a stone which he threw at a pack-horse with a "Hike you, there's plenty of scenery at the top."

Several delightful days were spent at the foot of Wilcox Pass where Bill initiated me into the art of securing wild mutton. His knowledge in this was most extensive and his experiences most interesting to listen to.

Once when we were climbing so as to overlook some perpetual ice where rams stay in the hot days to be clear of the flies, I pointed to the magnificent scenery around us and wished I had my sketching outfit with me. Bill grunted and said "I wish we had someone with us who could draw to my liking." Feeling piqued because I fancied he admired my sketches, I asked him what he fancied most. "Corks out of beer bottles," he said, moistening his lips with his tongue, and noting my wistful expression he laughed. Next day we camped in a little bend on the Sun Wapta. Bill said there were big flats below, but he wanted to look up a side creek for future reference. His plan was to keep the horses above us or they would go down to these flats for the goose grass which grew there, and this would occasion a long walk over the gravel flats, and several fordings of the river to get them for the next day. While he was away I kept them above camp, and when he returned his mood was peaceful. During the night our slumber was rudely disturbed. About midnight Bill awakened, yelled, tore the blankets off me, and le[a]pt out into the night. I heard him yell again, heard the sound of hobbled horses, a screach, a curse, a dull thud, and hoof beats going—which way? Hastily pulling on some clothing I ran out, and on rounding a clump of willows, half stifled groans and bad language reached me, and parting the bushes, I discovered Bill clad only in his shirt, and nursing one foot.

Between spasms he tried to explain, but it was not until I had the fire going and he was putting vasaline between his first and second toe, that I could make out what had happened. "Yes sir," he said, "I heard 'em sneakin' by, and was only just in time to head 'em off. I hopped around them bushes and run right into the "Rat." He was on the lead. He stopped and snorted, and I ran at him and yelled, flopped my shirt-tail, stubbed them toes, and flopped into a juniper bush." Lord, I feel as if I'm tattooed all over. Yes, laugh if you want to." In the morning, much to my discredit, I saw Bill take a halter and start after the horses. He had turned them back at the flats, but we could not hear the bell. However as he said they were probably in the timber and it would only take a few minutes to locate. I prepared breakfast, waited, had mine, waited and waited. About noon he returned almost too hoarse to talk. "They were scattered over 1700 acres," he said. "Two-Bits, Four-Bits, and Six-Bits were on top of the pass. The rest were up the left hand creek, and the "Rat" was almost as high as he could get." "Something scared them, you think?" I asked. He grinned. "MEBBEE they saw something in the night," [he said] as he sat down to his breakfast lunch. We started down the river, Bill driving the outfit, I on the lead. He had told me about a small muskeg that it might be wise to go around, but to size it up when we got there, and if not too bad, to go through it. I thought it looked fairly dry in the centre, and went over on foot to inspect it. Three pack-horses started to cross it, and all would have gone well had not one stopped to feed. The others crowded and the thing was done. I saw two stagger, attempt to gain dry ground, plunge forward and fall completely mired, one falling half across the other's neck. Bill yelled something un-intelligible, and wallowed thro. the worst of it to join me.

Together we started to unpack the mired horses, and carried the packs over when a commotion to one side attracted my attention. I saw "Six-Bits" reach for a bunch of grass, flounder, half recover, then sink on his side, completely unable to move. Bill wheeled and his eyes carried an electric shine as he surveyed this new disaster. He took his hat from his head, planted his feet firmly, and fixing his gaze on a passing cloud, prepared to follow his own teachings, when a new thought struck him. He walked over to the fallen animal and lifting the mantle looked at the pack. He buried one arm to the elbow in the black ooze and with a mighty heave, brought to light one end of the submerged side-pack. "Them pink silk things o'mine!" A six jointed adjective next escaped his lips. For my part the whole outfit might have gone right thro. that muskeg to the bottomless pit. I was too happy to care a continental and I expected to feel his fingers on my neck, but nothing happened. Without much bad language we got things straightened out and an hour after pitched camp at Jonas Creek. After every thing was unpacked and the kettle on, Bill got his dunnage bag and dumped the soaked contents on the ground. He spread out his once pink silk garments and regarded them critically, while I watched in silence. "Now would you look!" he said, a strange silence in his voice," if that wouldn't strike you stiff! I'll eat them things beginning right there at that baggy part. If that wouldn't———." But an uncontrollable happiness, which lasted until the coffee boiled over and doused the fire, had seized me, so I did not hear his concluding remarks. What became of them? Well, I asked him that one day a week after as he sweltered in the shade of a spruce, and if a fragment of his wish comes true, they'll decorate the hind quarters of "Six Bits" when he makes his final exit from this world; but as Bill concluded, "Its no use placin' any faith in wishes." To come down to the fine point, I guess they're still reclining at full length at the old campground on Jonas Creek, while old Sol scorches Hell out of 'em."

A Ptarmigan Story

It was a happy little family living in the spruces of a bit of high alpine country in the Rocky Mountains of Canada. A beautiful young cock-bird known as a ptarmigan had left his own people that spring, and flitting further and further up from the warm sunny, snowy valley in which he had wintered—parents, brothers, and sisters forgot—he searched for the mate his heart called for, yet had never seen.

As the hot May suns touched the great fields of snow they melted into thousands of little streams, the flowers hurried out, the young willows put on their new spring dress of tender green leaves, and little Mr. Ptarmigan found plenty to eat. Still following his quest, he ate of the baby willow leaves, of the tender green buds of the trollius, flew up occasionally to the high boughs of the spruces, nibbled off the young needles, and kept his bright eye open for the little wife for whom he was searching.

One warm bright day as he stood poised by one of the thousands of little streams trickling down the mt. side drinking his fill of the snow—[?], he saw a bush quiver, and then—from out among the scarce-covered twigs she stepped—a little lady clad in brown, all softly speckled except the tips of her wings which were snowy white—the little wife for whom he had searched. With no fear in her pretty face she hopped toward him, as he to her, and there with the mountain-stream to sing their wedding-bells, with the heather and lilies to deck their way, and the sun to brighten their path, they were mated. He told her how he had searched for her so long, how lonely he had been, and then he whispered, "Thou art my fair, yet different from what I had been searching. I knew thou wert mine when I saw thee, yet had I thought to find thee in white—in the dress my mother wore." "Sweet-heart," she whispered, "thou hast not seen many summers. Last summer when thou and I were born our mothers wore the brown suit like mine, and when the winter was coming, and I saw my mother's gown grow white, I asked her why. She said, "My dear child, when you are older you will learn we have many enemies. I have sheltered you and your brothers and sisters from all harm so far. The day will come when you must fend for yourselves. He who made us, gave us gowns for the summer wh. wd.

hide us from our enemies, and in the winter, He clothes us in white for the same reason. Foxes, bears, weasels are all our enemies, and many a time your little white dress will stand you in good stead."

I remembered my mother's words, Sweetheart, we will have our enemies, and when winter comes, thou and I will be ready for them. I remember my mother also said she had heard of another enemy, which she had never seen, but her mother's mother had told her, and she had heard of it from her mother, that there was an enemy much worse than the foxes or weasels, for it barked from a long way off, and then the ptarmigan fell dead.

But this is only hearsay, and I think if we watch the wicked ones my mother spoke of, we need not bother our heads about something of which we know nothing.

This is a happy valley—let us be happy in our new home. Where shall we build it?" And the little bride and groom, leaving the stream, jaunted away flying, hopping, twittering in sweet abandon of the morrow. Just below the last line of spruces, they built them a nest, nature in their breasts had told them they would have need of it for the little brood of chicks which would come with the July sunshine, their own hearts called them to the snowline, but snowline is no place even for ptarmigan babies, so in the spruces they must come, and the flight from there to their loved snowy haunts would be a short one for the little wings. One sunny day followed another and the little pair were happy as the days were long—and they were very long in that northern land—they wandered about, calling each other if out of sight a moment, and always returning to the home beneath the dark thick spruce, where even the raindrops could not search them out. One morning as the little wife rose and stretched her dainty wings, she smiled a gentle smile all to herself and said—"I won't tell him yet." But she had no need. As they returned to-gether, his quick little eye peered into the nest, and excitedly he twittered—"Little wife, little wife, here's a brown speckled egg. Did you know it?" How she laughed at him, and fluttered and nestled down on her one precious egg. Did she know it! How like a man! The days went on, two eggs, three eggs, four eggs could be counted in the nest. Then one morning he suggested she should stretch her wings, and "take more exercise." She sat at home too much he said. He was a good husband, but alas, he should have been less thoughtful on that particular day. Flying to a tall spruce, choosing the same bough, they let the wind rock and toss them as it would; with a happy home, with plenty to eat, with the whole world fair before them—what cared they for the future.

Suddenly Mr. Ptarmigan heard a sound he had never heard before—'twas a sharp yell—"Get out of that mud-hole, you Dandy!" then came a distant snapping of brush, a clatter, a regular stampede. "Do you think its a fox my dear?" he whispered. "That's not the way mother described them," replied the bride. We are quite safe here however, let's wait and see." And the two little innocents sat on.

Thro. the brush and the willows and the scrub came the enemy—pandemonium it was to the watchers who had never heard anything worse than a high wind or a mountain-stream; out into the open it swept—this awful noise. No not foxes, but horses, men, women, packs, and worst of all a little boy—with eyes as bright as Mr. Ptarmigan's eyes. "Jack!" He yelled, "what's that!" His eyes had seen the ptarmigan. "O Jack, I could get them, I know I could, you remember how I hit the tin-can better than any one else yesterday.

"Give me the 22 Jack, let me get them." The boy's pleading voice and eyes were too much for Jack. You must remember too, that neither of them knew of the wedding or the little home, or the eggs which would never again be cuddled under a mother's warm breast. Then for the first and last time the little ptarmigan heard the enemy of which the bride's mother's grandmother said she had heard mentioned in the old days. Those were the days when Indians had known and hunted the valley. This was the coming of the white man's rifle.

My Garden

With a charming invitation from your hostess, Mrs. Wright, to meet you on the 28th of April, and tell you something of another garden in another corner of the world than this, I find ill health permits me only the medicine of paper and pen to tell you a little, Oh! so little, of my own garden three thousand miles away. Mine?—by pre-emption. A garden?—because it is flowers, flowers, from lowly valley to sunny hill-top and bleak mountain fastness.

For hundreds of miles stretches this garden of mine, clasped in the snowy embrace of the great white Rockies. I must take you far and fast by train, on foot and with ponies, even then you will miss something.

No gardener tends my treasures, only the spring sunshine, which coaxes them forth, the summer rains which wash their dainty faces, and the deep, deep blankets of snow which cover the seeds, the bulbs, and roots, and cuddles them all close to warm Mother Earth's breast.

The spring in that far north country of the Canadian Rockies, comes with a silent rush of wings about the end of May. With the sweep of the chill March and April winds, the last snow-banks disappear in the open valley of Banff, and forth in thousands spring the rose-violet wind flowers (pulsatilla hirsutissima). All the plains for miles east of Banff are rollicking in this same joyous color, but we must not stop till we reach Banff, 'tis there my garden begins. These exquisite nodding, swaying bits of color are found most numerous in the open flats where the Bow and Spray Rivers join hands and wander east to the open country. By the first of June there is a whisper in the air that the little orchid calypso (cytherea bulbosa) has come. It is the darling of my garden, and all who see it. You must be quick of eye to find it, it is shy, and always nestles deep in the mosses of the spruce and pine forests. A whole mountain is scarce too great a range for the crimson-hooded, yellow-throated calypso. You will find the first specimens in the warm secluded nooks at the base of Sulphur Mountain, but as the June days advance, the little beauty flowers steadily spread toward the summit of the mountain, and daily during that month you may return to the hotel laden with the fragrant blossoms of which no one ever tires.

Before becoming so intensely interested in the Rocky Mountain flora, I remembered once finding some exquisite specimens of gentian (gentiana affinio) on the banks of the Spray River just below Banff Hotel. Remembering their existence when gathering photographs for future work, I sallied forth one sunny day in July to see if perchance they were blooming. Plodding up the bank on the river's right, I heard a sharp yell, and saw a man gesticulating violently as though ordering me back.

Be turned out of my own garden? and by a man? No indeed! I was after gentians and went on. We drew nearer, he still waiving his arms and yelling, but it was my ground before his, and he was welcome to get out, not I, I wanted my flowers. Over logs and bushes we both scrambled nearer each other, and then his words, previously lost in the noise of the chattering Spray, came to me quite distinctly. "You'd better go back! There's a smallpox camp here." Needless to say the gentians went temporarily out of my head, and I retreated with what small dignity I could muster. Two weeks later, hearing that the camp was dispersed, and all materials burned, again the blue gentians lured me. We reached the obnoxious camp with skirts gathered close about us, found we were fully a week too early for the gentian, but in the midst of that former camp of pestilence grew a most perfect bush of trumpet honeysuckle (lonicera ebractulata). They reminded me of my grandmother's garden, and as photographic specimens, not to be passed by. Against all sound judgment we gathered them, then watched developments for several days, but as nothing happened we concluded nature was an excellent disinfectant.

Last year I saw that all sign of the old camp was gone, but the honeysuckle and gentian still bloom for those who search there for them in the month of August.

Once upon a time after a stiff climb to the summit of Sulphur Mountain back of the Banff Hotel about the end of July, I found a dainty plant about three inches tall, with a tiny bunch of cream white flowers, smelling of sweet vernal grass. Tucking them into the band of my cowboy hat to preserve them, I descended to find the poor little jewel of a flower bore the uncompromising name of androsace carinata. After that, I concluded it to be a night alpine flower; and not till arriving at Banff one early day in June, did I see the androsace carpeting the ground near the railroad, and have since found it at most low altitudes throughout the mountains.

Here at Banff, is found also the white cypripedinno passerinum, or moccasin flower and the lovely pink orchio rotundifolia. They are most numerous on the road to the sulphur hot springs.

I remember in the early days of my enthusiasm, searching for the earliest and rare blossoms in a swamp where the overflow from these springs fell.

153

Down on my knees I was reaching through the bog for a blue lobelia almost out of reach. To gain poise I was putting one hand in the damp moss and found on the spot chosen a snake. Porcupines in camp hold no terrors, a wild cat is a treat to behold, a bear brings not a shiver, but a snake alas! is always too much. I arose to flee, minus my new lobelia, and saw possibly twenty snakes in all attitudes wiggles. With a few undignified bounds, I was out of that swamp, and the rarest plant would never call me back again. Since then I have covered thousands of miles but never again came across my enemy, the harmless little water snake. Before we leave Banff I will tell you where to find one of the secret spots of my garden and one of the richest.

Looking north from the station of Banff, one sees on the Stony Squaw (a mountain), what seems a tiny green meadow about two thousand feet about the valley. I followed a deserted trail one day about the end of June, and reached this meadow, to discover treasures un-numbered, and a garden more than worthy the climb. I do not remember all the flowers I found, but that which impressed me most were the beds and beds of low forgetmenots (myosotis). I sunk among them, just they and the bees and the butterflies and I in that brilliant northern sunshine. The wild mountain sheep and goats had strayed here, below I heard the tinkle of a cowbell, a humming-bird flitted here and there, and I and my rare garden were alone, with the great silent Rockies rising round us.

By this time you have but peeped into my garden. Now cross the threshold, and join me at Lake Louise, where the mengeoin lines the drive to the lake, three and one-half miles, where the [word(s) missing] is springing in the swamps. It was here I hurried early one spring (June 1st is very early for Louise), to search for the bloom of the Lyell's Larch, whom even our famous Sargeant did not know existed there till he saw it in a photograph. This larch is only found between Six thousand to Seven thousand five-hundred feet altitude, so that to obtain the bloom which comes with the first warm days of spring, one is apt to have rather uncomfortable snow banks to contend against to reach it. I remember that day how we toiled up, up in the heat, then reaching the melting snow, trudged on and on often knee deep, till the land of the larch was reached. It was plainly visible a long way off by the delicate band of green which encircled the mountain, the first young leaves coming forth. There we stood in its midst, big trees little trees, all about us. A delicious odor permeated the air, and over the boughs I saw the coveted crimson blossoms. It was one thing to see, another to obtain this rare bloom. The finest trees of course bore the finest flowers, but we could not climb. Then we piled up stones at the base of a small tree and reached—no good. Then a brilliant idea struck me. Opening a favorite knife which contained a saw, I tied it firmly to the end of my alpine stock—and—sawed. In a trice I held the rare blossoms in my hand and later photographed them. In the fall in this section of my garden, you may see near the summits of the mountains about Laggan, a golden ribbon, 'tis the larches foretelling the coming of winter.

But follow on; this great garden leads us into the Sebkiok Mountains where many of the plants of forest or open valley are different from the little friends just introduced.

The snow is going, going fast on the open slopes, and even in the distance a glimmer of sunshine which is not sunshine, is seen. We draw closer and suddenly you see it is the snow lily (hronium) of that country. Thousands of the golden blossoms are all about us. I shall never forget my first glimpse of this sight. Sinking down on a mossy bed, I touched, caressed, revelled in their odor, buried my face in their own bright petals, and half hidden among them, lay and watched the butterflies, dragon flies and bees, the little robbers stealing the honey from my great golden preserve. Near me still towered a great snow bank with yellow violets, spring beauties and the first tender of ferns forcing its edge. Up through the great spruce forests to the very tongue of the glacier you will find the Great Gardener of all has strewn the way with [word(s) missing].

[word(s) missing] and perhaps if you are fortunate you will see there is a little deniz[e]n of the hills who loves flowers too. He lives among the rocks toward tree line. We call him the marmot. His whistle of warning to his friends that an enemy is advancing is the long shrill whistle of a school-boy. Find his home, and before the entrance to his cave you will see bunches of fading flowers. It is supposed he dries them for winter use, but I like to think he loves the color as I do myself, and brightens his home with them as do we. But come with me now to another corner of this great garden. This time it must be with ponies. We go from the little station of Laggan with a pack train trailing behind us. Taking the Pipe-stone River trail we are soon on a march of the flowers, for our trail leads gradually up from about four thousand feet to eight thousand five hundred, where we reach the summit of Pipe-stone Pass. It takes us three days and we run the gamut of almost every plant the Rockies possess.

As papers seem long and time is short, I can only mention a few. But you must stop in the lowlands and look for a wee starry gentian. Its tiny blue eye closes with the descending sun, and buried deep in the bush grasses, it is hardly seen even in mid-day unless one searches diligently. But it is when the last steep slopes are being surmounted that I pridefully say "All yours and all mine for the coming!" Arnicas of a dozen varieties herald the carnival of flowers. The great mountains hung with glaciers sweep away on both sides the high valley, we plunge deep into color. Fancy trying to guide a materialistic pony's feet that he may not crush all this splendor beneath his iron shoes, knee deep in the tall forget-me-nots (lithosperiumum), whose blue eyes brush the rider's knee, he cranes his neck and snatches a mouthful of the most perfect crimson castilia or painter's brush you think you ever saw and you long to spank him till you realize it's only cake to him and that there are millions of other clumps of color just as rich and all about you. Up, up we climb in the crisp bracing air. The tall forget-me-nots are replaced by the low carpets of the other varieties. The masses of wild roses and columbines crimson and yellow, are left behind. The rosy moss campion, the alpine saxifrages, the humble [word missing] cover the way. And then we reach the summit. If words could only paint the "looking back." Far to the south are the hoary old monarchs about Laggan, noble peaks still nearer, above us on both sides bold rocky cliffs and sweeping from our feet to the valley far below such a carpet as man could never weave. It is the richest botanical section of which I know, in the many thousands of miles my pony and I have wandered in the blue hills of the Rockies, and some day I hope some of my listeners will share these treasures. One more flight, and we must hurry, for winter comes and then all these little people of the wild sleep the long sleep of the north. Two years ago we left the Laskatchenaw River and crossed to the Athabaska waters in search of a lake which only the Indians knew. They had called it [word(s) missing] (Beaver Lake), and had drawn a quaint map of the lakes, passes and mountains to be traversed to reach it. We were three weeks finding this sheet of water which even the Indians called beautiful.

A week's travelling was old ground to our now seasoned band of explorers, then two weeks we crept steadily on in a country where few white men had ever been, and at last we reached a pass one bright sunny day over which I doubt a white foot ever had passed. Our [word missing] said Seven thousand two hundred feet. Large patches of winter's snow still lay upon the ground, a tiny aquamarine lake just unlocking from the winter's ice lay partly exposed on the summit. A new [word missing] of exquisite purple pink and a small white composite were something to pay us for the trip, even if the mythical lake never materialized.

And now I wish I could lead you to the brink of that pass where with me you could look into the unknown beyond. Except for the sun and the flow of the rivers we had no knowledge of our whereabouts, nor did we care. Food for three months was on our faithful ponies' backs, and like the tortoise our home was with us. So, with not a care we gazed into the strange land. At our feet sprang the tender green mosses and ground willows of the Alps, all in their brightest spring jackets; then on the long descent and for miles and miles as far as the eye could reach, was an unbroken color scheme of green. Not a fire (that scourge of the Rockies), had left a scar in all that great range. As we slowly descended into the valley, our caravan marked its way by the crushed white blooms of the pulsatilla or alpine anemone, then the caltha blossoms were snapped hither and yon, and then under the feet of our horses fell hundreds of flowers of the sunny faced trollius. There was no avoidance of such a slaughter, our way was carpeted royally as though for a conquering hero.

Two days later we found this magnificent park led direct to the lake so long sought, and as we gazed on that sheet of water so long a hidden gem, we named it "Maligne," and turning to look back at the Valley called it "the green valley of the Maligne." It is the fairest of all the many valleys I have known in that vast country. It is a long and another story to tell you of our life; the life of the first white people on the largest lake yet found in the Rocky Range of Canada, of how we rafted it, and found such untold wonders; of the silence and the peace and beauty of it all.

One night on its shores, our tents were pitched in a garden of crimson. As I lay back by a tree near the camp fire, the evening breeze brought the odor of the countless flowers to me. I closed my eyes and in thought was back in Pennsylvania in clover time; then sounded the crash of an avalanche from a glacier opposite me, and far away came the whining cry of a coyote. No, it was not my Pennsylvania home, but my Rocky Mountain garden.

The Story of Revelstoke

It is many years now, twenty-three to be exact, since I first saw Revelstoke—at least I suppose I saw it. The Canadian Pacific trans-continental train stopped there, changed her tired engine for a fresh one and hurried on (no, not hurried, we took our time in those days) to our goal, the last "west" to be reached—Vancouver.

Nothing regarding the site of the town caught my eye in those days save a little red-brown hotel on a high bank overlooking the station (labeled with what was already to us magic letters—"C.P.R."), and a stray liver-colored dog wandering aimlessly about the platform in the early frosty air. No, I was not impressed.

My next visit was nine years later. There were several liver-colored dogs by that time, just as aimless and useless-looking as their probable ancestors. We stopped at the little red-brown CPR hotel, found it clean and neat, with good meals, and a magnificent view from its veranda of the Columbia valley, and far in the distance Mount Begbie with her snowy glaciers, and range after range of purple mountains in all directions.

There was very little for idlers like ourselves to "do" at that time, no nice nearby trips and but one "sight." It was suggested we go to see the "Big Bend." With much difficulty we obtained a team, and when it stood ready at the hotel for us, we could but wonder when we would reach the destination for which we were bound, as it was said to be five miles distant. The wagon was of the type used for hauling purposes, and the horses though handsome, were surely of the "dray" variety. Being slightly timid of horse-flesh in those days, I took comfort in thinking that if they ran away I might at least be able to run with them—they looked so fat and slow—so clambered to my high perch in the wagon with some sort of assurance.

After leaving the town and river we came upon the canyon of the Big Bend. We had gone about three miles and reached it evidently by a well-traversed road, a road resultant of many miners seeking the earth's wealth in that district.

Our sturdy outfit was halted a considerable distance from the point of interest which our driver had suggested we see, so we tumbled down cautiously and watched our phlegmatic beast being securely tied to a tree to await our return—such caution striking us rather unnecessary when we contemplated the amount of urging it had taken to get them thus far. Of the details of that first visit to the canyon of the Columbia I recall only a long walk with very doubtful footing here and there,with the river on our left boiling and seething between high rugged walls; and as I trudged along, I thought of the lives which I had heard the "old-timers" say had been lost in the rapids below us, of the hands which had laid the now-rotting timbers over which we were precariously making our way, and the many, many feet which had crossed and re-crossed that old highway. Where were they all? No answer. Only the rumble and roar of a great river fighting its way through a narrow, rock-bound channel came back to me—to me as to those whose minds bent on gold, gold, had probably been a blank to the organ-like tones of the waters, and whose eyes had seen no beauty in the hills about them. It was my first baptism in the sadness and the wildness and the beauty of the Canadian Alps. I had lived hitherto always within sound of the shrieking engines and passing trains of the mountain division, and the impression made, was one to last always.

Then I noticed the shadows were falling in long shafts across the gorge, the air growing chill, and we walked regretfully back over the rotting timbers, beneath the sturdy cedars—silent, listening to the river's voice—words were inadequate, useless. We came to the tree where the team had been so securely tied. Alas, no team was there at all! There was no broken strap dangling from the improm[p]tu hitching-post to proclaim a run-away, nothing, save in the dust of the road a nic[el]y turned wheel-track which continued on toward Revelstoke three miles away. Three miles was it! The sun was [s]inking toward the blue hills far away, the dust was inches thick; the forest, the river, the mountains, the lovely Columbia valley lost then and there all their charms, as, wearily packing our cameras and wraps, we set forth to reach the town before darkness caught us.

It was 1903 before we again saw Revelstoke. I was sitting in the tiny office of the Glacier House Hotel. A rather short, snowy-haired man was talking to a lady behind the desk. Though from "across the border," the land I love and have adopted unto myself, has long been keenly interesting to me, and when I heard the words "Palliser," "1857," "Kicking-horse," I had the ill manners to listen, then rose and slipping over apologetically asked if I might hear too. The kindly little lady knowing my greed for all this history of the hills, introduced me to "Sir James Hector." Here was a piece of good fortune I had not expected, and certainly did not let pass. He was a good talker and most willing to describe in detail the facts which all may obtain in Palliser's Journal—providing they are lucky enough to come across a copy.

Just as I slipped up to the desk he was in the midst of the following conversation. Bringing his fist down hard on the desk, he said—"Yes, it is my first visit into the Rocky mountains since 1861; I mean to go on to Golden and from there up the Kicking-horse river, and then to my grave! I know I can find it." "Your grave!" said the little lady in astonishment. "Yes, my grave! Oh, I suppose you don't know how that river received its name. Well, it was after we had won the good-will of the Indians of the foothills. They were very ugly at first, refused to let us go into the mountains at all, claiming that we only wanted to go there for game. I thought the expedition had about come to an end. Then dysentery attacked their camp. I went over to see what I could do for them. I gave them some medicine, changed their camp-site, the disease died out and after that they were willing to do anything I asked of them. They gave us guides to lead us over their trails and with a picked bunch of men we set forth to explore the mountains. We crossed what is now known as Vermilion Pass to the Kootenay river at its head, then down the Beaverfoot River to a river which joins it at the present station of Leanchoil, then followed the unnamed river to the eastward trusting it would bring us back to the permanent camp in the foothills. I think from the maps that the rail-road has issued, that the town of Field must be very near my grave. We were having our own troubles getting up this unnamed river, crossing and re-crossing wherever we could find any sort of footing for the horses. My own saddle-pony had anything but a pleasant disposition and he hated fording rivers, specially the kind this one was. I was having a good deal of trouble with him at one point, and finally went up behind him with a stick. I saw his heels fly up and then knew nothing more for hours. When I regained consciousness, my grave was dug and they were preparing to put me in it. So thats how the Kicking-horse got its name, and that how I come to have a grave in this part of the world." He was a most delightful old gentleman. No wonder that it was through his tact the stubborn Indians were conquered and Captain Palliser able to make some sort of report to the home government, even if that report did say there could never be a continuous route from the east to the west without passing through United States territory, "owing to unsurmountable obstructions on Canadian soil."

We spent a delightful evening talking to the last-known living explorer of Captain Palliser's day. But a shadow was to fall across our pleasant meeting. The next morning Douglas Hector, the young and brilliant son of Sir James, was reported ill. Dr. Schäffer diagnosed the case as one of advanced appendicitis. The young man was hurried to the nearest hospital—Revelstoke—but it was too late. In two days the bright young life was ended. Near his grave in Revelstoke we parted with one of the most delightful acquaintances we had ever made in the mountains. Sir James, broken in spirit, turned his way homeward to New Zealand (he never saw the land of his great triumphs again) while we with Edward Whymper—he of world-wide mountaineering fame—returned to Glacier. Thus ended under so dark a cloud my third visit to Revelstoke.

Nine years have come and gone. Little, quiet Revelstoke has kept calmly on her way, few from the great out-side world noticing her. Men who went there as boys, had an undefined faith in her and stood by her. I remember a number of years ago one of them sent me at Glacier a few peas grown in the valley, a note accompan[y]ing them fairly bursting with pride that his valley of the Columbia had grown those peas. As for me, I ate each pea individually, they tasted so delicious coming into a place where we had never seen so fresh a vegetable before—fruit and vegetables at that time all coming from Vancouver and California. Two years later the same person sent me a rosy-cheeked apple—"grown in Revelstoke." We passed the apple round and felt a reflected pride in the advancement of that particular valley. But when three years ago a whole dozen ears of delicious green · corn came up the hill to Glacier with the now familiar label—"grown in Revelstoke" attached to them, our pride burst all bounds, and we felt that Revelstoke's future was assured. And so it is. For not only have the most delicious vegetables been coming to cheer the hungry mountaineer, but rumors of wonderful nearby scenery discovered, so wonderful that the British Columbia Government finally took a hand and volunteered to assist to build the first aerial motor road to be attempted in all the vast expanse of the Rocky Mountains of Canada. On August ? 1912, beneath the great cedars on the shores of the Columbia River gathered all of Revelstoke . who could get there, the band played, speeches were made by noted men of British Columbia, all made merry. Then silence reigned for a moment beneath the stately trees as the first sod for the first alpine motor-road of the mountains was turned. By October of 1913 those interested hope to see the last spade laid down little at the summit of Mount Revelstoke, and Revelstoke's dream of the future an assured fact. Thus do I come to my fourth visit to the quiet town on the banks of the Columbia River.

It was a chill, biting air through which the train was hurrying me down the mountain slopes from Glacier one morning in the early part of September, 1912. The road threads its way from the birth-place of the Illecillewaet river, along its course at the base of green, wooded hills to within a short distance of its junction with the Columbia River, and every mile of that course lends itself to one beautiful view after another. The old scenes of the other days came back to me familiarly except that as the train glided gently along the last few miles, I caught glimpses of trees laden with crimson apples, interspersed with boughs bending low with ropes of purple plums. The silver glow of great patches of cabbages caught my eye as we whisked by, and the long leaves of the sweet-corn gayly waved me a passing greeting.

We glided into the station; the chill of the upper mountains was gone. I stepped out into warmth and sunshine, and an atmosphere laden with an odor reminding me of the tropics. A comfortable, up-to-date motor received my luggage (where Oh where were the dray horses of the years before!) and trundled me away on the mission for which I had come—to see for myself a rapidly growing city, a city which I had known so well in its babyhood. Was this Revelstoke? All was changed. Coming from a much higher altitude and being rushed pell-mell through streets lined with young trees of mountain ash in full berry, with gardens on both sides the highway aglow with sweet peas, nasturtiums, dahlias, asters, the walls and verandas of the pretty bungalows and cottages on every side aflame with the autumn colors of the Virginia creeper, I could but sigh—"'Tis not the Revelstoke I knew," nor could I realise that in such a latitude (51°) the fruit-trees could bear so enormously. And then to myself I wondered what kind of small boys they raised in that town that such an amount of fruit should hang in the main streets undisturbed, till I recognised the fact that even a small boy has limitations of capacity and that probably the supply was so great that even his appetite left no marked effect.

To live for months in the higher altitude of the mountains to the east where frost or snow may catch us napping any night of the summer months, and then to suddenly drop into the warm valley of the Columbia (1450 ft.) with all its conditions of a temperate zone, is a bewildering experience. But with mind re-adjusted and plans for the week laid, I slept that night in the original red-brown inn (now tan and brown) perched high on the bank above the station, taking a last look across the wide valley of the Columbia before turning in. How different it all seemed. Nothing looked familiar save the hoary head of old Mount Begbie in the south, the Columbia a winding thread of silver shimmering in the last glow of the sun and the purple hills to the south-west which marked the Eagle pass whence traversed the trans-continental road to the Pacific coast. Immediately below, instead of a sleepy, valley village, was a town ablaze with electric lights, instead of columns of smoke rising from the scattered and tumbling shacks of other days, could be dimly seen the unfinished dome of a $150,000 court-house, the rising walls of a fine hospital; among the darkening trees as far as the eye could see were private residences far above the average; nearer in view an avenue of twinkling lights proclaimed a shopping district worthy of a town of much greater dimensions. But it was immediately in the foreground I noted the greatest change of all. Where once had stood a half dozen engines fretting and steaming to be off to east or west, now panted and throbbed many, many more, while track upon track-ful of waiting freight-cars testified to the fact that instead of being merely a divisional point as in the old days, Revelstoke could now lay claim to being a distributing center of no mean importance.

Night was closing in. The fretting engines shunted noisily back and forth, the mountains slipped from sight in the coming darkness, and as I watched the twinkling lights in the vast valley stretched before me, I thought of that valley's future. Through it runs a great trans-continental rail-road whose payrol[l] in that one town alone is over $1,000,000 a year. It is anticipated that in the near future the same rail-road will bring a line from Beavermouth (on the main line east of the Selkirks) around by the Big Bend and connect with its original line at Revelstoke, while other roads which are crossing the continent in the north are casting envious eyes upon the Big Bend. Then I thought of what those two words implied—the Big Bend. Known since gold-rush days of '69 as a region of vast mineral as well as timber wealth, the country about the Big Bend of the Columbia River has practically lain sleeping for want of cheaper transportation of that wealth.

Revelstoke is the door to the Big Bend. On the river benches surrounding her and to the Arrow lakes twenty-seven miles to the south are thousands of acres of rich lands awaiting cultivation, and many more thousands of acres of magnificent timber land, which when cleared away will open the door to the fruit-grower. Yes, little town, as I compared you that night in the darkness to your condition as I first saw you, you were as a grown man to a child, but as I thought of your future, you seemed still in your infancy.

But trains and boats wait not for dreamers, and as I was to have a trip on the Arrow lakes the following day, it behooved me to leave Revelstoke to look after her own future, of which she seems quite capable, and snatch the hours remaining for sleep before I must be on the wing.

The morning dawned bright and clear—just the morning for a flight in the open. The neat little train of the Arrowhead and Kootenay River rail-road puffed fussily out of the station of the Canadian Pacific Road at 7.40, crossed the Illecillewaet River and passing through some wonderful forest growth (to me, though my escort said the cedars were nothing compared to other sections of the valley), was soon following the shores of the winding Columbia.

For twenty-seven miles we were drawn by the iron horse across a country filled with interest. The distant mountains in every direction were decked with caps of fresh snow; autumn's breath had touched the aspens with gold; the leaves and berries of the mountain ash stood out against the background of deep green cedars in flaming crimsons; the bracken here and there had turned a golden brown on the banks of the winding, twisting, hurrying Columbia and the conductor called—"Arrowhead! All change for the boat!" before we thought we were half there. The boat, a stern-wheeler, proved to be neat, clean and manned by officials who were courtesy itself. The season was late and tourists few, but those who sailed the Columbia that sunny morning of September on the Rossland, enjoyed every moment of the day.

I had been to West Rossland in those "early days" of 1898 and it was interesting to note the change which had taken place in so few years in this newly opening land. Where in 1898 we had paddled the live-long day between silent and apparently unpeopled banks with only an occasional glimpse of some Indian habitation, in 1912 we passed many a deserted logging camp, many a logging camp in full swing, small clearings where a few head of cabbage bespoke the beginner, large clearings where the long-leaved corn waved, upon hill-sides where the sun beat down on trees crimson with their weight of apples and plums, a couple of fine health resorts, and last, but very numerous—collections of houses, which if their names be any guarantee of fitness, may some day be important towns. At scheduled intervals our small boat would plunge her nose toward shore, plow into the mud thereof, her gang-plank be thrust forward like a small boy showing his tongue to the Dr., the passengers would rush to the side of the boat and then all hungry-eyed, watch boxes of plums, peaches, apples or fresh-plucked corn being taken aboard. The reflections of the surrounding mountains in the water, the occasional "narrows," the constant change of scene, made us all regret the fact that we must take time to go in and eat, but the table was loaded with the good things of the region, and there was thus some consolation.

As evening closed down upon the water and the chugging little boat, the signal of a swinging lantern turned her nose to shore where on the map was printed no high-sounding name of some future flourishing city. As her nose ground into the sands of the beach, the search-lights of the boat showed a solitary hunter standing there. A short distance away lay his rifle—at his feet—a beautiful, dead deer.

Oh, that March of Progress! The small ranches which in no short time will be large ones, the luscious fruits growing beside the wild, wide lake, the magnificent timber which is being sent in great quantities out into the busy world, are pictures to contemplate, but—there is another side to those same pictures—the wild creatures of the forest will be swept from existence. Progress brings much of sadness with her.

About eight o'clock in the evening, the boat slid quietly up to the wharf at West Robson. Business men, ranchers and their wives, tourists and sportsmen departed for points to the south, or like ourselves, remained aboard to return to Revelstoke. By nine o'clock I was sound asleep in an immaculate berth aboard the "Rossland," only rousing at midnight to notice the fact that the boat had turned about and had begun her homeward journey in the darkness. By two o'clock the next afternoon we had landed once more at Arrowhead, made our way to the waiting train and in another hour had passed under the shadow of Mount Begbie, saw Mount Revelstoke ahead, and pulled into the station—tired, but infinitely pleased with one of the finest and most picturesque boat-trips that the Canadian Rockies offer.

The next morning I woke to the fact that the day was cloudless and to the pleasant realisation that a friend the evening before had said that if I would be ready by nine o'clock, it was quite probable we could cover all the motor roads leading out of Revelstoke at the present time in the one day—in another year it will take longer than that. This *was* exciting; for I had come from a land of horses, motors were to me a novelty in the mountains, and I was to delve into byways where so few years ago even the strong dray-horses could go but a distance of three miles without reaching unsurmountable obstructions. "Let it be the Big Bend first," said I, "and don't go too fast, I want to see if I can remember any of it, and to know how it feels to glide unfatigued over a trail where once I trudged weary and footsore to get home before dark." Armed with cameras and memories, I took my seat in a roomy motor. Again we drove through the flower-grown town; paused through the sho[p]ping section, saw churches, opera-house, fine Y.M.C.A. building, the dome of the new court-house being placed, passed a fine public-school building fairly embowered in flowers, the tennis grounds, and at last came to the old, familiar road over which we had trudged the night of the "joke."

"Progress" has entered the valley of the Columbia and marked it for her own. She claims the wide, sunny benches for ranching purposes, she claims the great river for drawing her share of the grain from the prairies to the coast, the mineral wealth to market, the lumber to the outside world, but she can never claim the rugged beauty of the Big Bend.

There are rumors that the near future will see a railroad seeking footing among the bold crags that mark the Columbia's course, tying the traffics of the Yellowhead country to that of lower Canada, opening the vast mining region of the Big Bend to the world, erecting transportation for miles and miles of standing timber. Let it come, it can be but a thread of steel after all among those massive hills; the wild Columbia will flow the same, "Progress" can never dim the grandeur and nobility of the Bend.

I wish I might use colors for the picture of the drive on the old trail of the Big Bend that sunny autumn day. The rotting timbers which we had crossed so gingerly on our first visit in 1898 had been replaced by new ones. I confess I held my breath at first on general principles as the big motor rumbled over them, then sanely settled down to enjoy every inch of it all, every moment. The air was crisp and redolent of cedar and the dying vegetation, the surrounding growth was rich and rank as though we had plunged into the tropics; here and there many shades of crimson mingled with warm browns and lit up the deep green of hemlock and fir—all silent and cool.

At last we reached the "gorge," the spot we had visited in days gone by, that point of the river where so many adventurous lives had been lost in the greed for gold. It was just as magnificent, just as cruelly beautiful as ever. We stopped and watched it in silence, and then were reminded that we still had five miles to go to reach "Silver-tip Falls," so the busy motor took up the trail again.

Reaching the falls we found the wide roadway went no further, but the old trail led on as far as eye could see, and I longed for tepee, guides, outfit and a couple of weeks that I might go on, on, till via the Canoe River I might reach the Yellowhead Pass.

Try it, Oh you, who would know the spirit of the trail! "Progress" is steadily marching on and the day is coming when there will be no secret wilderness left. The Big Bend offers much to-day; to-morrow, what?

A short climb through primeval forest brought us to the base of the falls we had come to see. They came splashing down with a musical ring in a deep, dark glen, too dark for a good photograph to be made at that time of the day, but well repaid us for the scramble we had just made, and seemed a fitting climax to the first motor ride I had ever taken in the Canadian Rockies. But the sun peering down at us from among the forest growth reminded us that time was slipping by, so regretfully turned about and descended to the motorroad, looked regretfully at the well-marked trail winding away indefinitely to the north, climbed back into the motor-car and started for Revelstoke.

I was telling my companions of the drive, of the night when we were forced to make our way back to town afoot and how much more preferable was this form of locomotion, when—came a bump, a halt, a last gasp from the machine—the motor stopped dead, as though it had been listening to the conversation. All the visions of an eight mile walk in the heat of the day danced before my eyes, was history to be repeated here and now? Conversation ceased, the polite chauffeur requested us to rise, as our seat was the toolbox, so we crept in silence from the motor and sat dumbly on the bank wondering what misery was in store. But that blessed chauffeur knew his business. With a few mysterious tools he opened this, shut that, took a twist on something else; the silent motor began to hum inwardly, we stood not on the order of our going, but climbed back at once and in a short time were safely back in Revelstoke, seeking to appease a ravenous appetite before going on the road again. The motor road of the Big Bend will in the future be one of the features of the mountains. Kept in repair by the British Columbia Government, which collects in timber and mine licences $340,000 a year from this Section alone we can expect each year to see a few more miles of roadway added to the original trail route and perhaps eventually be able to call in motors on friends living at the Tete Jaun Cache.

Our drive in the afternoon led us along less stupendous ways. For an hour and a half we threaded valley roads beside the Illecillewaet River and among small ranches where strong hands had rescued the acres from virgin forest. The ground thus obtained is rich and the crops remarkably heavy. We then climbed to a higher bench, found that busy hands had been at work there too, then stopped at a charming cottage all embowered in flowers, from whose veranda the whole sweep of the valley could be seen. A kindly hostess invited us to enter, and in a few moments asked us if we would enjoy a glass of buttermilk. Buttermilk! Just think of it! Why only the other day there was not a cow in all the Rocky Mountains.

Soon bidding adieu to the lady of the flower cottage, we again took our seats in our vehicle, and someone said—"Let us go over to Greely." Where was Greely? A new name to me. Our motor crossed the main line of the railroad and went to mountain-climbing in earnest on the bluffs of the Illecillewaet. We climbed from bench to bench only to find large tracts of land already wrested from the wilderness. We halted at the homestead of an "old-timer," bought some delicious corn from him, plucked his rosy apples, tramped through cucumber beds to the plum trees, ate till we could eat no more, and with pockets filled, headed again for Greely. From the high roadbed we looked down and saw a train puffing its way breathlessly toward Glacier. What a change it all was in so few years! It kept me in a state of bewilderment. We never got to Greely. We had dawdled so long among the alpine ranches, had stopped so often to take in the constant panorama, that the sun's shadows were growing uncomfortably long, the evening wind sharp, and so regretfully turned about—for there were other sights for the morrow.

The morrow? Yes, for even though I had seen so much, they had saved the cream of the surrounding scenery for the last. Directly north of the Canadian Pacific rail-road station rises a rugged, unprepossessing hill. Some one climbed it one day in the past and reported great alpine meadows, innumerable lakes and wonderful flower growth. It did not seem possible. Doubting ones went up to see if it were true. The water supply of Revelstoke was becoming inadequate to the fast-growing town—those interested climbed there in search of springs. The great park-like lands, 4600 feet above the town quickly became an accepted fact and with her usual aggressive attitude, Revelstoke grasped the idea of bringing those alpine stretches within easier reach. This was done by building what is known as the Lindmark trail, a trail about five miles long. More residents, surveyors, and tourists then climbed to the alp-land at the door of the coming mountain city. But many of the moving spirits of Revelstoke were still dissatisfied. Some could walk, some could ride to this greatest scenic point of all, but many, many more could do neither or had not the time to devote to it. Nothing daunts the Spirit of the West, so—someone calmly said—"Let us have a motor road to Victoria park," (as these heights are now called). The suggestion was as calmly taken up as though it was a mere foot-way to be cut into the forest. The interest of the British Columbia Government was enlisted, and after many details which I cannot mention here, the survey was made and the first aerial motor road of the Rockies of Canada begun in the summer of 1912.

For me, I was to take the Lindmark trail, and glad to do so. "Progress" follows the motor road—I preferred to see it all as nearly as Nature had made it and rejoiced. They apologised that I "would find the trail rough and crude." Having covered pretty well all trails in the region between the Canadian Pacific road and the Yellowhead pass, I can say it was the best kept trail I have ever been over. Free of stones in the main, free of fallen logs, free of muskegs, a steady grade, there is no better engineered trail in the mountain system—to my mind. Starting at an elevation of 1450 feet and rising to 6150 feet in five miles, the grade suggests to him who knows anything atall about, that it is no easy trail for the horse that carries him, but with all the minor obstructions obliterated and the horse given his own time, the trailer has a happy, a glorious trip ahead of him.

At nine o'clock, all set, I mounted my pinto pony and with four others started ahead of our solitary pack-animal and its care-taker. The first half mile impressed me little. The forest growth had been destroyed by fires, and the ground was too arid and dry to have brought forth a second growth; the slope was very steep, the sun hot. Then the view of the great valley we were leaving behind us came into sight. We had now something to watch and every five minutes someone would call out to the stranger in the party—"Look, that is the Eagle pass through which the rail-road winds its way to the western coast." Again—"Look to the right, that is where the Jordan flows," and "Do you see those lakes coming into view?" etc., etc. We took it all slowly, we had to, for the sake of our patient beasts. Someone saw a grouse and the entire cavalcade had to stop till the poor innocent was secured to satisfy the vulgar appetite which we knew would be in all evidence at dinner-time on the top. After about two miles' of climbing, we came to wonderfully brilliant dyed maples, and then from then on, the autumn tones were wonderful. The blue-berry bushes had turned a purple crimson, and the mountain ash vied with them in glory.

We had passed the steepest portions of the trail and were among the last growth of blue-berry bushes (whose enormous fruit is so luscious), when he who was ahead, called sharply—"Look up there! Its a big brown bear!" Our eyes followed his pointing finger to a mass of tumbled rocks twenty yards above our heads, and there, peering down at us was the face of an inquisitive bear. He took but a moment to study the situation, then with a clumsy plunge, was off leaving only the suggestion of a black streak on our minds. Had he but known we h[a]d nothing with us more alarming than a "twenty-two," what a good time he might have had stampeding the entire outfit; but he did not know and the situation was gracefully saved.

After just three and a half hours' quiet climbing, after passing two charming mountain lakes, we came out on Balsam lake and the shelter which was our destination for the day. The warm breath of the valley below had long given place to the crisp and invigorating air of the mountains and no doubt was reason enough for the fearful inroad which then and there took place in the bacon supply. The noon meal over, we set forth—cameras in hand—and wandered over meadow after meadow. The flowers were all dead, killed by the frost, but any novice could see that but a few days before it had been a fairy-land. As we closed our eyes in tired and delicious sleep that night in the little log shack, one of the many guardians with us, called through a crack—"Don't leave anything near that window you don't want the bears to get. The trail-gang says (that body was even then working on the mountain) they're thick here, and have twice put their paws in through the window and stolen all there was in reach." I cast around one eye, there was a bunch of frying-pans within a proper radius of stealing and a half-burned candle; my shoes were my pillow that night; I had lived too long in the land of bears, I was too deliciously weary to care if a dozen of them had poked their noses or their paws in that uncovered window, and we were off to the land of dreams with no terror in our hearts. By six the next morning we were all awake and all alive in spite of the bear-stories of the night before, and all wondering where our steeds were that were to carry us five miles further to Eva Lake, the largest lake in the alpine park. Of the seven here was but one visible, and it only there because the owner thereof had had the foresight to tether her the night before. The problem seemed a puzzling one (for the guide had been out three hours searching for them) and someone suggested I walk to Eva Lake and if the horses were found in time they would be along to pick me up. It was five miles there and five miles back; I demurred, with an eye on the tethered pony. Her master as politely said if I would ride his pony, he would accompany me on foot. There was a tone in his remark which made me say, "Anything the matter with her?" "No, she's mostly all right, she fired a lady off last week." "Why?" "Well, the lady tied a tin can to the saddle to have something handy when she was thirsty; it rattled and Dolly is slightly nervous, and the lady went off her suddenly." I felt that Dolly had legitimate reason for her actions and decided to go thirsty and use Dolly's legs for those next five miles and back.

The hunters of horses started off to search the meadows to the right, I with the doubtful Dolly and her master on foot, to the left—bound for Eva Lake. Up and down the rolling alp-land we made our way. The air was as clear as crystal; the Gold range came into view and disappeared. We wandered on, wondered where the horses were and were discussing the fact that we had come about three miles, when from my vantage-point on the back of Dolly, I looked into a sunny pocket of the hills to behold the delinquent ponies staring up at us, while Dolly—all ears and curiosity—stared back. We held a caucus. I knew what was the only thing to do and knew I had to suggest it—my companion being entirely too polite to do it himself. Without the quiver of the voice or a suggestion of hesitation, I said—"We can make better time if you will take Dolly and drive those stray-aways back to camp. I will keep on the trail, and you can return and join me when those aggravating beasts are once more in the clutches of the law." Did I say "fear" to him or "bears"? No, not once; but what I failed to say, I thought.

I stood and watched him disappear with Dolly and his charges over the next hill and I? I walked on alone. There was certainly no use standing there, I was just as liable to see a black, lumbering body topping one of the many rises where I stood, as when moving, so I moved. Perhaps it does not sound specially un-nerving to be walking alone on a mountain-top where bears are of daily occurr[e]nce, with no rifle in case of emergency, but it is a solemn fact that it is very hard to refrain from dwelling on the uncomfortable subject, and I did a good deal of "dwelling." I looked at the trees I was passing to see if they were of the climbable variety—they were the most unpromising specimens I ever saw. It was deathly silent all about me and I caught myself listening for the returning foot-steps of Dolly. Then a chipmunk chattered at me from a nearby tree, a marmot whistled his sweet note from a great rock-slide; the terrors of the trail died away, the spirit of the wild came back, and I hurried ahead to see what I might see. So beautiful was it all, I had no more time to waste on thinking of bears. I stopped to listen to the marmot, I paused to hear what a saucy whisky-jack had to say about it. A little further, a mountain torrent was thundering its way to the Columbia directly beneath my feet, hidden from view by bowlders from a great crag towering above my head. I passed on; the noise of the torrent became a gentle murmur, which was suddenly pierced by a far-away "Halloo!"

I was very glad to see my returning protector and Dolly, but bears having been finally eliminated from my mind, I think that of all the lovely mental pictures I have stored away of Revelstoke and her surroundings, that mile and a half alone, hand in hand with Nature and her little folk, is the prettiest one. We three finished the five mile journey to-gether. We wandered by the shore of the glass-like lake, looked across at the white-capped Gold range, over to the serracs of Gordon glacier and to-gether decided that those in whose hands is the fate of the first mountain motor road, should themselves journey to that wonderful "look-off" at the mouth of Eva lake and say if the new road should remain thirteen and eight tenths miles long as at present planned, or eventually carry the tourist to this look-off. The sun was at his highest in the blue heavens as we reluctantly turned our faces back to camp, leaving the crags, the canyons, the many lakes, the glaciers, the little people of the alp-land to their peaceful kingdom; for the long hill was to descend before dark, even the idea of lunch intruding itself amidst all the splendour about us.

On arriving at the Balsam lake shack, it was rather a comforting sight to see all the horses well tied, each to his own tree, leaving no dismal prospect of having to tumble down the long hill to Revelstoke on foot.

One of our guardians had spent a busy morning with the "twenty-two," six grouse hanging to the rafters of the shed by their toes testified to his zeal as a hunter. We quickly skinned them, cleaned them and popped them into a frying-pan with plenty of butter—no "mulligan" for us such as we had seen the trail-gang preparing the night before from six other grouse. The delicious lunch of fried grouse, coffee, peanut-butter and jam over, the party mounted, soon turned the bend which hid from sight the lakes, and meadows of a great upland playground, an alpine garden, and jogged slowly down the mountain trail into the town of Revelstoke just as darkness fell. Tired! Certainly. But very, very glad that it had been our privilege to see Victoria park in her virginity. The day when thousands of others will know Revelstoke and her surroundings as I learned to know them in one short week, is coming, coming soon. I had but a week to give, there is at least another week's pleasure to places where I had not the time to go. I had many friends who helped me to make the best of my time, many will go to this new playground who cannot be so fortunate I was, so have I penned these few, inadequate words trusting they may reach the eye of the stranger who enters Revelstoke's hospitable doorway.

Tepee Life in the Northern Hills

There has been running in the Saturday Evening Post of the spring months of '24 a series of articles entitled "Diary of a Dude Wrangler" by Struthers Burt, which has probably interested this writer quite as much as any of your other readers.

To begin, I might refer to Mr. Burt in the language, who in his extreme youth, had been naughty as small children are apt to be at times. Hav[ing] sprung from a solid old Quaker family where obedience was the first law of the household, and his proper mentors not being present, I had administered first aid to naughtiness. With his big brown eyes snapping, he looked at me and said: "You have no right to correct me." I replied: "I think I have a perfect right to correct you as I am your aunt, (his father being my brother"). This was adding fuel to his small furnace of wrath and he replied scornfully: "Well, you are only my aunt by marriage."

It is thus I could introduce myself to Struthers Burt. I am literally only his cousin "by marriage." He must have been just about dreaming of long breeches when I last saw him, and though it is a strictly "marriage" connection, it seems odd that each of us has taken seriously to the "wilds."

One brackets that word these days, for except to him who traverses only fifth Ave. of New York, Chestnut St. of Phila. or the Boston Commons, there is really no "wild" left. In fact if you happen to have a little money about you, the above places are much more "wild" than the places of which I write.

There are glorious open spaces in the far west to which one can never make monetary claim or else so empty of anything but game and rocks and rivers in the summer and filled with snow in winter, that Nature just naturally takes care of our thriftless dispositions.

In going faithfully over Mr. Burt's "Diary," which I have done from a pure love of the whole subject, I think he has swung wider the door to general opinion than he had any idea of doing.

There is undoubtedly a great drifting to the west. ENNUI may have much to do with it (for the wealthy) and a lack of funds has shown many people what a great place the west is and how they may live without thought of high rents, expensive clothes, electric light bills, so long as a Ford will carry a few pounds of bacon for them and include a tent and the dog.

I am inclined to fancy an article written by Wallace Smith entitled: "Dood Wrangling" may have had its inception in Mr. Burt's first bit of "Diary," but that may be only a coincidence.

That there is a spot "where men are men" can never be denied by those who live among them & understand them, and for those who wish to have a taste of that which to the writer is merely our daily bread, we should give generously and refrain from smiling openly when we see them decked in broad, checked shirts, with chaps which have no mortal use in my particular locality and a few other things on which I mean to touch gently.

Mr. Burt's pen has sketched all round about my own particular life but not of it though I have known a good deal about it much longer than he has. While his breeches were short, my skirts were long and the first time I was hurled by train across the continent, I own to-day I had a nice little revolver which I was sure I would use, though why I should think I could ever master its interior, is more than I know now. At that time I doubt if I could hit a tomato can at ten feet, but after all the written yarns of the west, it was really a comfort to carry it and gaze on it whenever there was cause to open my grip.

I am also willing NOW to admit that when I struck the real west, my eyes opened further than my grip. There was no west according to books. People spoke excellent English, they were well educated and I felt an inclination to weep when I knew after all there was no real west left.

I managed a few thrills and shivers when I saw Indians wrapped in their gay blankets at various little stations and watching the "dude" traveler with hardened and critical eye, but they never once attempted to cut our throats.

Remember this was long ago when I was just a girl and since then a lot of common sense has drifted to the east through our magazines and by some of us who have shown with our lantern slides and word sketches that there is no "tough" country left if I can now ever believe there was much that was "tough" in the men who saw our country first.

While Mr. Burt was passing through Princeton and learning all the things which were to fit him for "dude wrangling," the writer was a pretty busy woman studying the west at its source as well as from books.

To begin, I really crossed the Rockies at a date which I now consider indelicate to mention in public and in spite of the fact that I had entree in the east to art circles, musical circles—all that goes to make a city life adored by those who are willing to endure the black dust of rail-roads, clanging of cars twenty-four hours of the day, puddles of mud on rainy days, broiling heat of summer, etc., my heart turned ever to my memory pictures of the Rockies and open spaces. No sweltering heat was there, where by pure accident, I had found my first "location," only the distant toot of a train at odd moments, only the singing birds, the chatter of busy squirrels, an occasional deer passing fleet and frightened into the brush beside the trail, and if we were specially lucky, at times a perfectly live and frightened bear would go tumbling out of sight at the pace of a race horse, whose speed they can equal for a short time. He had probably been disturbed while tearing up an old log for the ants of which he is inordinately fond, or skirmishing for berries. Never have I seen a bear of any kind which wished to court the company of a human being—unless as a cub he had been accustomed to be fed.

But remember, my words are for the real wilds as we think of them, not the animals which we have coaxed to our doors with dainty bits. A tame, wild animal is to be avoided. If a tamed bear has received all he is to get, then the kind feeder had better "get"; if its a deer, you want to watch out when the last bite is gone, for in his impatience he takes no cognisance of kindness and is in many instances ready to strike with his front foot or to use his horns.

But to return to the days of the written wilderness in which I was so disappointed. I had been studying botany in a rather desultory way—a delicate girl, not staunch enough to attempt some of the "first climbs" of which I was hearing daily or to penetrate some of the "new" valleys of which others spoke, but satisfying myself in gathering the wild flowers which at that time had not been studied scientifically and bringing them back to one to whom botany meant so much and who was in himself a true botanist. Of horses I had a wholesome horror. They were all of Indian breed in the land I had chosen as my place for recreation, and to my city eyes, they all looked tricky and vicious. Mountain climbing for the sake of saying I was the first person on a certain peak, had no charms for me. I admit I was scared stiff at rocks and precipices (and firmly believe that there are those who have gone to great heights with their hearts in their mouths, so to speak) and neither had I the physical endurance which such work entails.

Just so far as my feet and strength would take me, I went, gathered my specimens, sketched them and added to the knowledge of botany to such small extent. The thought of bears was ever a shadow in my mind, but I never came across one when alone. Nothing more terrible was ever encountered in my botanical walks than the marmot, or as some folk say "whistler." They are lovable little creatures, about the size of an eastern ground-hog, and easily tamed by simply whistling back to them the notes with which they seem to warn the rest of their special colony that something strange is in sight. They always live in the higher slopes and every summer if you whistle your way into their timid hearts, you may note any amount of wilted flowers round the holes down which they dive if one presses her personality on them too closely or suddenly. I have been told by those who have watched them that those same wilted flowers are dried in the sun and used as winter vegetables, and see no reason why that may not be the case. We believe what we see, and then divide it in two. Its a sound rule in any part of the globe.

There came a day when gathering flowers for play ceased and necessity forced me to make what use I could of my smattering of botany, to study in solid earnest, to gather and press, sketch and photograph the rare specimens of the northern wilderness.

It all sounds so easy on paper, but its one thing to do what you know how to do and another to do something of which you are perfectly certain you have but the merest rudiments. To know your terrible ignorance is a great handicap, but I had reached the point where I knew I must lay down the playing with botany and take it up in seriousness for I had touched the place where there was no longer the companion to help me in my work and I knew I must face the future alone.

I looked at the many sketches and photographs and decided that if money would pay for the brains, I would go on with a preconceived botany which till that time had been but a dream between my companion and myself. I was perfectly well aware of what my part of the work meant but distraction was to be my salvation. It is a bore to attempt to tell of my first experiments to sit a cayuse on high alpine ridges where a vivid imagination showed me death staring in my face from below, but where the precious rare plants could be found and where my small strength would not carry me afoot, but its no bore to say I finally succeeded in mastering my fright to a certain extent on an Indian pony.

I was forced to sit with beating heart as a tiny atom of horse-flesh made his way up some impossible looking place, to learn to balance myself as my live vehicle took an unexpected leap over some soft place where a treacherous stream might have sunk us both to the neck in mire, to attempt to look wise in horse lore before the critic who was ever with me on these botanical hunts and to absorb with sickening knowledge the fact that he knew I was a "tenderfoot" of the worst type when he would casually tell me the manner in which I held my feet in the stirrups was not atall right.

But work, and hard work at that, is a great panacea for broken threads in life, and to come across a new and undescribed primula or anemone, was, in time, to feel a glow which helped life's path immeasurably. What is more, while I went through case after case of heart failure (all unknowing to my guide and mentor) I finished that botany, learned a little more about flowers from a scientist's point of view, learned considerably more about Indian ponies and learned a GREAT deal more about the people who lived three thousand miles from what I had always held sacred as civilisation.

Remember I am not describing Wyoming but another bit of the far west not so many miles from that state "as the crow flies," and that I have seen the west from a completely different point of view from my "cousin." I want specially to mention our horses at a different angle from the sketches Mr. Burt has made. All these long years we were compelled by necessity to use Indian ponies, for the simple reason that they were the only transportation obtainable. My first attempt to ride an Indian pony long antedated the botanical struggles. It was in 1893 that a party of nine decided to make the plunge and see for themselves a lake known as Louise. Its wonders had been hailed by trappers, timber-cruisers and in fact by anyone who had had the luck to get to its shores. We engaged ponies which at that time had to go eighty miles to the station of Louise to meet us, as they came from an Indian reserve known as Morley. I have often wondered whoever had the bright idea to suggest that we go our own forty miles to Louise on the top of a box car. But we were so eastern we simply reveled in it and the mountain scenery, taking very little note of the belching smoke and cinders forward.

As we descended from our high and dirty perch on the freight train we were welcomed by the sight of tepees, horses in plenty, two braves, two squaws and children innumerable running about amidst the stunted pines like rabbits.

No "dude wrangler" of the present day would have cared to speak to us, so utterly grimy were we from our novel ride. That we must have been of a certain amount of interest to the Indians, there could be no doubt, but they had nothing on us for curiosity. I only know we showed ours, while they acted as though they had seen such crazy folk before. Goodness, but we were black!

The horse inspection took place first and to my eastern eye there was nothing of charm about them and much of trickery. It was "Hobson's choice" to me as to which I took, so I picked out a good half dollar and showed it quietly to "William Twin," their owner. As quietly (you see an Indian is not slow) he pointed to one of the worst looking of his ponies and I mounted it trusting to that half dollar. In a few moments we were started on the Great Adventure. To stop and consider that day in the years so long gone, is funny. Those poor animals, the squaws and babies had been dragged eighty miles for the nine "tenderfeet" to ascend a moderate slope whose length was but three miles. When we reached our destination, I could have fallen off my horse with surprise, so suddenly had the great experience come to an end. Still, we had a sensation of having "done something." For a few of us it was really breaking the bonds of the east in time.

[word(s) missing] and my heart went out to "William Twin" for his wink at the steadiest pony of the whole lot. (Perhaps he also had a warm spot for my half dollar). For about five minutes I was in terror of the beast, then my heart slowly warmed to him, for he behaved in such a gentlemanly manner. He did not wander all over the trail munching a bit of grass here and there as did his pals, but stalked ahead in a businesslike manner, so that though his bones may be reposing peacefully on the old Stoney reserve to-day, his memory will always remain green in the heart of the first "tenderfoot" who probably ever mounted his bony back. Just here it comes to mind his name—biblical of course—Joshua. Well, Joshua, you have many equals in my heart but no peers amidst the many Indian ponies I have ridden since.

I have just been reading of the terror a horse feels when his saddle turns. That is no doubt correct regarding a very large percentage of horses but let me make a plea for the horse which has lived so long within my adopted surroundings.

Saddle-turning is no doubt extremely disagreeable to the party wearing the saddle as well as to the one who is riding, still I prefer an Indian pony if the process must take place as it will in the best regulated families. Once I had wished onto me some sort of a cinch which was so lightly and airily described to me that I had no doubt I would know what to do with it when it came to doing it.

At that time I was riding a good old soul called Buck, who had certainly missed his life's calling which should have been that of a circus horse as he was so wise and understanding. One day, without bothering anyone, I calmly threw on the blanket and saddle, took a look at the queer looking cinch and went off with mind quite easy. I think we had ascended an easy slope of a mountain for about two miles when I had a premonition that I might not have fixed that cinch according to Hoyle. Leaning over, I took an extra reef in it, finding it decidedly loose. About two hundred yards further along, I was suddenly astonished to find I was lying directly under the pony, the back cinch somewhere round his tail and the other one gaily flapping to the breeze. The moment I had a chance to know what had happened, I looked up to see a perfectly puzzled expression on old Buck's face, which was enough to make anyone laugh. Picking myself from the dust of the trail, I replaced the blanket, adjusted the saddle, studied the new-fangled cinch, sought a stump, and decided to return home till I learned how that cinch was meant to go. We went in perfect balance down the mountain and Buck and the new cinch were poked unceremoniously into the corral till I learned how to fasten the thing properly. It was a most scientific arrangement and perfectly safe if anyone knew anything about it. I never learned, I never tried to learn. Just a plain cinch finished off with a strap pun-ctured with the necessary holes is all I deem desirable for riding a cayuse. At another time two companions and I had climbed quite a fair mountain. This day I was on one named Eva. (Funny how a "tenderfoot" loves a name for her steed.) The ascent was perfectly easy so long as a tiny set of feet picked the way and the rider did not mind a few gullies and precipices. We eventually reached the summit of the mountain in perfect safety and looked into the goal for which we had come—a valley recently discovered at that time and later known as Ptarmigan Valley. The friends with me did not know Eva's physical imperfections any more than I did. Most ponies are rounded where cinches are supposed to go, but in Eva's case we were to learn that she grew exceptionally flat toward dinner-time. I should judge from results that Eva had either fed very early that morning or else lightly, but we were all unaware of anything but the marvelous scenery, the new valley in the distance and our own excitement at a reco[n]noitre there within a few days. With our heads in the clouds, figuratively, we began our descent. Eva certainly had all the qualities of a cat for getting about in rough places, so in my ignorance, I trusted her as completely to get down as she had done in hauling me up. Suddenly something told me that all was not well and I exclaimed: "O Mr. Blank, don't you think I am getting very close to Eva's ears?" There was not time for another word. I was suddenly off over her head like a frog with my left spur nicely caught in a big, wooden stirrup.

Looking round from my ignominious position, there was Eva down on her knees with the blanket utterly obliterating her head while the two friends sat horrified and mute for the moment. The gentleman naturally jumped as quickly as his wits recovered, took a ghastly look at me, when he found I was in fits of laughter and then after a long struggle released the spur. Eva in the meantime behaved as not a mare in a thousand would be supposed to behave. She squatted quietly till cinches and blanket were removed and then rose like the perfect lady she was.

Understanding what had caused the whole trouble, the cinches got an extra hitch to which my lady objected by attempting to blow herself up like a balloon, but she was a mite too late. It was a great lesson to an amateur equestrian. I never failed to take cognizance of cinches after that, specially on Eva, whether before or after feeding time. These minor details are not exciting to anyone who has not played the part, but they have been recalled because I have recently read: "Indian ponies are to be avoided," by a practical man who knows the west. The same flower grows differently in different environment, perhaps Indian ponies do the same. I simply know nothing about ponies except those of Indian origin and after piling up miles and miles into the thousands on said variety, after living with them several years on the trail, studying their funny characteristics, I shall always recommend that "getting-back-to-nature" stuff. Into my mind comes the remembrance of one, Pinky by name. He followed or led our big band of horses for one season, the summer we swam the Saskatchewan and Athabaska Rivers to reach our goal—the Tete Jaun Cache. He had obtained his name because his eyes, ears, nose and hoofs were pink.

I think his price at that time was all the way to $5. I do not think there was a spot in his whole body that was more than two feet thick through but he was as like a human being as possible—"little but O my!" His one occupation was to carry our air beds. He was very sensitive, and showed an excessive amount of brains for a horse. Though his load was light, he was usually the last in our large outfit to be loaded. Sometimes he was far in the rear, sometimes far ahead. The one who had the horses in charge, never bothered his head about Pinky. Pink knew his own job and could be trusted to perform it. I often noticed he was never far from the rest of the band when grazing but he always gave me the impression of complete exclusiveness. He was certainly no "mixer."

One day when we were on the search of the Columbia Ice-fields, there was no visible trail and so we would be in the river one moment, then out on shingle-flats, then up on high ground—that perfect trailing when one did not know what the next moment would bring forth. No one had given Pinky a thought for more than an hour, for he was back of us "over the hills and far away." Then we came on a rather trying corner, where our leader decided it best to veer to the right into a scrub forest to avoid what appeared to the naked eye as a rather deep hole in the small river we were ascending to its source.

There were plenty of scratches from the scrub to endure by both man and beast but we quickly came out onto a solid bit of shingle flat. Then we saw Pink's white hide ambling through the distant brush and suggested waiting to see what he would do. He arrived at the brink of the hole, looked studiously at it, turned and noticed the way the rest of the band had gone to reach that nice flat of pebbles and after due deliberation, decided to take a short cut.

He and his bags suddenly took a plunge and out of sight they went. I thought he would never come up, but he did, and the sight of that wee, bedraggled and dignified piece of horse-flesh emerging with all the dignity washed out of him, caused us all to burst into laughter. He took no notice of any of us till quite on the shingle-flats, then giving everyone a withering look, he stalked off up the stream choosing the way he deemed proper, and when we emerged under the shadow of Mount Alexandra, there stood Pink.

He had already performed his usual stunt of placing his head close to a tree as though tied, which every other horse in the outfit needed to be, and was waiting for his beds to be removed. I do not recollect his ever being tied up in the numerous months he was with us, but Pink meant to be treated like the man he was, so if no one else did it, he did the best he could for himself. We all felt rather sheepish over that laugh and would have apologized if we could, as it was no one ever after laughed in Pinky's presence again. "Horse sense?" Well, if you could ever locate Pinky, (for he went back to the Stoney reserve after his days of usefulness were over with us), anyone would admit those two words mean a great deal. I have had well bred horses before and since but never have I encountered such brains as those of the little cayuse of the northland, for whom I make my plea.

I am quite willing to bow to the opinion regarding his brothers and sisters further south, but we have never met on any such social platform as I have encountered in my own land.

But I want to return to a couple of words which left so strong an impression in reading "Dude Wrangler." If there is such a thing as a motor road leading to the land from whence came those papers and if their owner will let me in for a night, I want to see that part of Wyoming, where that phrase seems so common.

In my part of the globe "dude" has a most unwholesome sound. To use it in the face of any visitor would be more or less shocking and as is often said: "It simply is not done" up here. Then to use the word "wrangler" in my part of the country seems to infer a general muss-up with your horse and to apply it to my district (I take the whole responsibility of this) would be to infer that he who "wrangled" was not much of a horse-man. We have as fine horses as the west knows, but he who undertakes to manage a horse makes him mind, or knows the reason why. We have any number of women who can ride into a bunch of horses, cut out those they desire with as great skill as a man but its done with the utmost ease and no "wrangling." I have lived (with various winter lapses) in the west since 1912 and but once have I ever heard the word used.

Several years ago there was a large party of eastern girls expected for a short vacation in our wilderness. The day was Sunday. I was driving down the main street with my own roadster, when out of a cloud of dust appeared their official caretaker. He was arranging for a very modern camp on the shores of a beautiful lake several miles west of the little mountain village which is now my home. He had been dressed for the part in an eastern city, though I think if he had dared to wear what I saw him in, in his own home town, they would have arrested him. He was looking so wild and excited that I stopped my team to see what had possibly occurred. His hat had struck me in the distance as he came madly dashing along … You may buy a hat for the more northern part of this continent, which, for all I know may look very out-of-place in Wyoming and though some of the finest hats worn in Mexico are Yankee-made, you may not buy them in Yankee-land, you must get them in Mexico. To wear anything but the tall peaked hat in Mexico would leave you a marked man to yourself as well as to the Mexican. My friend was rather stout, his pony not over-weight, and altogether I did want to laugh. To my enquiry, he burst out: "My horse wrangler has been hurt!" If he had answered me in any foreign language, I could not have felt more astonishment than his suddenly saying "horse-wrangler." The said "wrangler" was a fine rider, knew every trail in miles and miles of wilderness, had been born in the heart of the great west and was a part of it, but I who knew his whole family, knew they could pass muster with the best the east could offer. His father, a native of New York, had drifted west called by that glamour which comes to so many and his life and his knowledge had woven themselves into the heart of the new country—the great, clean wilderness. He had led the life of the frontiersman, had imbibed a love for something bigger and broader than what a city of the mere east could give and it was left for me to hear his son called a "horse-wrangler." I shall never forget it because that word is so utterly out of our ken. It just goes to show that though the miles of distance may be very short, one needs to use a different vocabulary across certain invisible lines. The word "dude" is equally unfortunate to use here, at least I have never heard a native express himself to a tourist thus for fear of offence, though I can well believe there are times and occasions when a man's soul almost reaches the breaking point where he would like to use it and perhaps within himself he uses plenty of "frills" which would sound far worse if cast to the western winds.

As a matter of fact, I have found the real westerner patient under the most trying circumstances and taking all his trials and tribulations out on the boys around the camp-fire during the evenings when he turns his troubles into jests.

In the summer I live among tourists from morning to night and thousands of them at that and they come all togged out by eastern shops till our lips twitch and then I look back to the days when I felt a small revolver the very essence of my existence in a woolly west. One simply must live for a space of time in a land so different from "home" to know exactly what he should have, do, or wear.

It's not such a fearfully long time ago since I found myself a complete misfit in the land I was beginning to love and one day I came across a book which was my salvation for the time. It was entitled "A Woman Tenderfoot." The author had really done the things of which she wrote and though the chapter which particularly enthralled me is no longer necessary owing to a complete change in the minds of women generally, it was of keenest interest then.

It was the sketch of a skirt which a woman riding cross saddle, would find invaluable. It buttoned at will both hind and fore. When you mounted your steed you unb[u]ttoned just enough to give your pommel full play in front and the cantle of your saddle behind. You then advanced amidst the public looking respectability itself. As soon as the village and critics were well left behind, you poked the old thing into your duffel bag and that was the end of anything but the modern breeches, till you hailed back to civilisation. To-day,—well to-day or rather a few weeks ago I saw a girl arranging her bobbed hair in one of the largest rail road terminals of this continent without an eye of the many hundreds passing taking the slightest notice of her. She might as well have been arranging for a long tour on horseback and she looked so free and comfortable that I thought in spite of all we have to say about the old world's faults, this girl had struck simplicity, but the best of it was that no one seemed to mind.

All the "dudes" of to-day are very far from being men, in fact its the women who have the most time to play and now they play wholesomely and sanely. No longer do they wander with long, annoying skirts or get caught by intruding trees in their voluminous garments. They have reached out for an equality in clothing and have got it.

There is one thing on which I do not agree with my "cousin by marriage." He thinks the life of the wilds must be headed by "an educated Eastern man with a great deal of experience." Well, where are we to find that eastern man with his education ready-made, so to speak? One need not go so very far west of Chicago to find a young and inexperienced land compared to the days of Indian fighting or Indian living.

In this small place I call "home," there are men who never saw the east atall and who could, if so inclined, beat an easterner at any trick he might suggest. From the Atlantic to the Pacific we are all foreign[e]rs so far as that goes and not one of us but must claim our original ancestry to the other side of the Atlantic. Even the Indian is a modern invention when spoken of in the aeons and aeons of time. But also those men who were the first to adventure into the west, have left children and grand-children and with those descendents they have left a love of the hills and the plains, they have left an inheritance with which no eastern education can cope.

They have taught them not to starve where apparently no food exists, how to locate themselves when everything looks about alike.

Though "dude" ranching is not a large business within my special vicinity, owing perhaps to the physical condition of the country, I should not be too critical. Ours is the land of the cattle ranger, the timber cruiser, the trapper and the camper. The latter is about the only trick I know but I do know a little about it except the diamond hitch. I have lived with that hitch for months at a time but never mastered it, partly because I was sure it would master me first and partly because I never had the strength which it involves. I have never insisted on my woman's rights when it came to laying the bacon and flour, the kitchen utensils and blankets slap up against the sides of the patient beast which is to bear the burden or to throw the tarpaulin over all, then adjust a tangle of rope that holds everything in shape till the next stopping place, with not a sore shoulder from a shifting saddle. At this point in camping I have always resigned my rights as a woman and what is more, when we travel hundreds of miles, I am willing to follow blindly the man who chooses the best horses, who knows at the beginning, how to make out his list of "grub" for the months ahead, who knows how to find a ford in the deepest rivers (if there is one) and if not to abide by his decision if he says: "Swim!"

I have taken to a swollen river with a man who perhaps did not know what a dictionary was. I have been weeks with a man who learned from the Indians how to put up a tepee and switch the poles on the inside till the draft sent the curling smoke into its proper place—heaven itself. I have been long weeks with a man who made the best pie one day and dropped a grizzly the next with his first shot, but I doubt if he could pass through the first grade spelling book. But at this point I am willing to weaken. If I want a perfectly glorious trip, I do want a man at the head of the party who can talk on any subject at the camp-fire in the evening, providing his brains are equal to assisting the man of the country born, who is cautious in nasty places and who always keeps a cool head. But for "savvy" in my adopted country I care not a fig if he ever saw an eastern college or not. It is "savvy" which has always pulled us through some trying situations with the least discomfort and no dictionaries, geometry, trigonometry, or foreign languages can translate the above word which is so invaluable on the unknown trails—the old hunting trails of the Indians of days long gone.

As pictures never to be forgotten, I can go back to the nights round a blazing log fire, when we listened to the yarns of the trapper, the REAL trapper who spent his lonely winters going from trap to trap and never a soul to whom to speak for months at a time, to the nights when we listened to a particular man who had followed a precarious living by driving the mailcoach in hostile Indian country as well as plenty of bandits to hold him up if the Indians were not on their job. His English was all frayed at the heels because he had had no occasion to use his own tongue for fifteen long years; where a white man was a novelty and a white woman had not crossed his path in all that time. That last was a delicious experience, just to watch the courtesy he offered us which must have been taught him at least fifty years before and though his English was limited, he retained the innate elements of a gentleman. Doubtless to those who took us on the long trails, we were "dudes" in a sense, but they never used the word or I think I would have immediately taken the back trail. Both I and my companion were exceedingly sensitive on the subject generally, but we absorbed to the best of our ability the proper way in which to hold our reins, how to plant our feet in the stirrups, how to leap a log (O the times I have wanted to let my horse make his own leap while I got down and crept under any obstruction, but pride forbade and in some marvelous way I always managed to get over without a spill), how to get up when the dishpan rattled for breakfast and to attempt to be useful about camp. I never knew the latter to end but in one way: "You two go off and play now" which was certainly disconcerting when one saw twenty-odd horses to be put in shape for the next drive. We did so adore being useful on the trail but I can only recollect that the berries we brought in for supper and a stock of amiability ever made the slightest impression on our care-takers in those long, delightful days when we knew not what the next hour held in store for us. After one very long expedition we decided we would try taking some dried vegetables on our next expedition as an asset to our daily bacon, but it ended in growing sorry for our stomachs, so rank was the cabbage, so soggy the spinach and the potatoes a monotonous diet. To gather a hatful of wild strawberries and roll out a pie with the vinegar bottle was a red letter day. To find a patch of wild raspberries was to hold a banquet. Grouse and fish and coral mushrooms broke a certain monotony and made us all love our daily bacon the more.

We were too busy covering ground to stop for goat or mountain sheep for the summers of the northland are all too short as it is, though many a time I have grown hungry indeed watching a bunch of wild sheep on some distant point—the daintiest bit of wild meat the American continent knows.

I have spoken of ourselves as "dudes" in the eyes of those who would bother themselves with two women in an unbeaten country & I have used the word because I never quite got over the fact that it might be a little "dudeish" to use air beds. But we both had seen so many nightly choppings of spruce or pine boughs, gummy and scratched hands, not to mention the times we have wakened in the night to find a knob sticking uncomfortably somewhere into a tired body, that we braved all ridicule and bought those beds for our next big hike. We never regretted that investment. Pumping up a couple of waterproof beds where we might sleep in a swamp if need be, letting them out in the morning, saved much that was tiresome after a long day in the saddle. We stood the stigma (if ever there was one) for the comfort to ourselves and the cutting down of labor to those who watched over us. I can always recommend an air bed—and its price—with perfect safety.

If one is sleeping in such absolute comfort as the above, with a sound tepee and a real little tepee fire to wink one to sleep, there is no hotel I have ever entered which has such charm—barring of course the bath-tub. A certain writer speaks of Lewis and Clark taking to a cabin and a four poster if they could have found them when crossing the continent over one

181

hundred years ago. A cabin! Well poor dears, I do not think air beds were made at that time nor could they have carried them, but I have passed or staid near cabins in my various wanderings at odd times and the mere sight of one was all I needed to see my tepee go up on nice, clean ground, the air beds blown up and then compare our living quarters to a place where squirrels, porcupines, and skunks had held parties at various times. No, I have faith that neither Lewis or Clark would have exchanged the sweet ground for a mouldy shack. Many a time have we been forced to camp in burnt and scrubby timber, put up our tents wherever a bit of level ground could be found, set our house in order for the night, be covered with charcoal next day, but going off singing, knowing our horses had had a wonderful feed. A camper's safety is his horse and if all the ponies are in the best of shape, one may go on as long as the larder holds out. I am certainly interested in this "dude community" business just because I have tried it in the slightest kind of a way. In camping its "the fewer the better," but in "dudeing" it may be "the more the merrier."

For Instance: In my very green days of camping I was arranging to take a charming Boston girl as far as the Saskatchewan River, a distance of about seventy miles I think from our starting point.

It stood out then as a great adventure and of course we had to talk about it. I advise anyone who has any particular notion of his own on which to practice, to keep his plans to himself.

In the midst of our preparations, a quiet, little eastern woman asked if she and a companion might join our small party. At that early date it truly meant to me—the "more the merrier." Then another party asked if she might join us. O ye who think five women, no matter how excellent they be, can all be of one mind on the trail, take a tip from me. In three days from starting, the little woman and I were occupying one tent while the other three had the second. I do not think one unkind word was ever uttered by any one of the five, but we had separated as oil and water figuratively.

When the little new friend and I heard the pan beaten for breakfast, we walked out all ready for the day, ate what was set before us and listened to the giggling and laughter of those who thus would keep the whole procession held up. It meant a real trial to the spirit to note the horses being brought in, packed and left waiting while the others were beginning "to sit up and take notice."

Thus began a silent friction and we two who loved every moment of the day, every mile of the trail, knew the others were beginning to think the whole jaunt a perfect bore. In spite of these minor annoyances, we had many funny happenings as far as the Saskatchewan River, trailed westward on its shores and reaching a corner in the bend of the river locally known as Bear Creak, felt that the inevitable was about to happen. In fact the shock came when one of our party openly said: "Only three days and we will be back to a bath-tub." I looked with sickening feeling at the new, but understanding friend.

When we retired that night, I said: "Well, think of that! Three strangers, my party, yet they intend cutting our only too short two weeks down by three days, all for the sake of a bath-tub." The other, mild and gentle, replied: "I do not see that we can do anything, do you?" A bright idea, born of despair, struck me—anything for a few more days in God's playground. "Yes, I have it! Watch me to-morrow morning" and we said goodnight.

Bear Creek Corner is in the heart of a great garden of the mountains, of glaciers and rivers—a place in which to play, to fish, to loiter, to LIVE. The following morning, she who longed the most for the flesh-pots of civilisation, said: "Well, to-morrow we will be well on our way to Bow Summit and from there only one day to a tub and a cake of soap." I looked at her as mildly as a guilty conscience well could and replied: "That won't be possible." She was a much larger woman than I and with quite as much determination and I seemed to feel my leather shoe-strings rattle with fright. "Why not possible?" she enquired with an icy air. "Well," I replied with far more firmness than I felt, "to-morrow is Sunday and I never travel on Sundays."

What a collapse was there! All three of that group had openly said they would never travel on Sunday by trail while the little new friend and I had often whispered to each other: "Surely its best to travel on Sundays when man and beast are depending on food."

We staid out our three extra days, but they were tinged with regret at such fraudulent behavior and I think we both wished I had not taken such drastic measures to get what we wished.

We arrived back at the land of bath-tubs in due course and we two friends made all sorts of plans for the future, but firmly decided to keep our numbers down to two. We never broke our rule after that. We never had a riffle of disagreement in the thousands of miles we meandered with ponies, we had daily pleasures in spite of rain and snow, heat and mosquitoes and heavenly days piled in between.

Use an old camper's advice, never take but one tried and true friend with you, before you ever risk a crowd of five women, as well as men. I don't care whether they are male or female, it is always the same, camping brings out either the best or the worst. This sounds a very rambling sort of article to offer to the Public, but when you are camping you surely are rambling and as the door swings wider to those who are appreciating more and more the real outdoor life, perhaps some words from a "tenderfoot" camper who has gone into the game rather exhanstively may contain something worthwhile.

When Kipling wrote "east is east and west is west" could he ever have had a shadow of an idea of our own great continent?

I know from long experience that there is a large element of the east which dreams of the country west of the Mississippi as a crude place with very crude people inhabiting it. Just in my own small environment I have found it utterly untrue that the native of the far reaches speaks a language not accepted by the effete east and yet I picked up a paper recently in which were these lines. "Its a dood, thats what it is! A white-haired snoozer of a pie-eatin' awful dood. You seen the critter, etc., etc." Is not that sort of language enough to dampen the ardor of anyone going themselves or sending boys or girls for a summer into our big west? It would settle my mind completely even if I had a half dozen restless boys under my feet for whom I would want a summer training in the wilds. There is nothing like the best of roughing it to make a man or woman of a spoiled boy or girl of the east. I do not mind dirty hands and face, plenty of soap will settle that, but after an experience beginning in 1893 of meeting anyone who came along (and I have met all kinds) I still insist the west speaks exceptionally good English with lapses here and there as we will find in any part of the globe. Living the lonely life of a distant ranch naturally causes a man to adopt many local phrases, but in almost every instance I have found the polish of the east below the surface, a bit of real England and above all else a heart of gold. So many authors seem to enjoy painting their word pictures with rather too vivid colors or else, in many instances, they have gathered their intimacy with the west at second hand.

For instance: Several summers ago, our little party of four had completed all we could do in the line of mapping (out for the fun of the open air to be truthful) and were homeward bound over Howse Pass. By this time the packs were quite empty of the "grub" we had taken for the summer. Our tents, blankets and duffel bags were about all we could boast. We came down from the distant hills onto a real road after miles and miles of trail or no trail atall. Two of us were "dolled to the nines." Our caretakers had never started out with chaps, kerchiefs or flapping hat-brims. That sort of stuff was too old a story for them. On our last day in the open from one of the greatest picnics I had ever known, we all gathered round for a personal bonfire. Our worn and bent boots were laid solemnly on the last camp-fire we would know for that season; a few abandoned hats went into the same firey discard. In fact these same feminine hats had not seen the light of day for weeks and weeks—they had been bought in the east and we felt far more foolish in them than in our own bare heads. In consequence our faces must have been about the color of a well-tanned Indian. As for the men, the less said the better.

Mollie and I had dug out from our duffels the last bit of finery for the great finale. She had covered her generally worn appearance with a handsome buckskin coat bought from a squaw in the far north and showed the complaisance she had a right to feel. I hunted out a new pair of moccasins made by the same lady and fished from the bottom of my duffel the last treasure in perfect dress. It HAD been a gorgeous red silk hankie, but it had met with somewhat of a disaster owing to our tent catching fire and leaving both it and the tent with several holes in them. The tent had been sewed up with some extra shoe-strings, but the hankie had not gracefully taken to shoe-strings. However I laid out my finery as though I was to be presented at court and folded and folded till not a hole was visible.

Our two friends had wasted no more time than it took to use lather and a razor. But we were used to them thusly and they looked quite all right to us. Extinguishing our last camp-fire and wishing with all our hearts that winter would never come to this great playground, we started off, quite assured of ourselves and the impression we would make when we burst on the public eye.

About noon we came out on a main highway which led to a well-known lake and my special pony touched for the first time in his life a real road. He had been born and bred on a ranch in the far north. It was something which puzzled him for a moment, but we strung out as we had so often done on the trail and I popped off Nibs' back because my knees wanted one last, good stretch. Thus were we moving along in silence when around a bend in the road trotted a collie dog. It meant the heralding of the first white people we had seen for nearly five months. It was a most unexpected shock, for in a flash I saw ourselves as I knew others must see us. The red hankie, so carefully folded and re-folded a few hours before to hide the unfortunate holes, did not in the least carry the conviction that it had been bought originally in a high-class shop in the east, the moccasins in all their spotlessness, both looked and took me back to the tepee from whence I had bargained for them in tea and I knew we all resembled specimens of well tanned leather.

Hopping back into the saddle, I whispered to Mollie: "Do you mean to look when those people pass?" "Indeed I do not," she indignantly replied (you see we knew there must be people coming if a dog was trotting round in that district).

They very soon followed the dog and were sitting in a buckboard with heads and necks craned just as everyone does when an outfit comes along.

No, I did not look at them, just took a glimpse out of the tail of my eye without turning my head. I knew the driver was a student of an eastern college of high standard who drove tourists in the summer to help out his expenses. About the man tourist there was something slightly familiar and the little woman beside him had iron-gray hair. They were both gazing intently, the man through a specially thick pair of glasses, but I was far more taken up with being caught togged in the garments which had recently looked so elegant and with my burnt face than with the people who looked so spick-and-span.

We reached the little station where all were to disband and where, though grief-stricken at the play-days being over for that year, I was longing for about six fresh boiled eggs—one always longs for something special after such a long hike as we had just made. Our many friends greeted us as though we had just encircled the earth and returned, preserved by a kindly Providence, when in fact we had been having the time of our lives and had no slightest wish to see a hotel and shuddered that we must return to the hum-drum of life—all but the boiled eggs. Then someone said: "You

must have met Kipling as his rig drove to the lake only a half hour ago."
"Indeed, was that Kipling? Well, he certainly took a good look at us and
our outfit," and he passed completely from my mind. I was thinking far
more of parting with our horses, a real bath-tub, the aforesaid eggs and
some nice garments which I donned as soon as the occasion permitted.

In the evening it was a perfect joy to put on a real evening gown. That
there was a well defined line of white and dark flesh, did not mar a certain satisfaction that I was rid, for the nonce of the out-door smell of a
khaki shirt.

Though I saw Kipling wandering about the rotunda of the hotel, it never
entered my head to speak to him, any more than the notion would probably
enter his to address us. For once in my life I was reveling in fine feathers,
a thing which is really not a part of my make-up any more than to eat six
eggs usually at one sitting.

Mr. Kipling is probably to-day what he was at the time of which I speak.
I fancy he never has had any love of playing "lion" any more than I would
wish to make him roar. I had been posted by mutual friends of his characteristics and respected them. For a couple of hours I switched round in my
gay garments. There was no intentional disloyalty to the khaki breeches,
the hob-nailed boots, or the dried potatoes, just a short love of change, for
within my soul my hills would be forever calling me back to them.

The next morning the Kipling family moved west by train and a short
time later I was looking on the flesh-pots of Philadelphia and the new
fashions which had rolled in while we had been having a perfect time in
the wilderness where there is no soil on which fashions may grow.

Stopping in a special business office to see and report to an old friend,
he suddenly said: "So you met Kipling?" "No," I replied," I did not meet
him, I knew better. I saw him, walked all round him and studied him as
anyone would study the only Kipling who ever was born, but I did not
exchange a word with him." My friend looked rather astonished and said:
"But you must have met him as he was telling me all about your work." I
smiled and replied: "O well, author's license," and forgot the incident in
five minutes. The following spring being in Boston, I mentioned passing
Kipling when we were such an unsightly party and how my friend of the
east had insisted we had met him. My cousin laughed and said: "Then it
must have been you of whom he wrote when publishing certain articles in
an American magazine after his return to England." She then kindly hunted
up those same articles that I might have the satisfaction of knowing how
so great a man viewed two very humble campers. There was no doubt he
had written of the right parties, but not in his usual wonderful strain. Who
could wonder? He was passing through a great country on a red plush seat
and anyone knows that red plush, a dining-car, a bumpy bed at night, and
a buck-board are not conducive to hailing the muses to your side. I felt
sorry for the part he had been forced to miss. Had Kipling gone into the
places where we had gone, the world would have been the richer for his

songs. OUR tongues and brains had not been adequate to tell in verse the joys of the nightly camp-fire, while he would have left a lasting and beautiful memory of some of the wonderful snowstorms in the hills, the roaring rivers, the sweet, calm days in the many sunny valleys. Perhaps he would even have found a way to say a good word for the pestiferous mosquito which drives the northern explorer wild. Even a buckboard had silenced the sweetest of singers and I found none of his usual charm in which I so delight. The only thing which really interested me was what he found to say about our unexpected camping party: "Indians on the move?" said I. How characteristic. (There was not an Indian camping or living within eighty miles of where we had our momentous passing.) As the women jolted by (O to see in print that I had "jolted" after the miles of experience on one of the best and easiest riding ponies I ever had) one of them slightly raised her eyes and they were doubtless the comprehending eyes of the civilised white woman which moved in the berry-brown face! "Yes" said the driver, "that will be Mrs. So-and-so and Miss So-and-so. They mostly camp hereabout for three months every year." There was a little more in the same strain, but that is enough to emphasize my point. I have found writers and writers who long to give local color to their sketches of the west and even my admired Kipling did not spare the man who was in his last year at one of the great Eastern colleges.

I cannot assume I am living in an effete west and though much of the language is simple it is almost invariably grammatical and pleasant.

It is not one writer but many who put the most astounding language into the mouths of those who live by hunting or chasing the "dudes" over the hills during the summer that they may add to their account for the following winter in some eastern college. That they absorb a wonderful vocabulary of profanity I have no slightest doubt. If I had to make a living for a few months of the year by keeping the average cayuse on an average trail, I wonder if I could stick to the plain clean English so splendidly as the men do who have taken me into the fastnesses.

Twenty-odd years amidst this type of man has taught me that solitude breeds refinement. I have entered many a bachelor shack to find the best books of reference, the best of poets (among them Kipling is never forgotten) good writers, plenty of the best music and above all, the best specimens from the brushes of famous artists.

Does not the writer owe it to his readers to sketch the man of the west at his best? I have heard tourists who felt actually defrauded because the man who takes him on the trail acts humanly and does not use the language as is so often dished out in print. I have just come from threading the streets of several large eastern cities and I can truly affirm that amidst the madding crowds, I heard quite an amount of exceptionally ungrammatical as well as unrepeatable language which would not be tolerated in my hills.

The man who lives closest to Nature—in my experience—is just about the cleanest living man I have ever met. I am not including his frills when he has a bunch of aggravating cattle or horses to handle (I might be able to locate a few terms myself if driven to it) but if I am looking for a REAL shock, I run down east where chewing-gum runs rampant or you are puzzled whether a silk stocking is silk or something else.

At one time here we had living on a famous ranch a man who knew all there was to know of either cattle or horses. He was not a young man and he might have been here in the buffalo days for all I know. I will give him the name by which he went to all who loved him and he was certainly a man of few enemies. "Fred." He had but one eye, but O what that eye could see! His voice was low and soft. He always appeared at the "Old Timers' Dances" in a dress suit perfectly up-to-date. He had hailed in the long ago from the east, and when he returned there to meet old friends, he was the pride of all the fashionable clubs. They gloried in him and his slow smile and speech, for there never was but the one "Fred." On his own authority I have this story of "Fred" who has long gone to the land of all clean living ranchmen. He had been on one of his few visits east and was quietly listening to a number of the younger club-men who did not know that the rather ill-fitting morning suit covered the massive body of one of the shrewdest men of the west.

Some of the crowd wore mon[o]cles, some spats of perfect date, while others wore tweeds from "the old country" and for want of something better to do, they were impressing a man of whom in their youth, they knew nothing. One of them had been to Lord-so-and-so's place in England, when he "was home last," one of them was on the most intimate terms with the Duke of such-and-such. Fred kept perfect silence for a long time, for Fred probably knew more dukes and things than all of them put to-gether as his ranch and his hospitality were known from coast to coast. They kept up their chatter of impressing this man of the west till his temperament would stand no more, and when finally addressed so as to bring him into their elite circle, he drawlingly said: "Your talk reminds me of when I was visiting Queen Victoria." The crowd gazed in astonishment, but his face was utterly without expression other than kindly & "Yes, I had a most pleasant time at Windsor. When I was in London she most graciously invited me down. Of course I went as I had known her when a much younger woman. It grew a little dull for me after living so long on the range, so one night I said: "If you don't mind, your Majesty, I think I'll take a little run up to London. Be back about eleven o'clock." "All right, Fred," said the Queen, "the butler is usually on hand, so you will have no trouble getting in." I went up to London, got among some of my old pals and by jove, it was twelve o'clock before I got back to Windsor. I found the front door locked and it was an excessively chill night. Fortunately I knew which was the Queen's window, so I stepped into the driveway and threw up pebbles on the glass till she came to see what was the matter. Then she said: "Is that you, Fred? Well, just wait till I put on my crown and I will come down and let you in."

O that I could put into his repeated words the drawl, so gentle, so distinguished, and the fun glittering in his one bright blue eye as he told me the tale. "Whatever did those men say, Fred, after such a story?" "Say?" "Say nothing! They saw my point and I never heard of dukes or lords from that day while staying at the club." Twenty years must have passed since I heard the famous story of Fred visiting Windsor but there must be many yet who remember his joke on a bunch of boys who worked so hard to impress a westerner. "You see," he added "they have a mighty restricted outlook on life as compared to us who have all out-doors to keep us clean, we are not forced to elbow our way on trams or mix even in the slightest way with the worst of civilisation, and we have a bigger chance of being men, real men." This lovable Fred had entertained (no doubt many a time to his sorrow) hundreds of famous men and women from every part of the globe and though I know he must have been courteous, I venture to say he would many a time have liked to consign them to some other spot than his own ranch. In his own inimitable way he had silenced—well, a type of man who would have starved to death if left to his own resources in the Great West.

Mr. Burt's "Diary" is of inestimable value to the constantly increasing numbers who are finding out the fact that the west holds in its hands (and is ready to give for the asking) health, wealth and happiness to him who will seek. He talks of bears as only one who has lived in their haunts and knows them harmless if let alone. He speaks of small frictions which are apt to occur when too many are congregated to-gether—a sample of which I gave before.

Life is the same whether on a ranch, a range or the trail. A few nights ago I sat on the train reading a portion of his "diary" and I could not but take violent exception to one thing he said. I was sitting beside a man who knows what "dude wrangling" is by experience and he also knows what a true wilderness is. I said: "You know my work after a fashion. How many miles do you think our various outfits have traveled in a complete and unmapped country in the course of all the numerous summers?" "Well," said he, "I never was with you but counting thus and so and all the extra valleys, I should say you have gone into at least two thousand unexplored miles." "Just read this then," and I pointed to these words: "The man who says he never was lost or can't be lost is a liar." Why I felt utterly angry. Don't think for one moment that I take the slightest credit to myself that we never were lost but I doubt after my long experience if anyone could lose me under average conditions.

I can well remember the day when I could have been lost in five minutes, but after studying how rivers run, how the north star is located, how the green moss clings to the north side of the trees, and that the sun is mostly on his job, I cannot for the life of me see why anyone should ever endure more than a short bewilderment.

I can count twenty men off-hand who have gone off in the late fall with their snow-shoes, a side of bacon, some flour and trapped the whole winter, living at times under trees, burrowing for a few hours' sleep in a great snow-bank and came back laden with pelts, perhaps no sun for days, with rivers frozen solid, and arrived in our midst whole, healthy, happy and never gone a half mile out of their way. I never heard anyone express themselves that these men had done anything remarkable, neither did they ask praise for the doing.

Of course in our own particular instance it has been a different matter. We have always carried sufficient food in case our unknown destination might be four or forty miles—whether we might strike a nasty muskeg or an impassible river. One never can tell what is ahead when there is no slightest information obtainable. All we have ever required was a river, for the smallest of rivers will be looking for a larger one and with patience, time and plenty of food one is bound to get through any place. LOST! Why we took one whole summer in a new lot of valleys and rivers to attempt to locate a special lake whose beauty even the phlegmatic Indians painted in exciting terms. We could never say we were lost but there was not a day in all that untracked country when a single one of us would have failed to back-track if any sort of accident had occurred. To be sure we did not locate the lake that year, having misunderstood a certain detour from one of our red friends, but we had any amount of fun mapping a perfectly good piece of ground more than three hundred miles in length which the hunters and trappers had never considered for a moment in their line of business.

Often and often has come to me the title of a lecture by an old man speaking to a bunch of small children of which I was one. He was dry as dust so far as keeping our minds on the valuable things he was attempting to tell us, but the title of his talk was: "There is nothing new under the sun." Haven't I had plenty of chances since to know the old chap was quite right? To think of the miles and miles we ferreted out only at the end of a long day to see some rotting tepee poles, the little triangle of a prospector's camp-fire, a long-discarded wickiup, something or other which bore into our minds: "Don't think you were ever the first in this place."

To go back to our illusive lake. It was late the same fall when an Indian visited us on the Kootenai Plains and though he must have been at least thirty years of age, he had gone on a hunting trip with his family when he was about fourteen to the lake for which we had been so valiantly searching and he drew for me one of the grubbiest maps (at least they were memory sketches) it has ever been my privilege to behold. But we clutched that sketch as something more priceless than the gold it took to reach it and vowed we would never rest till that lake was located on our map.

Early the following spring, with all our family—the horses making up a most affectionate portion, the air beds in shape, the food packed, we practically made a "bee line" to our desired lake through the help of the dirty map, the understanding qualities of those in whom we trusted and the driving motive of that for which we had sought so long.

Just two weeks from the day of starting we located our long elusive treasure, another summer surveying its tortuous shores, finding it eighteen miles long, eighteen miles of as great beauty as the Indians had said. I shall never believe but that an Indian has a love of the beautiful in his soul. He would think you crazy if you told him such a thing, but never in all our wanderings have I found either old or new camps which did not indicate a love of the beautiful. He looks for water, he looks for grazing ground, but his tepee always seems to stand where it speaks aloud—"The world is mine."

We hear of people being lost in blizzards in great cities, but what have they to guide them? Out in the wilderness is a far safer place to wend your way. You may feel the up-hill or down-hill on your ponies if caught in heavy snow. The man of the hills buries himself with some wood for cooking, his blankets and his frying-pan and bides his time till the storm breaks, leaving the sunshine and rivers to act as guide-posts. We (I mean always those who have had the lives bothered out of them by us) have tried it all in a modest way, but the husky trapper has tried it in earnest and I know of no case where he has failed.

LOST! Goodness, that's a part of the game in our part of the country and until I read the quotation in the Saturday Evening Post I had never heard of such a catastrophe happening a man who was practical. But as none of the hundreds of miles of our country are alike in the great west & I am perfectly willing to concede such a thing may happen in some other part of our vast country and perhaps I have been more lucky than I know in having chosen a place for a home in the west where such things are unknown in my limited experience.

A New Year in the Wilds

It was New Year's eve. The old Year, with his ragged cloak clutched tightly in his cold hands, was bidding adieu to the world—our mountain world—a shrieking, howling, lusty, new-born infant of a year crowding rudely in behind him to gain the position he was so reluctantly giving up. The winds from the very polar regions themselves had searched out the village of Banff and finding one lone, little bungalow crouched among the pines, high on the mountain-side, screamed at its shuttered windows and threw itself upon the doors as a hungry wolf. Inside all was cheery. Around the walls of the large living-room lanterns burned dimly and softly, a great fire of pine logs snapped and roared up the wide chimney and I and my dog, alone, dreamed dreams of the outside world and its doings. No angry, little New Year could touch us in our retreat, no howling wind-wolves intrude a fang within the tightly barred casements.

The tempest rose and fell; with a howl of rage it hurled a fine, sandy snow upon the window-panes, then impotently sobbed, and died away among the pine-tops. Silence reigned and my little companion and I sat watching the showers of sparks scurrying up the black throat of the chimney till another blast struck the bungalow and fought to reach us even by way of the chimney itself.

The little dog could have no fancies—it was his first New Year, his first experience of a great storm raging in the heart of the Canadian Rockies. Stretched before the bright logs on a soft Navajo blanket, his mistress whom it was his duty to guard, safely beside him, he yawned and slept. Alone I watched the pictures of other New Year nights forming and fading in the pine smoke; some were clouded some were bright. The storm without brought voices long unheard, some were merry and sweet, some sad as the moan of the passing wind in the pine-tops, but all—memories, memories.

The old, high clock, a bit of HOME from the east, ticked solemnly in its newly adopted corner, ticked relentlessly the hours nine, ten, eleven, into the passing year, into eternity. Then in a lull of the storm, of the fretting shutters, of the cre[a]king, grinding trees, it gave the warning click—and to my listening ear, borne on the clear north wind, came the first faint tones of our village church-bell. The old clock, which had tol[l]ed over a century's knells, joined its heavy ring with the village voice and for us in the mountain fastness a year was gone, a year was come.

With toes on the fender and eyes gazing into the fire, but thoughts three thousand miles away, the old, old saying came to me—"How very little one half the world knows of how the other half lives." Such perfect peace in the heart of a storm, in the heart of a wilderness, but the WORLD knew nothing of us! The lives of those who elect to live in the land of the Frost King seem but a series of deprivation and hardship to those who have never known the fierce splendour and savagery of our country, but its very wrath and cruelty only endear it all to us, and each rare, sunny day is brighter for the clouds that intervene. And here was New Year's eve! I had thought it was to take courage to remain in the frozen north-land that I might see for myself the greatest winter play-ground of our continent, and here I was, snug and warm and happy, and eagerly looking forward to the morrow for the greatest treat of all, a treat of this country which had been promised me for years, but which had never been fulfilled. I had been bidden to the New Year feast of the Stoney Indians at their reserve at Morley, a small wayside station about [word missing] miles east of our own small village. But would it be possible to reach Morley in such a blizzard? would the long-desired visit come to pass after all? No use to surmise ten hours ahead in this land of fickle weather. I had watched the old Year out by my "ain" fire-side, the morrow and the young Year would give me what they chose when the morrow came. Out went the lanterns, the faithful dog crept to his blanket, the dying embers lit up the brasses of the fire-place, and the ghostly face of the old clock; in ten minutes storms might rage, the coyotes' cry reverberate through the wild hills, I was sleeping peacefully and perhaps dreaming of the real nerve it would take the next day to eat my share at the Indian feast.

It was nearly nine o'clock the next morning before sufficient light had filtered in the windows to waken me. There was no breath of the wind of the night before, not a cloud in the sky, only a great, unbroken pall of snow covering everything. Behind Mount Rundle the sun was shyly steal-ing, too early in the year for it to look bravely in before 10 o'clock. Across the smooth lawn of snow went foot-prints—fresh ones—and my sleepy eyes followed them to the scrub and pine beyond the drive, where I saw what I knew I should see—three deer pawing in the soft, fluffy snow for breakfast—a buck, a doe and a fawn. "Lonely" say you who live in that other world from our's? Lonely, when we have such visitors, who shyly crane their necks to our windows and start ever so slightly when they catch a glimpse of themselves reflected? when we may go but a mile from our own door and see the mountain sheep in their haunts? speak a wandering coyote by the wayside? and even see an occasional bear in the springtime as he slips silently into the bushes, his motto—"best to keep out of trouble than to get out"?

But New Year morning and an Indian feast and a glorious day were no combination to allow one to idle away the precious moments before train-time thinking of so-called loneliness or watching the pretty callers. The morning, was cold, clear and still, and the engine of the east-bound train a hoary monster of frost as he puffed into the station, gobbled up a bunch of merry hockey players bound for Canmore and me for Morley, then hurried on toward the open prairie and the vast, frozen wheat-fields of the interior.

Mile by mile we rushed past the great snow peaks that form the gate-way to the entire Rocky mountain system, then leaving them standing white, clear and stern against the cold, blue sky, we shaped our course among the rugged, rolling foot-hills. With the mountains always beckoning the stranger's interest, these foot-hills of the Rockies often are passed quite unnoticed by the stranger coming to our land for the first time. But let him see them when the wee ground roses are in full bloom, or that first flower of the spring, the purple anemone dyes all the slopes in mauve,—each little blossom rollicking nodding its head in the soft breeze,—and many other prairie flowers which spring up in rapid succession, and he would almost aspire to be a ward of the government—a Stoney Indian—and idle away his life among the hill flowers and beside the Bow River.

But in January only frost flowers are to be seen huddled among the dead stalks of the golden-rod, the leafless rose-bushes and an occasional tuft of brown buffalo grass, which has struggled to hold its head to the sweeping winds, even then the foothills are picturesque. But magnificent as it all was, my thoughts remained of the earth, earthy, and with the steady, rhythmic turn of the wheels of the train, the refrain flew round in my head—"What do you eat at an Indian feast? What do you eat at an Indian feast?" over and over, till I was ready to take a back train for fear I should weaken in doing my part. Then, "on the dot," we pulled up at the station of Morley, I grabbed up camera and bag and in another moment stood on the platform among waiting friends, the engine gave a busy whistle, the train slid off to the east, the windows showed a row of mystified faces looking out at three human beings who seemed to be voluntarily remaining behind in "the wilderness." O the traveler of the every-day, how very little he knows of our northern life, as he profoundly rushes "on schedule time" from ocean to ocean. I know it from my own experience. Time and again have I been carried past Morley with not an idea of the life there, time and again looked across those rolling foot-hills, gazed hungrily at the Indian tepees with their threads of blue smoke curling from them in the frosty morning air, or in winter at their wee, crude houses tucked in the notches of the hills, and wished I might wander round among them and study closer the life of our "vanishing race." And the day had come at last. Those meeting me, hurried me, sans ceremony, to the picturesque shack of the Indian trader, where I met first his wife, then a wee daughter, and then—a glorious turkey done to a turn and flanked with all the goodies known to the world I had just abjured. It was a comforting sight, but with the keen edge of a ravenous appetite finally dulled, the song of the train wheels came back to me and I remembered this was not the feast for which I had come.

I began to feel impatient, I was a little afraid of missing something. Out on the distant highway an occasional team passed and still the good things of civilisation were marshalled to the trader's table. Then there came the clatter of wheels close to hand, and an open rig, driven by a stalwart Indian drew up to the house. That finished all thoughts of turkey. Three or four squaws and a half dozen pappooses seemed to be piled in the ancient rig without much idea as to order and all of them clad in the very dyes of the rain-bow itself. I hurried to the window and immediately recognised my friend Jonas Benjamin and his squaw. The wind was screaming straight from the mountains, but I flew forth to shake hands, and take if possible, a photograph showing the social side of Indian life. The women in their sweet, musical voices called pleasantly "Happy New Year!" the kiddies peeked, then ducked shyly under the blue, pink, purple, green blankets, and a tiny pappoose, tied to its mother's back, shrunk out of sight and out of the force of the icy wind.

My friend Jonas, whom I had met before at more civilised functions, it seems was a 'north-side' Indian (living on a portion of the reserve north of the rail-road track) and with his family was just returning from his official visit to the Indians of the south side. We passed a few complimentary remarks and smiles to each other, but as I was not clad in warm, Hudson Bay blankets, the conversation was quickly brought to a close, and I ran back to shelter in the stout log shack. Standing by the window, I looked out upon the phase of life I had come to see. Far away in the distance I could mark where the shacks of the Indians stood, by the threads of blue smoke curling to the sky; along the prairie roads crude, rickety wagons, filled with decorous occupants and drawn by typical Indian ponies, moved, some bound for the north side, some for the south; red, blue, yellow and green emphasized the passing scene, as each lady clad in the very best she possessed, sat [proud], straight and unsmiling beside her lord and master—each bent on the one social event of the year. "Not so different from the white man and his New Year calls," thought I.

Within my shelter, the windows of the little shack rattled, the wind found an unused chimney somewhere in the room and howled and shook and fought for entrance; I wondered how we were ever going to stand that prairie wind, it was my first experience. Then the rig was announced and muffled to the eyes, we all emerged, receiving a blast in the faces which cut off breathing for an instant. I eyed the team. It had a "frisky" appearance. I warily watched my host take the ribbons, he grasped them with that skill which sends a wave of confidence to the doubting heart and we shot out before the whole exposed valley. I remarked on the fine type of his beasts—"Yes, pretty good goers. Haven't been out of the stable since Christmas." I could well believe him! I had so often gazed longingly from the train windows at those prairie roads as they wound their way inconsequentially up hill and down dale, behind hummocks, then away into the blue haze of the horizon, so often wondered if I might ever follow them, that for the instant life was but a dream.

But away we sped, the unreality died. There was no dream in the movement of those horses. So far as I could see, my host merely held a taut rein and let them go. We were quickly on the main highway, skimming over the hard ground, topping a rise, plunging into a coulee, swaying from side to side with the natural rise and fall of a road-bed which was only a prairie trail in reality. Behind us tore the wind, piling up our own dust in clouds before us; no one spoke, my hat settled over dust-filled eyes, and we crouched in silence before the hurricane which was materially assisting our advance to the Council house of the south side, where we drew up with a flourish and a sigh of relief from all hands.

Descending to the ground, I had my first chance to look round and see where we were. In various directions stood the small shacks of the Indians, their natural home, the tepee, being too cold a residence during the rigid winters of the foot-hills now that they must be made of canvas and not the warm buffalo hide of the old days. Coming over the hills were fluttering bits of color—the squaws in their best—men in beaded garments stood about and small boys hopping round in moccasins to keep warm looked respectfully at the white visitors coming to the feast. The door of the Council House was bravely decorated with spruce boughs and above the building waved a large English flag. My partial eye caught sight of "the stars and stripes" floating gayly over an unpretentious dwelling a short distance away, and I eagerly asked why its presence, "O, all flags look alike to the Indian," said my informant, which quite settled all patriotic thrills for me.

The horses securely tied, everyone was glad to seek shelter from the persistent wind, and we entered the Council hall. The other members of our party being friends of long standing of the tribe, our entrance caused no flutter of undue curiosity. The hall was about forty feet by twenty-five feet, the walls were of unplaned boards, three windows on each side, which had never seen soap, bravely let in all the light they could, a rude pine table stretched its gaunt length from side to side at the far end, and an old rusty box stove held its honorable position in the centre of the room. To us just hurled into shelter by the bitter wind, this last object was a most welcome sight. Its old sides were a glowing red from the stoking it was constantly receiving at the hands of innumerable squaws who were squatting quite within scorching distance of its intense heat and who seemed to be testing its abilities by frequent expectorations on its sizzling sides. Just beyond the fire ring sat other squaws, their little ones of three to five tumbling over and among them, their pappooses either swaying in their arms or slung in the gay blankets on their backs. A few men stood about smoking vigorously at cigarettes or old black pipes and evidently acting as hosts for the occasion. The few attempts at conversation were being carried on in low tones, there was little or no laughing or jesting, the greater amount of noise heard, being whimpers and wails from the infant element who cried "just like white folks."

And this was the New Year feast of the Stoneys! The greatest day of the year to the Indian! It all struck me as a very good lesson in politeness and self-restraint to their higher cultured brothers and sisters who pretty universally are under the impression they are made from more superior clay. As soon as I had grown accustomed to the heat, the closeness, the semi-gloom of the room, the thick smoke from the innumerable ancient pipes, I looked across at the rough table. On it were a few tin plates, a partly used can of condensed milk and an old sugar bowl. Then one of the Indians, a fine, manly fellow stepped to and whispered something. The white man turned to us and said,—"Allow me to introduce Chief MacLean and he wishes us to step forward and have something to eat." It had come. Past the gay colors and through the un-curious throng of up-turned faces and restless little folks we made our way, noting each object as we went. A huge, square tin vessel, which had originally had coal-oil consigned to its keeping, was bubbling away busily on the red-hot stove, doubtless contained the tea. Were we to be served tea? We stepped round a large, wooden bucket sitting on the floor which contained boiled rice liberally mixed with raisins. Were we to have rice and raisins, and if so, why had I been doomed to behold the kiddies playing leap-frog over it and almost in it? Then we slid to the places appointed by the Chief and after all the years of desire, I sat at an Indian feast.

The festive board was bare but neat. In front of each was a tin plate liberally supplied with pieces of "pemmican," at each place an enamelled cup of strong tea, and before us the can of condensed milk and the bowl of sugar. It was my first taste of "pemmican." We think of it to-day as a diet invented for polar explorers, but it is really an Indian recipe, and at the Indian feast I first tasted his national dish, made as his grandmothers and great-grandmothers had prepared it.

In the past fall the bucks had brought in the deer meat, which the squaws had dried. This dried meat had then been pounded—probably in some of the stone basins of old, then packed in crocks and hot beef suet poured over it. It looked on our plates like chunks of rock salt and took nearly as much energy to masticate. The flavor of it was not atall bad and I have seen one or two occasions in my life when it would have been a most welcome addition to our camp larder. The tea was very good indeed, and was most refreshing to a body that had been chilled to the bone in a zero breeze. Some of our party who had eaten Indian pemmican before kindly saved us the annoyance of finishing what was on our plates by reaching across the table and clearing our tin plates for us, and I, for one, rose satisfied at last at having witnessed a portion at least of the Indian New Year. Rising we sauntered back among the seated crowd, speaking to some low-voiced squaw, admiring the beautiful beadwork displayed in both masculine and feminine toilets, noting some specially fine type of manhood. The women quickly lose their claims to good looks owing to early child-bearing and to all the rough work of the lodge falling upon their shoulders; but the men remain handsome, dignified, stalwart even to extreme old age—so much for being a man among the Indians.

As we gathered our warm wraps around us and filed down the room among our seated hostesses, grimy, daintily formed hands were held out and many a murmured "Happy New Year" in low voices, lingered with us as the door closed behind us.

"We will have to visit the Council house on the north side now," said my driver-host, "it would never do to go to one and not the other." "How far is it?" I asked, as the blast from the north pole hit me. "O, not far, just a short distance over the track, back there in that bunch of hills." Sounded pretty near, and I did so want to see it all. The day was darkening fast, too dusk already for the camera to be of the slightest use, but even the devotee of a camera may be permitted memory pictures.

We all "piled" into the rig, drew the rugs well up, Mr. W. untied the now thoroughly chilled and restive team from the flag-staff, made a dash for his seat. Instantly we bounded out into the open prairie, where fortunately, there wasn't a thing to fall over or run into, then turning the horses' heads scientifically and facing the icy winds, we went tearing madly toward the "north side." What a drive that was! Those who were with me were too accustomed to it to see anything out of the ordinary in it, but to me it was freighted with all the wildness and romance of that wild country in the past. It was to this bit of section had come the first Protestant missionaries

197

fifty years before, it was here had met in peace and war the Sarcees, Bloods, Crees, Blackfeet. The low, surrounding hills and their sheltered coulees had been homes for the Indians perhaps for centuries. The great Douglas spruces and feathery poplars had given them heat, the valleys flowing with clear streams had given them drink it was a country as fruitful for game as for man, before the advent of his white brother, the Indian had few wants unsupplied in the valley of the Bow.

But the streams were locked in the ice grasp, the poplar boughs stood like ghosts and the rugged spruces were as black spectres against a ragged, angry sky. Our team, warmed to its work, bounded (ran, I would prefer to say), across the rail-road track, tore down a long hill-side, stopped for nothing as we rattled across the Bow River bridge, tackled a steep slope as though they had nothing but themselves to pull up there, and then avoiding the main highway, which Mr. W. thought too slippery to follow, started on the wildest drive I ever had. All road whatever was abandoned, our way led over virgin prairie; the horses, never stopping for breath, went to their work and the hills as though it was all play.

Rounding one very steep portion, we faced not only the hurricane, but all the Rocky mountains themselves. The wind shrieked and struck us, tore at the robes and threatened to behead us, but there lay a sight which no wind could blow from us. The sun had just slipped behind the long range leaving a trail of red, gold and brown streamers flaunting above the purple peaks. To the south glistened two steel threads, their sinuo[u]s way soon lost in the distant shadows, and beyond them column after column of smoke rising from the humble homes of the Indians.

But the wind, with re-doubled force, whipped the fine snow into our eyes, we gave up the magnificent view, with half-blinded eyes, I looked round to see if that second Council house was within sight—there was nothing save more hill to climb. I grabbed my hat, my fingers ached with the cold, enthusiasm was rapidly departing. Mr. W., in a lull of the blast, said he had never gone that way before, "but it could not be much farther" and we kept on climbing. Another rise and the mountains were almost obliterated by the oncoming night, and except that I knew our pilot of the wilderness pretty well, I might have done much more thinking than I did regarding our return drive. We reached a level, the horses trotted gently under a clump of poplars, and I knew we had reached the Council house. It was a chilled and stiff enthusiast who crept over the wheels to the ground and made her way in the dusk to the shack just visible. Jonas Benjamin met and welcomed us, but we were too late. The little hall was growing cold, the guests had departed, the fire burned low, one old coal-oil lantern burned dimly and smokily and barely lit up the pitiful decorations of paper garlands. Outside, far and wide could be had the boughs of spruce and pine and kini-kin-ic with its scarlet berries, but the un-aesthetic hearts of our red friends had turned to fluted green and red tissue paper and big, fat bells made of the same. Alas, alas! To what is civilisation bringing us!

But night with black wings, was hurrying across hill and valley. Mr. W. had done his duty by presenting himself and we had done ours by coming with him. There was no lunch left to offer us, a fact over which we felt more or less resigned. Jonas informed Mr. W. that "there was so much grub left, they would feast the following day and perhaps the next, so come again," then we all said "Happy New Year" and groped our way back to the rig.

I do not know but that the drive home in the dark was almost as hair-raising as any of the rest of it. The wind had not abated perceptibly, we descended to the valley via the coulee which we had avoided going up and our horses reach[ed] level ground more by miracle than otherwise, as it was ice from top to bottom with a stream of good dimensions flowing over it.

What does an easterner know of horses or the driving of them? Or what is an eastern horse compared to one bred in those hills? No comparison can be made, they are separate elements. And one whose school in horse flesh has been in the east, finds much left to learn. I certainly went to school behind those two horses. After much bumping, swaying, slipping, sliding—after catching breath twenty times as we pitched toward some slippery precipice or seemed in imminent peril of turning into one grand toboggan slide, the welcome twinkle of station lights shone through the blackness and our team swept round the curve to the door of the little shack.

How good it felt inside that wee, prairie home, how the wind howled and tore about it as we sat around our hostess' pretty table, and how I longed to say—"I have had enough!" But the pow-wow at the south-side Council house was to come off at eight o'clock and as invitations to pow-wows in the past had been exceedingly limited, it seemed imperative to make one last sacrifice to the elements. No, however appreciated the shelter, curiosity came first and at eight o'clock sharp, the restless stamping of the horses at the door and a brisk call from outside—"All aboard for the pow-wow!" spurred our still shivering and reluctant bodies into our warm wraps. Emerging into the pitch-black night, each was individually picked up by stalwart arms, tossed over the wheels and deposited once more among the masses of robes. The driver sprang to his seat, the horses plunged forth into the black night and I can safely say nothing but faith, FAITH spelt thus, kept me from slipping to the ground and back into the shack, for we seemed to be heading straight for—well, somewhere that looked very doubtful to me. But the hands on the reins were steady, the wild little team knew their master, he knew the road and so did they and in ten minutes, all safe, we drew up at the now-familiar flag-pole by the Council house, where, the horses quickly tied and blanketed, we settled our plumage straight and quietly opened the door to the festivities.

A hot blast of somewhat used air struck our faces still tingling with the frost, then one by one we wriggled through the narrow opening and slowly found foot-room inside. If the hall had seemed full in the afternoon, by this time it resembled a sardine box. Everybody seemed present and not an extra inch of space visible. We stood there taking in the scene. Huddled to-gether on the floor, with their gay blankets drawn over their heads, sat women and children—unsmiling, absorbed. At the far end on a series of steps ranged against the wall, sat the heads of the band in feathered and beaded attire, below them, on old packing-boxes, four braves pounding vociferously on a crude drum and accompanying the music(?) thereof with a curious chant. A very gay, young buck, with eagle-feather head-dress, with paint splashed over his countenance, with a fine string of horse-bells wound round from ankle to knee, with Christmas-tree tin[se]ls attached to his ears and otherwise "fetchingly" disposed about his person, was going through the "chicken dance." Occasionally another buck would rise and imitate the "star," but "star" he was and "star" he remained, none could perform the figures he did. None of our immediate party could explain the dance, but in the end it seemed as though the chicken's head had been chopped off and he expired in agony. As he and his bells and his imitation tail sank breathlessly to the floor, an Indian came forward and escorted us to seats politely made vacant by some of the great, and for an hour we sat in the midst of a real pow-wow, unnoticed by the actors—apparently. One dance followed another in rapid succession, the only music(?) being the dried cow-skin drum beaten upon vociferously by the four braves and the ever-repeated chant. This chant or song is quite impossible to describe; it is as wild as the race from which it sprung. There is the cry of the wild animal in it, the roar of the rivers, a song written by Nature herself for her people and none other could sing it. In a pause of the programme, the master-of-ceremonies spoke a few words in a low tone, when squaws here and there all over the room slowly rose. Throwing off the cumbersome blankets, depositing their infants in their moss-bags on the floor, they ranged themselves in one solid circle, thereby enclosing the red-hot stove, the orchestra, the chicken "star" whose supercilious expression showed plainly what he thought of his own work, and others of the masculine element huddled near the heat. The drum pounded, the drummers took up their chant, and heel-to-toe and toe-to-heel, the great circle of broad-backed, massive-hipped squaws began their slow shuffle. Round and round, shoulder to shoulder, they kept their way, their moccasinned feet making no sound, not a ripple of fun or nonsense on their placid faces. Occasionally a hungry baby sent forth a wail, proclaiming the need of a mother, but for the time, her social duties called louder than her motherhood, no one had thought for aught but that everlasting shuffle.

Perhaps ten minutes were consumed in this wild hilarity, when from a sign of the "floor-manager," they and the drum and the chant ceased, the fair dancers returned to their positions on the floor, picked up the discarded moss-bags, and the braves went to posturing harder than ever.

Probably an hour had been consumed in this manner, the braves of course, having the largest slice of time allotted to them, when the head man of the tribe rose and spoke with great dignity at some length, his words being greeted with hand-clapping and sounds to which I gave a free translation of "Here-here!" Then turning with the air of a man-of-the-world and certainly one quite accustomed to leading men, and bowing gracefully to my host he said in very good English—"Mr. W. I am just telling my friends how good you have been to us (Mr. W. had contributed a whole beef to the festivities), how well you have treated us in trade and they have just given you a vote of thanks." Mr. W. stepped forward, made a few complimentary remarks, which I judge lost nothing in strength in the mouth of George MacLean, for his words were received with clapping and cheers, and then retired to his seat by the wall. Ah, it was a sight worth seeing! A sight that cannot endure many years longer. Sitting in the seats of the mighty were men who must have remembered the days of the buffalo and heard from their fathers of the day of the tomahawk. With their long gray locks thrown back from seamed copper skins, with lids half-drooped over almost sightless eyes, smoking the old, hand-carved pipes, nodding sagely at their leader's words, there was a picture before us, which all too soon will be no more. The intense heat, the racket of the drums, all faded away. Before me was a picture which carried me back to the tales of childhood, here was the same drama which had been enacted thousands of times on the wide prairies, for the moment the Indians were again a free race, the white man and his reservations forgotten. In the smoke of the pipes I could see those other feasts, not of the new year (that is a touch brought by the missionary) but the feast of plenty when the buffalo roamed the foothills, when no white hand stayed the arrow, when the tepee was made of warm skins, when they danced in a huge lodge about a wood fire. Into my rever[ie] intruded a voice—"Have you had enough? Shall we go home?" Enough? Enough of dreams? Perhaps. As we threaded our way among the seated squaws low, musical voices whispered "Happy New Year! Happy New Year!" Someone opened the door to the night and the storm; the chicken dance was starting, with a sob of wind came the last whisper "Happy New Year" and we were back in the present. Far away in the east came the head-light of an engine, with a rumble muffled in the scream of the wind, it parted its way among the elements, and rushed with its many sleeping souls into the darkness of the west. Again came to mind the old saying, "How little one half the world knows how the other half lives."

Complete Works of Mary Schäffer Warren

Published Books

Alpine Flora of the Canadian Rocky Mountains. New York: G.T. Putnam's Sons, 1907. (Illustrations only; text by Stewardson Brown.)

Old Indian Trails of the Canadian Rockies. New York: G.T. Putnam's Sons, 1911.

Untrodden Paths in the Canadian Rockies. Minneapolis: Powers Mercantile Company, n.d. (pamphlet).

A Hunter of Peace. Banff: Whyte Museum of the Canadian Rockies, 1980. (Reprint of *Old Indian Trails* with an introduction by E. J. Hart and including "The 1911 Expedition to Maligne Lake.")

Published Articles

"The Burial of Cheronkee." *Rod and Gun in Canada* (1904).

"First Ladies to Visit Cave." Clipping (August, 1905).

"The Flora of Canada." Clipping (1905).

"The Valleys of the Saskatchewan with Horse and Camera." *The Bulletin of the Geographical Society of Philadelphia* (April 1907): 108-114.

"Flora of the Saskatchewan and Athabasca River Tributaries." *Canadian Alpine Journal* 1: 2 (1908): 268-70.

"Untrodden Ways." *Canadian Alpine Journal* 1: 2 (1908): 288-94.

"Among the Sources of the Saskatchewan and Athabasca Rivers." *The Bulletin of the Geographical Society of Philadelphia* (April 1908): 48-62.

"A Recently Explored Lake in the Rocky Range of Canada." *The Bulletin of the Geographical Society of Philadelphia* (22 July 1909): 123-34.

"Haunts of the Wild Flowers of the Canadian Rockies." *Canadian Alpine Journal* 3 (1911): 131-5.

"Hunting a Lost Lake." *Travel* (May 1911): 321-3, 364.

"Attractions in the Canadian Rockies." *Banff Crag and Canyon* (4 September 1911): 6.

"The Finding of Lake Maligne." *Canadian Alpine Journal* 4 (1912): 92-7.

"America from the Front." *New York Times* (30 April 1916): 18.

"Americans at the Front." *New York Times* (25 October 1916): 10.

"Sergeant Sidney J. Unwin—Canadian Artillery." *Canadian Alpine Journal* 8 (1917): 130-2.

"The Byways of Banff." *Canadian Alpine Journal* 10 (1919): 78-91.

"Ptarmigan Valley Twenty Years Ago." *Trail Riders of the Canadian Rockies Bulletin* 10 (16 July 1926): 1-3.

"A Personal Touch of One of the Great Trail Riders of the North." *Trail Riders of the Canadian Rockies Bulletin* 14 (May 1927): 4.

"A Short Synopsis of the Work of the Palliser Expedition." *Trail Riders of the Canadian Rockies Bulletin* 14 (May 1927): 8.

"Palliser's Expedition: Some Intimate Glimpses." *Calgary Herald*. Clipping. n.d. Whyte Museum of the Canadian Rockies. M79: 8.

"The Infinite Variety of the Canadian Rockies." *Rod and Gun in Canada*. Clipping. n.d. Whyte Museum of the Canadian Rockies. M79: 9A.

"With the Hairy Ainus." *Travel and Exploration*. Clipping. n.d. Whyte Museum of the Canadian Rockies. M79: 9A.

Unpublished Articles and Lantern Slide Shows
(All housed in the Whyte Museum of the Canadian Rockies, Banff, Alberta, Canada.)

"A Glimpse of the Head-hunters of Formosa." 1908. M79: 2.

"The Monarch of the Plains." ca. 1908. M79: 2.

*"My Garden." 1909. M79: 2.

"An American Boy in the Canadian Rockies." 1912. M79: 4.

* "The Story of Revelstoke." 1912. M79: 5.

Untitled history of Howse, Yellowhead and Athabasca passes. 1912. M79: 5.

"Trail Life at Lake Louise." ca. 1915. M79: 5.

"Story of Famous Ride of Doctor Red Deer Valley." ca. 1916. M79: 5.

* "Tepee Life in the Northern Hills." 1924. M79: 6.

* "A New Year in the Wilds." ca. 1925. M79: 6.

"The Beginning, the Middle, and the End of a Hunting Trip." n.d. M79: 5.

* "A Chapter of Accidents." n.d. M79: 7.

* "A Ptarmigan Story." n.d. M79: 7.

"Fairy-land of the North." n.d. M79: 7.

"Jonas." n.d. M79: 7.

"Lake Louise of Early Days." n.d. M79: 7.

"The Heart of a Child." n.d. M79: 7.

Untitled poem. n.d. M79: 9A.

"In the Heart of the Canadian Rockies with Horse and Camera, Part I." n.d. M189: 7.

"In the Heart of the Canadian Rockies, Part II." n.d. M189: 7.

* Published in this volume.

Bibliography

"Advertise Banff When Writing to Friends." *Banff Crag and Canyon* (8 May 1925): 1.

"Aged Pioneer Celebrates His 99th Birthday." *Banff Crag and Canyon* (25 November 1932): 1.

Akrigg, G.P.V. and Helen B. Akrigg. *British Columbia Chronicle: 1847-1871*. Vancouver: Discovery Press, 1977.

Alice Fulmer fonds. Whyte Museum of the Canadian Rockies. Banff, Alberta. M70.

Anderson, Bart, ed. *The Sharples-Sharpless Family*. Vol. 1. West Chester, 1966.

Anderson, Bart, ed. *The Sharples-Sharpless Family*. Vol. 2. West Chester, 1966.

"Anyone who has not read…" *Banff Crag and Canyon* (2 September 1911): 8.

"Are You Doing Your Bit?" *Banff Crag and Canyon* (10 June 1916): 8.

Baltzell, E. Digby. *Puritan Boston and Quaker Philadelphia*. New York: The Free Press, 1979.

"Banff and the I.O.D.E." *Banff Crag and Canyon* (28 October 1927): 1.

"Banff Skiers Will Compete in U.S. Championships." *Banff Crag and Canyon* (5 April 1935): 1.

"Banff Tenders Reception To New Premier-Elect." *Banff Crag and Canyon* (29 August 1930): 1.

Benham, D.J. "Jasper Park in the Rockies: Canada's New National Playground." *The Globe Saturday Night Section* (15 January 1910): 4.

Benjamin, Philip S. *The Philadelphia Quakers in the Industrial Age, 1865-1920*. Philadelphia: Temple University Press, 1976.

Berger, Carl. *Science, God, and Nature in Victorian Canada*. Toronto: University of Toronto Press, 1983.

"Botanizing in the Canadian Rockies." *Proceedings of the Academy of Natural Sciences of Philadelphia Vol. 58 (1906)*. Philadelphia: Academy of Natural Sciences, 1907: 429-30.

"Boys at Front Write Interesting Letters Home." *Banff Crag and Canyon* (2 March 1918): 1.

Brown, Robert Craig. "The Doctrine of Usefulness: Natural Resource Use and National Park Policy in Canada, 1887-1914." *The Canadian National Parks: Today and Tomorrow*. Vol. 1. Eds. J.G. Nelson and R.C. Scace. Calgary: The National and Provincial Parks Association of Canada and the University of Calgary, 1968: 94-110.

Brown, Robert Craig and Ramsay Cook. *Canada 1896-1921: A Nation Transformed*. Toronto: McClelland and Stewart, 1974.

Bumsted, J.M. *The Peoples of Canada: A Post-Confederation History*. Toronto: Oxford University Press, 1992.

Burt, Nathaniel. *The Perennial Philadelphians: The Anatomy of an American Aristocracy*. Boston: Little, Brown, and Co., 1963.

Caesar, Terry. *Forgiving the Boundaries*. Athens: University of Georgia Press, 1995.

Calgary Public Museum file. Glenbow Archives. Calgary, Alberta. 2111: 13.

Cavell, Edward and Jon Whyte. *Rocky Mountain Madness: A Bittersweet Romance*. Banff: Altitude, 1982.

Charles Reid fonds. Whyte Museum of the Canadian Rockies. Banff, Alberta. M413: 2.

"Christmas Tree Very Successful." *Banff Crag and Canyon* (27 December 1924): 1.

"Citizens Pay Last Respects to Late Dr. Harry Brett." *Banff Crag and Canyon* (15 May 1925): 1.

"The Cleanest Bunch." *Banff Crag and Canyon* (20 October 1917): 1.

"Col. Moore Gave Interesting Lecture on Columbia Icefields." *Banff Crag and Canyon* (8 November 1935): 5.

Coleman, A.P. *The Canadian Rockies, New and Old Trails*. Toronto: Henry Frowde, 1911.

"A complete and beautiful…" *The Dial* 44 (1 June 1908): 355.

"Consider Well Before You Vote." *Banff Crag and Canyon* (16 August 1935): 2.

"Constructive Policy Needed." *Banff Crag and Canyon* (14 August 1931): 4.

"Continues the Work." *Banff Crag and Canyon* (4 June 1904): 5.

"Contributions to Banff Wolf Cubs." *Banff Crag and Canyon* (4 December 1925): 8.

Cope, Gilbert. *Genealogy of the Sharpless Family*. Vol. 1. Philadelphia, 1887.

Cope, Gilbert. *Genealogy of the Sharpless Family*. Vol. 2. Philadelphia, 1887.

Daem, Mrs. Mary, Rita Crick and Mr. J. Daem. Taped interview with Maryalice H. Stewart and Ted Hart. 26 March 1974. Whyte Museum of the Canadian Rockies. Banff, Alberta. S1/95.

Dempsey, Lisa. *Gender, Ethnicity, and the Narrative Persona in Early Canadian Travel Writing*. M.A. Thesis. Edmonton: University of Alberta, 1993.

"The disappointing news…" *Banff Crag and Canyon* (9 July 1904): 4.

"Do Some Boosting." *Banff Crag and Canyon* (6 April 1928): 2.

"Essay on Pants." *Banff Crag and Canyon* (18 September 1920): 1.

"Expedition to Maligne Lake." *Canadian Alpine Journal* 4 (1912): 64-83.

"The Fighting Spirit." *Banff Crag and Canyon* (20 April 1918): 1.

Forster, Merna M. *Maligne—Valley of the Wicked River, Jasper National Park*. Ottawa: Parks Canada, 1979.

Foster, Janet. *Working for Wildlife: The Beginnings of Preservation in Canada*. Toronto: University of Toronto Press, 1978.

Francis, Daniel. *The Imaginary Indian: The Image of the Indian in Canadian Culture*. Vancouver: Arsenal Pulp Press, 1992.

Fraser, Esther. *The Canadian Rockies: Early Travels and Explorations*. Edmonton: M. G. Hurtig Ltd., 1969.

Fraser, Esther. *Wheeler*. Banff: Summerthought, 1978.

"Friends of Mrs. W. Warren…" *Banff Crag and Canyon* (2 May 1930): 1.

Fuley, J. Smith and Gilbert Cope. *History of Chester County, Pennsylvania*. Philadelphia: Louis H. Everts, 1881.

"Funeral Service for William Warren Held at Vancouver, Fri." *Banff Crag and Canyon* (23 July 1943): 1.

Glacier House Scrapbook, 1897-1910. Whyte Museum of the Canadian Rockies. Banff, Alberta. M352.

"Good Form." *Banff Crag and Canyon* (30 November 1912): 5.

Gowan, Elsie Park. *Jasper Story*. Unpublished manuscript. University of Alberta Archives. Edmonton, Alberta. 87-123, Box 1, Items 1-12.

Gowan, Elsie Park. "A Quaker in Buckskin." *Alberta Historical Review* 5: 3 (Summer 1957): 1-6, 24-28.

"The Great War Veterans…" *Banff Crag and Canyon* (1 June 1918): 5.

H., A. "In Memoriam." *Canadian Alpine Journal* 28: 1-2 (1939-40): 108-10.

Hall, Margaret Ann. *A History of Women's Sport in Canada Prior to World War I.* M.A. Thesis. Edmonton: University of Alberta, 1968.

Hart, E.J. *Diamond Hitch.* Banff: Summerthought, 1979.

Hart, E.J. *Jimmy Simpson: Legend of the Rockies.* Banff: Altitude, 1991.

Hart. E.J. *The Place of Bows: Exploring the Heritage of the Banff–Bow Valley, Part I to 1930.* Banff: EJH Literary Enterprises Ltd., 1999.

Hart, E.J. *The Selling of Canada.* Banff: Altitude, 1983.

Heilbrun, Carolyn G. *Writing a Woman's Life.* New York: Ballantyne Books, 1988.

Hentschel, Ingo. *Expectations and Perceptions of the Wilderness Travel Experience.* M.A. Thesis. Edmonton: University of Alberta, 1988.

"History of Banff Taken from Crag & Canyon Files." *Banff Crag and Canyon* (3 May 1935): 10-16.

Humphrey Toms fonds. Whyte Museum of the Canadian Rockies. Banff, Alberta. M429.

"Hundreds Gathered For Brett Golden Wedding Anniversary, Tuesday." *Banff Crag and Canyon* (29 June 1928): 1.

"In Memoriam—Julia W. Henshaw, FRGS." *Canadian Alpine Journal* 25 (1937): 128-31.

"In Memory of Banff Pupils." *Banff Crag and Canyon* (29 May 1920): 1.

"Indian Committee Will Break Even." *Banff Crag and Canyon* (2 August 1924): 1.

"The Indian Day…" *Banff Crag and Canyon* (14 June 1919): 1.

"Interesting Lecture." *Banff Crag and Canyon* (15 August 1914): 8.

"I.O.D.E. Entertain—Historical Lecture on Matters of Local Import." *Banff Crag and Canyon* (30 January 1915): 1.

"I.O.D.E. Rose Ball." *Banff Crag and Canyon* (22 April 1927): 6.

J. Monroe Thorington fonds. Whyte Museum of the Canadian Rockies. Banff, Alberta. M106: 36.

"Jas. I McLeod…" *Banff Crag and Canyon* (14 May 1921): 1.

"Jas. I. McLeod…" *Banff Crag and Canyon* (9 June 1923): 1.

Kipling, Rudyard. *Letters of Travel (1892-1913).* London: Macmillan and Co., 1920.

"A large and appreciative audience…" *Banff Crag and Canyon* (23 January 1915): 1.

"The Last Rock." *Banff Crag and Canyon* (21 February 1914): 1.

"The late Dr. Charles Schäffer…" *The Nation* (3 September 1908): 217.

"A lecture…" *Banff Crag and Canyon* (12 January 1918): 8.

"Life Carries on at Mary Schäffer Warren's Historic Home." *Bow Valley This Week* 8: 23 (6-13 June 1995): 1, 5.

"A light-hearted account…" *A.L.A. Booklist* 8: 2 (October 1911): 72.

Lillian Gest fonds. Whyte Museum of the Canadian Rockies. Banff, Alberta. M67.

Lippard, Lucy R. "Introduction—Part II: Doubletake: The Diary of a Relationship with an Image." *Partial Recall.* Ed. Lucy R. Lippard. New York: The New York Press, 1992: 34-43.

"List of Members." *Canadian Alpine Journal* 1: 1 (1907): 182-96.

Lord Beaverbrook. *Friends: Sixty Years of Personal Relations with Richard Bedford Bennett.* Toronto: Heinemann, 1959.

Lothian, W. F. *A Brief History of Canada's National Parks.* Ottawa: Environment Canada, Parks, 1987.

Love, Currie. "Pushing Ahead of Trails." *Canada West Monthly* (August 1911): 273-9.

Lowenthal, David. "The Place of the Past in the American Landscape." *Geographies of the Mind*. Eds. David Lowenthal and Martyn J. Bowden. New York: Oxford University Press, 1976: 89-117.

Luxton, Eleanor G. *Banff: Canada's First National Park: A History and a Memory of Rocky Mountains Park*. Banff: Summerthought, 1975.

"Maligne Lake: One of World's Beauty Spots." *Edmonton Daily Bulletin* (9 August 1911): 3.

"Married in Vancouver—Three Cheers." *Banff Crag and Canyon* (3 July 1915): 2.

Mary Schäffer file. Glenbow Archives. Calgary, Alberta.

Mary Schäffer fonds. Whyte Museum of the Canadian Rockies. Banff, Alberta. M79.

Mary Wright fonds. Whyte Museum of the Canadian Rockies. Banff, Alberta. M248.

McCabe, James D. *The Illustrated History of the Centennial Exhibition*. Philadelphia: The National Publishing Company, 1876.

McCowan, Dan. *Hill-Top Tales*. Toronto: The MacMillan Company, 1948.

Millan, Nancy. "Quakers' Stress on Equality is Unchanged." *Calgary Herald*. 6 December 1980: A20.

Minnie Nickell fonds. Whyte Museum of the Canadian Rockies. Banff, Alberta. M8.

Minute Book. Philadelphia Academy of Natural Sciences Archives. Philadelphia, Pennsylvania.

"Monument Unveiled in Local Cemetery to Honor Old Pioneers." *Banff Crag and Canyon* (30 July 1937): 1, 4.

Mount Rundle Chapter I.O.D.E. Minute Books. Whyte Museum of the Canadian Rockies. Banff, Alberta. M366.

"Mr. Aberhart..." *Banff Crag and Canyon* (23 April 1937): 2.

"Mr. and Mrs. Warren..." *Banff Crag and Canyon* (25 September 1920): 8.

"Mr. and Mrs. W. Warren..." *Banff Crag and Canyon* (20 October 1917): 8.

"Mr. and Mrs. W. Warren..." *Banff Crag and Canyon* (17 May 1919): 8.

"Mr. and Mrs. W. Warren..." *Banff Crag and Canyon* (16 September 1922): 8.

"Mr. and Mrs. Wm. Warren..." *Banff Crag and Canyon* (14 August 1915): 4.

"Mr. and Mrs. Wm. Warren..." *Banff Crag and Canyon* (18 October 1924): 8.

"Mrs. Charles Schäffer..." *Banff Crag and Canyon* (29 May 1909): 6.

"Mrs. Dr. Schäffer..." *Banff Crag and Canyon* (30 May 1908): 4.

"Mrs. Mary T. S. Schäffer..." *Banff Crag and Canyon* (23 September 1911): 8.

"Mrs. Schäffer..." *Banff Crag and Canyon* (22 April 1905): 4.

"Mrs. Schäffer..." *Banff Crag and Canyon* (10 June 1905): 7.

"Mrs. Schäffer..." *Banff Crag and Canyon* (9 September 1905): 2.

"Mrs. Schäffer's Survey of Maligne Lake..." *Geographical Journal* 40: 3 (September 1912): 334-5.

"Mrs. Shaefer Tells of Rocky Mountains." Clipping. 1907. Whyte Museum of the Canadian Rockies. Banff, Alberta. M70: 91.

"Mrs. W. Warren..." *Banff Crag and Canyon* (3 September 1921): 8.

"Mrs. W. Warren..." *Banff Crag and Canyon* (28 July 1923): 1.

"Mrs. Wm. Warren..." *Banff Crag and Canyon* (17 February 1917): 8.

"Mrs. Wm. Warren..." *Banff Crag and Canyon* (1 March 1924): 8.

"Mrs. Wm. Warren..." *Banff Crag and Canyon* (4 December 1925): 8.

"Mrs. Wm. Warren..." *Banff Crag and Canyon* (19 March 1926): 6.

"Mrs. Wm. Warren..." *Banff Crag and Canyon* (23 September 1927): 8.

"Mrs. Wm. Warren Banff Oldtimer and Explorer of Rockies Passes." *Banff Crag and Canyon* (27 January 1939): 1-2.

Nash, Roderick. *Wilderness and the American Mind*. New Haven: Yale University Press, 1973.

Nash, Roderick. "Wilderness and Man in North America." *The Canadian National Parks: Today and Tomorrow*. Vol. 1. Eds. J. G. Nelson and R. C. Scace. Calgary: The National and Provincial Parks Association of Canada and the University of Calgary, 1968: 66-93.

"New Flowers." *Banff Crag and Canyon* (9 July 1904): 4.

Nicol, J.I. "The National Parks Movement in Canada." *The Canadian National Parks: Today and Tomorrow*. Vol. 1. Eds. J.G. Nelson and R.C. Scace. Calgary: The National and Provincial Parks Association of Canada and the University of Calgary, 1968: 35-52.

Nolan, Edward J., ed. *Proceedings of the Academy of Natural Science in Philadelphia*. Philadelphia: Academy of Natural Sciences, 1889-1910.

"Notice of Dissolution." *Banff Crag and Canyon* (29 September 1923): 8.

Oldham, Vera. Letters to Esther Fraser. Whyte Museum of the Canadian Rockies. Banff, Alberta. M517: 91.

"The Other Side of the Story." *Banff Crag and Canyon* (18 March 1916): 4.

Palmer, Howard with Tamara Palmer. *Alberta: A New History*. Edmonton: Hurtig Publishers, 1990.

Panzer, Mary. *Philadelphia Naturalistic Photography, 1865-1906*. New Haven: Yale University Art Gallery, 1982.

Pennsylvania Census, 1900. National Archives. Philadelphia, Pennsylvania.

Philadelphia and Birmingham Monthly Meeting Minutes. Friends Historical Library. Swarthmore College, Pennsylvania. MR-Ph368.

"Philadelphia Woman Names New Mountain." *Edmonton Evening Journal* (8 August 1911): 1.

Phillips, Patricia. *The Scientific Lady: A Social History of Women's Scientific Interests, 1529-1918*. London: Weidenfeld and Nicholson, 1990.

"Pioneer of Banff, Mrs. Warren, Dies." *Calgary Herald* (24 January 1939).

"Planning a Visit to Mountain Lake." *The Edmonton Capital* (5 June 1911): 4.

"Promise Should be Fulfilled." *Banff Crag and Canyon* (12 May 1933): 2.

"R.B. Bennett..." *Banff Crag and Canyon* (1 May 1915): 2.

Raymond Zillmer fonds. Whyte Museum of the Canadian Rockies. Banff, Alberta. M8.

Reichwein, PearlAnn. *Guardians of a Rocky Mountain Wilderness: Elizabeth Parker, Mary Schäffer, and the Canadian National Park Idea, 1890-1914*. M.A. Thesis. Ottawa: Carleton University, 1990.

Reichwein, PearlAnn. "Guardians of the Rockies." *The Beaver* (August/September 1994): 4-13.

Report of the Rocky Mountains Park of Canada Part V. Annual Report 1908. Ottawa: Government Printing Bureau, 1909.

Robinson, Bart. *Columbia Icefield—A Solitude of Ice*. Banff: Altitude, 1981.

Russell, Mary. *The Blessings of a Good Thick Skirt*. Toronto: William Collins Sons and Co. Ltd., 1986.

Sanderin, Walter S. "The Expanding Horizons of the Schuylkill Navigation Company, 1815-1870." *Pennsylvania History* 36: 2 (April 1969): 174-191.

Sandford, Robert. *Yoho: A History and Celebration of Yoho National Park*. Banff: Altitude, 1993.

Sandford, R.W. *The Canadian Alps—The History of Mountaineering in Canada*. Vol. 1. Banff: Altitude, 1990.

Schaeffer file. Philadelphia Academy of Natural Sciences Archives. Philadelphia, Pennsylvania. Collection 241.

Schaffer, C. clipping file. Chester County Historical Society Archives. West Chester, Pennsylvania.

Schäffer, M. clipping file. Chester County Historical Society Archives. West Chester, Pennsylvania.

Schäffer, Mary T.S. "Among the Sources of the Saskatchewan and Athabasca Rivers." *The Bulletin of the Geographical Society of Philadelphia* (April 1908): 48-62.

Schäffer, Mary T.S. "The Finding of Lake Maligne." *Canadian Alpine Journal* 4 (1912): 92-7.

Schäffer, Mary T.S. "Flora of the Saskatchewan and Athabasca River Tributaries." *Canadian Alpine Journal* 1: 2 (1908): 268-70.

Schäffer, Mary T.S. "Haunts of the Wild Flowers of the Canadian Rockies." *Canadian Alpine Journal* 3 (1911): 131-5.

Schäffer, Mary T.S., E.J. Hart, ed. *A Hunter of Peace*. Banff: Whyte Museum of the Canadian Rockies, 1980.

Schäffer, Mary T.S. "Hunting a Lost Lake." *Travel* (May 1911): 321-3, 364.

Schäffer, Mary T.S. Letter to Dr. Nolan. 9 December 1903. Whyte Museum of the Canadian Rockies. Banff, Alberta. M517: 91.

Schäffer, Mary T.S. *Old Indian Trails of the Canadian Rockies*. New York: G. P. Putnam's Sons, 1911.

Schäffer, Mary T.S. "A Recently Explored Lake in the Rocky Range of Canada." *The Bulletin of the Geographical Society of Philadelphia* (22 July 1909): 123-34.

Schäffer, Mary T.S. "Untrodden Ways." *Canadian Alpine Journal* 1: 2 (1908): 288-94.

"Schäffer, Mary Townsend Sharples." *Who Was Who in America*. Vol. 4. Chicago: Marquis—Who's Who, Inc., 1968: 833.

Schäffer, Mrs. Charles file. Philadelphia Academy of Natural Sciences Archives. Philadelphia, Pennsylvania. Collection 567.

Schäffer, Mrs. Charles. *Untrodden Paths in the Canadian Rockies*. Minneapolis: Powers Mercantile Company, n.d.

Schäffer, Mrs. Charles. "The Valleys of the Saskatchewan with Horse and Camera." *The Bulletin of the Geographical Society of Philadelphia* (April 1907): 108-114.

"Schäffer-Sharpless." *Friends' Intelligencer and Journal* 46 (3 August 1889): 488.

Scharff, Robert. *Canada's Mountain National Parks*. Banff: Lebow Books, 1972.

"School Library Fitted With New Furniture." *Banff Crag and Canyon* (8 May 1925): 1.

Sharpless Family family history folder. Chester County Historical Society Archives. West Chester, Pennsylvania.

Sharpless, A. clipping file. Chester County Historical Society Archives. West Chester, Pennsylvania.

Sharpless, E. clipping file. Chester County Historical Society Archives. West Chester, Pennsylvania.

Sharpless, F. clipping file. Chester County Historical Society Archives. West Chester, Pennsylvania.

Sharpless, H. clipping file. Chester County Historical Society Archives. West Chester, Pennsylvania.

Sharpless, J. clipping file. Chester County Historical Society Archives. West Chester, Pennsylvania.

Simpson, Jimmy. Taped interview with Catharine Robb Whyte. September 1972. Whyte Museum of the Canadian Rockies. Banff, Alberta. M88/S28.

"Ski Club's Whist Drive and Dance." *Banff Crag and Canyon* (24 February 1928): 1.

Smith, Cyndi. *Off the Beaten Track*. Lake Louise: Coyote Books, 1989.

Smith, Margot and Carol Pasternak, eds. *Pioneer Women of Western Canada*. Toronto: The Ontario Institute for Studies in Education, 1978.

"Social Credit—Does It Fit the Bill?" *Banff Crag and Canyon* (15 March 1935): 2.

Society of Friends of Canada. *Society of Friends of Canada Discipline*. Toronto: 1881.

Spears, Betty. "Mary, Mary, Quite Contrary." Paper presented at North American Society for Sport History. Vancouver, May 23-26, 1986.

Squire, Shelagh J. "In the Steps of 'Genteel Ladies': Women Tourists in the Canadian Rockies, 1885-1939." *The Canadian Geographer* 39: 1 (Spring 1995): 2-15.

"St. George's Bazaar Big Success in Spite of Rain." *Banff Crag and Canyon* (13 August 1926): 1.

"St. George's Church Entertainment." *Banff Crag and Canyon* (13 September 1913): 4.

Stearns, Sharon. *Hunter of Peace*. Victoria: J. Gordon Shillingford Publishing Ltd., 1993.

Stewart, Maryalice H. "The Mountains in Maps." *Canadian Collector* 11: 1 (January/February 1976): 41-5.

"They Did Well." *Banff Crag and Canyon* (6 July 1918): 5.

"This is a story…" *Geographical Journal* 39: 1 (January 1912): 65-6.

Thompson, John Herd. *Canada 1922-1939: Decades of Discord*. Toronto: McClelland & Stewart, 1985.

"Ticket No. 23…" *Banff Crag and Canyon* (13 January 1917): 8.

Tindall, George Brown. *America: A Narrative History*. New York: W. W. Norton & Company, 1988.

"To Again Visit Mountain Lake." *Edmonton Daily Bulletin*. (5 June 1911): 6.

"Tom Wilson Celebrates 73rd Birthday at Louise." *Banff Crag and Canyon* (26 August 1932): 4.

Tom Wilson file. Glenbow Archives. Calgary, Alberta. W753A.

"The Tourist Who Stayed: Mary Schäffer Warren." *Builders of the Rockies*. Whyte Museum of the Canadian Rockies exhibit. Banff, 1993–2003.

"Trail Riders Hold First Pow-wow." *Banff Crag and Canyon* (9 August 1924): 4.

"Trousered Women Scale the Heights of the Rockies." *Bow Valley This Week* 6: 39 (28 September-5 October 1993): 8, 12.

"Two of the most…" *Banff Crag and Canyon* (9 August 1919): 1.

"Two Women in an Untrod Land." *New York Times* (16 July 1911): 443.

Van der Bellen, Liana. *An Essay on Personal Accounts of Travel in the Canadian Rockies and the Selkirks, 1754-1914*. M.L.S. Thesis. Montreal: McGill University, 1967.

Vance, James E. Jr. "Democratic Utopia and the American Landscape." *The Making of the American Landscape*. Ed. Michael P. Conzen. Boston: Unwin Hyman, 1990: 204-20.

Vaux family fonds. Whyte Museum of the Canadian Rockies. M107.

Vaux, George. "The Vaux Family's Scientific Pursuits." *Frontiers: Annual of the Academy of Natural Sciences in Philadelphia* III (1981-82): 57-63.

Vaux, William Jr. Glacier Notebook. Whyte Museum of the Canadian Rockies. Banff, Alberta. M107: 8.

"Vote Early Thursday For R.B. Bennett Vote Early." *Banff Crag and Canyon* (28 October 1925): 1.

"Vote for Van Wart..." *Banff Crag and Canyon* (26 August 1911): 1.

W., M. S. "Attractions in the Canadian Rockies." *Banff Crag and Canyon* (4 September 1911): 6.

Ward, Mrs. Humphrey. *Lady Merton, Colonist*. Toronto: The Musson Book Company, n.d.

Warren, M. clipping file. Chester County Historical Society Archives. West Chester, Pennsylvania.

Warren, Mary S. "Americans at the Front." *New York Times* (25 October 1916): 10.

Warren, Mary S. "The Byways of Banff." *Canadian Alpine Journal* 10 (1919): 78-91.

Warren, Mary S. "In the Heart of the Canadian Rockies with Horse and Camera, Part I." Unpublished manuscript. Whyte Museum of the Canadian Rockies. Banff, Alberta. M189: 7.

Warren, Mary S. "In the Heart of the Canadian Rockies, Part II." Unpublished manuscript. Whyte Museum of the Canadian Rockies. Banff, Alberta. M189: 7.

Warren, Mary S. "Sergeant Sidney J. Unwin—Canadian Artillery." *Canadian Alpine Journal* 8 (1917): 130-2.

Warren, Mary Schaeffer. "A Personal Touch of One of the Great Trail Riders of the North." *Trail Riders of the Canadian Rockies Bulletin* 14 (May 1927): 4.

Warren, Mary Schaeffer. "A Short Synopsis of the Work of the Palliser Expedition." *Trail Riders of the Canadian Rockies Bulletin* 14 (May 1927): 8.

Warren, Mary Shaeffer. "Ptarmigan Valley Twenty Years Ago." *Trail Riders of the Canadian Rockies Bulletin* 10 (16 July 1926): 1-3.

Warren, Mrs. William. "America From the Front." *New York Times* (30 April 1916): 18.

West Chester... Past and Present. West Chester, ca. 1900.

Wheeler, A.O. *The Selkirk Range*. Ottawa: Government Printing Bureau, 1905.

Wheeler, Arthur O. "The Congress of Alpinism at Monaco." *Canadian Alpine Journal* 11 (1920): 65-8.

"When you see..." *Banff Crag and Canyon* (13 August 1921): 8.

Williams, M.B. *The Banff Jasper Highway*. Saskatoon: H.R. Larson Publishing, 1948.

Williams, M.B. *Jasper National Park—A Descriptive Guide*. Vancouver: H.R. Larson Publishing, 1949.

Wilson, Thomas Edward. Taped interview with Maryalice H. Stewart. Whyte Museum of the Canadian Rockies. Banff, Alberta. S1/69.

"Women Who Have Revealed Hidden Paths." *Edmonton Journal* (5 June 1911).

"Years ago..." *Banff Crag and Canyon* (13 October 1917): 4.

"The young women..." *Banff Crag and Canyon* (11 September 1920): 8.

Endnotes

The Average American Girl?

1. Mary Warren, letter to Humphrey Toms, 13 December 1933, Whyte Museum of the Canadian Rockies, M429.
2. Mary Warren, letter to Lillian Gest, 23 May 1938, Whyte Museum of the Canadian Rockies, M67: 8.
3. Mary Warren, letter to Humphrey Toms, 2 April 1938, Whyte Museum of the Canadian Rockies, M429.
4. Mary Schäffer, "The Heart of a Child," unpublished manuscript, Whyte Museum of the Canadian Rockies, M79: 7, 5.
5. Mary Schäffer, "Tepee Life in the Northern Hills," unpublished manuscript, Whyte Museum of the Canadian Rockies, M79: 6, 3.
6. Mary Schäffer, "The Heart of a Child," 7.
7. Ibid.
8. Ibid., 8.
9. Ibid., 12.

Westward Bound

1. Though some sources have Mary and Charles meeting at Glacier House courtesy of Mary Vaux, a recently available manuscript, "Lake Louise of Early Days," indicates Mary's first sight of the Rockies was not until 1889, after she and Charles were married.
2. Mary Schäffer, "Lake Louise of Early Days," unpublished manuscript, Whyte Museum of the Canadian Rockies, M79: 7, 1.
3. Ibid., 2.
4. Schäffer, *A Hunter*, 16.
5. Mary Schäffer, "Tepee Life in the Northern Hills," unpublished manuscript, Whyte Museum of the Canadian Rockies, M79: 6, 3-4.
6. Mary Warren, letter to Minnie Nickell, 13 December, n.y., Whyte Museum of the Canadian Rockies, M8.
7. Mary Warren, letter to Humphrey Toms, 26 November 1937, Whyte Museum of the Canadian Rockies, M429.
8. Mary Schäffer, "Tepee Life in the Northern Hills," 4.
9. Mary Schäffer, "Lake Louise of Early Days," 2.
10. Mary Schäffer, "Tepee Life in the Northern Hills," 8.
11. Walter Wilcox, qtd. in Elsie Park Gowan, "A Quaker in Buckskin," *Alberta Historical Review* 5:3 (summer 1957), 2.
12. Schäffer, *A Hunter*, 16.
13. Ibid.
14. Ibid.
15. Mary Schäffer, "The Story of Revelstoke," unpublished manuscript, Whyte Museum of the Canadian Rockies, M79: 6, 2.
16. Ibid., 3.
17. Mary S. Warren, "Palliser's Expedition: Some Intimate Glimpses," *Calgary Herald*, clipping, n.d., Whyte Museum of the Canadian Rockies, M79: 8.
18. Charles Schäffer, letter to Tom Wilson, 1 May 1903, Glenbow Archives, W753A.
19. Mary S. Warren, "Palliser's Expedition."

From House Plant to Wildflower

1. Mary Warren, letter to Humphrey Toms, 25 May 1935, Whyte Museum of the Canadian Rockies, M429.
2. Ibid.
3. Ibid.
4. Mary Warren, letter to Humphrey Toms, 1 February 1934.

5. Mary Warren, letter to Humphrey Toms, 25 May 1935.
6. Mary Warren, letter to Humphrey Toms, 9 April 1937.
7. Mary Schäffer, "Tepee Life in the Northern Hills," unpublished manuscript, Whyte Museum of the Canadian Rockies, M79: 6, 4.
8. Ibid., 5.
9. Ibid.
10. Ibid., 6.
11. Mary T. S. Schäffer, "Hunting a Lost Lake," *Travel* (May 1911), 321.
12. Mary Schäffer, "Tepee Life in the Northern Hills," 6.
13. Ibid., 7.
14. Mary Schäffer, "My Garden," unpublished manuscript, Whyte Museum of the Canadian Rockies, M79: 2, 2-3.
15. Ibid.
16. Ibid.
17. Schäffer, *A Hunter*, 16.
18. "First Ladies to Visit Cave," clipping, 10 August 1905, Whyte Museum of the Canadian Rockies, M79: 9A.
19. Mary Warren, letter to Raymond Zillmer, 12 April, n.y., Whyte Museum of the Canadian Rockies, M8.
20. "First Ladies to Visit Cave."
21. Mary Warren, letter to Tom Wilson, 15 August n.y., Glenbow Archives, M1322/f19.
22. Schäffer, *Untrodden Paths*, 16.
23. Mary S. Warren, "In the Heart of the Canadian Rockies with Horse and Camera, Part I," unpublished manuscript, Whyte Museum of the Canadian Rockies, M189: 7, 9.
24. Ibid.
25. Mary Schäffer, "Tepee Life in the Northern Hills," 23.
26. Schäffer, *A Hunter*, 70.
27. Mary Schäffer, "Tepee Life in the Northern Hills," 7.
28. Schäffer, *A Hunter*, 80.

Into the Unknown
1. Schäffer, *A Hunter*, 16.
2. Ibid.
3. Currie Love, "Pushing Ahead of Trails," *Canada West Monthly* (August 1911), 279.
4. "Two Women in an Untrod Land," *New York Times* (16 July 1911), 443.
5. Schäffer, *A Hunter*, 16-7.
6. Ibid., 17.
7. Ibid.
8. Ibid., 18.
9. Ibid.
10. Ibid., 76.
11. Mary T.S. Schäffer, "Flora of the Saskatchewan and Athabasca River Tributaries," *Canadian Alpine Journal* 1: 2 (1908), 268.
12. Schäffer, *A Hunter*, 22.
13. Ibid., 31.
14. Ibid., 33.
15. Ibid., 35.
16. Ibid.
17. Mary T.S. Schäffer, "Untrodden Ways," *Canadian Alpine Journal* 1: 2 (1908), 288.
18. Mary T.S. Schäffer, "Old Indian Trails: Expedition of 1907," 56.
19. Ibid., 60.
20. Ibid., 62.
21. Mary T.S. Schäffer, "Untrodden Ways," 292.
22. Schäffer, *A Hunter*, 74.
23. Ibid., 75.

Life on the Trail
1. Schäffer, *A Hunter*, 27.
2. Ibid., 56.
3. Mary S. Warren, "In the Heart of the Canadian Rockies, Part II," unpublished manuscript, Whyte Museum of the Canadian Rockies, M189: 7, 3.
4. Mary Schäffer, "Tepee Life in the Northern Hills," unpublished manuscript, Whyte Museum of the Canadian Rockies, M79: 6, 18-9.
5. Ibid., 20.
6. Schäffer, *A Hunter*, 38.
7. Ibid., 46.
8. Ibid., 47.
9. Ibid., 48.
10. Coleman, *The Canadian Rockies, New and Old Trails*, 251.
11. Schäffer, *A Hunter*, 49.
12. Ibid.
13. Mary Schäffer, "Tepee Life in the Northern Hills," 17.
14. Schäffer, *A Hunter*, 50.
15. Mary Warren, letter to Minnie Nickell, 21 September, n.y., Whyte Museum of the Canadian Rockies, M493.
16. Mary T.S. Schäffer, "Untrodden Ways," *Canadian Alpine Journal* 1: 2 (1908), 294.
17. Schäffer, *A Hunter*, 75.
18. Kipling, *Letters of Travel (1892-1913)*, 188.
19. Ibid., 189.

Unlocking the Treasure
1. Mollie Adams, trip journal, unpublished manuscript, Whyte Museum of the Canadian Rockies, M79: 10, 12.
2. Mary T.S. Schäffer, "The Finding of Lake Maligne," *Canadian Alpine Journal* 4 (1912), 92.
3. Mollie Adams, qtd. in Schäffer, *A Hunter*, 90.
4. Schäffer, *A Hunter*, 91.
5. Ibid., 92.
6. Mary T.S. Schäffer, "A Recently Explored Lake in the Rocky Range of Canada," *The Bulletin of the Geographical Society of Philadelphia* (22 July 1909), 126.
7. Schäffer, *A Hunter*, 92.
8. Ibid., 93.
9. Ibid.
10. Ibid.
11. Sid Unwin, qtd. in Schäffer, *A Hunter*, 93.
12. "To Again Visit Mountain Lake," *Edmonton Daily Bulletin* (5 June 1911), 6.
13. Mary Warren, letter to Minnie Nickell, 12 November 1936(?), Whyte Museum of the Canadian Rockies, M8.
14. Schäffer, *A Hunter*, 97–8.
15. Mary Warren, letter to Raymond Zillmer, 28 February 1928, Whyte Museum of the Canadian Rockies, M8.
16. Schäffer, *A Hunter*, 96.
17. Ibid., 105.
18. Ibid., 114.
19. Ibid.
20. Mollie Adams, trip journal, 71.
21. Lewis Swift, qtd. in Schäffer, *A Hunter*, 117.
22. Schäffer, *A Hunter*, 120.
23. "The young women…" *Banff Crag and Canyon* (11 September 1920), 8.
24. "Essay on Plants." *Banff Crag and Canyon* (18 September 1920), 1.
25. Schäffer, *A Hunter*, 123.

26. Ibid., 124.
27. Ibid.
28. Mollie Adams, trip journal, 87.
29. Schäffer, *A Hunter*, 126.
30. Ibid., 130.
31. Ibid.

To Asia and Back

1. M.T.S. Schäffer, "With the Hairy Ainus," *Travel and Exploration*, clipping, n.d., Whyte Museum of the Canadian Rockies, M79: 9A, 378.
2. Ibid., 380.
3. Ibid.
4. Ibid., 384.
5. Ibid., 382.
6. Ibid.
7. Ibid.
8. Mary Schäffer, "A Glimpse of the Head-hunters of Formosa," unpublished manuscript, Whyte Museum of the Canadian Rockies, M79: 2, 3.
9. Mary Schäffer, letter home, 19 December 1908, Whyte Museum of the Canadian Rockies, M79: 1, 4.
10. Ibid., 5.
11. Ibid., 6.
12. Ibid.
13. Ibid.
14. Mary Schäffer, "A Glimpse of the Head-hunters of Formosa," 7.
15. Mary Schäffer, letter home, 19 December 1908, 7.
16. Ibid.
17. Mary Schäffer, letter home, 27 December 1908, Whyte Museum of the Canadian Rockies, M79: 1, 11.
18. Ibid., 12.
19. Mary Warren, letter to Minnie Nickell, 21 September 1936(?), Whyte Museum of the Canadian Rockies, M8.

Adventures With a Pen and Paper

1. Schäffer, *A Hunter*, 19.
2. Mrs. Charles Schäffer, "The Valleys of the Saskatchewan with Horse and Camera," *The Bulletin of the Geographical Society of Philadelphia* (April 1907), 41.
3. "First Ladies to Visit Cave," clipping, 10 August 1905, Whyte Museum of the Canadian Rockies, M79: 9A.
4. Ibid.
5. Mrs. Charles Schäffer, "The Infinite Variety of the Canadian Rockies," *Rod and Gun in Canada*, clipping, n.d., 747.
6. Ibid.
7. Ibid., 751.
8. Ibid.
9. Schäffer, *Untrodden Paths*, 23.
10. Schäffer, *A Hunter*, 20.
11. Ibid., 19.
12. Ibid.
13. Schäffer, *Old Indian Trails of the Canadian Rockies*, v.
14. Ibid., vi.
15. Schäffer, *A Hunter*, 25-6.
16. Ibid., 52.
17. Ibid.
18. "A Woman in the Rockies," clipping, n.d., Whyte Museum of the Canadian Rockies, M79: 9A.

19. "Another boom…" *New York City Sun* (24 June 1911), clipping, n.d., Whyte Museum of the Canadian Rockies, M79: 9A.
20. "Anyone who has not read…" *Banff Crag and Canyon* (2 September 1911), 8.
21. "Two Women in an Untrod Land," *New York Times* (26 July 1911), 443.
22. Ibid.
23. Mary Warren, letter to Minnie Nickell, 13 December, n.y., Whyte Museum of the Canadian Rockies, M8.
24. Mary Warren, letter to Raymond Zillmer, 12 April, n.y., Whyte Museum of the Canadian Rockies, M8.
25. Ibid.
26. Ibid.

Maligne Lake Revisited

1. This chapter and the next incorporate research data and interpretations from Reichwein (1990 and 1994).
2. Mary T.S. Schäffer, "The Finding of Lake Maligne," *Canadian Alpine Journal* 4 (1912), 93.
3. Schäffer, *A Hunter*, 133.
4. Mary Schäffer, "An American Boy in the Canadian Rockies," unpublished manuscript, Whyte Museum of the Canadian Rockies, M79: 4, 1.
5. Ibid.
6. Ibid., 2.
7. Schäffer, *A Hunter*, 132.
8. Ibid.
9. Mary Schäffer, 4.
10. Ibid.
11. Schäffer, *A Hunter*, 133.
12. Ibid.
13. Mary S. Warren, "In the Heart of the Canadian Rockies, Part II," unpublished manuscript, Whyte Museum of the Canadian Rockies, M189: 7, 13.
14. Ibid.
15. Schäffer, *A Hunter*, 147.
16. Ibid., 141.
17. Mary Schäffer, 16.
18. Schäffer, *A Hunter*, 144.
19. Mary T.S. Schäffer, "The Finding of Lake Maligne," 94.
20. Ibid.

An Activist Emerges

1. "Philadelphia Woman Names New Mountain," *Edmonton Evening Journal* (8 August 1911), 1.
2. Ibid.
3. Mary Schäffer, "The Story of Revelstoke," unpublished manuscript, Whyte Museum of the Canadian Rockies, M79: 6, 13-4.
4. Schäffer, *A Hunter*, 36.
5. Ibid., 63.
6. Mary T. S. Schäffer, "Haunts of the Wild Flowers of the Canadian Rockies," *Canadian Alpine Journal* 3 (1911), 131.
7. Schäffer, *A Hunter*, 140.
8. Mary S. Warren, "In the Heart of the Canadian Rockies with Horse and Camera, Part I," unpublished manuscript, Whyte Museum of the Canadian Rockies, M189: 7, 9.
9. Mary S. Warren, "In the Heart of the Canadian Rockies, Part II," unpublished manuscript, Whyte Museum of the Canadian Rockies, M189: 7, 13.
10. Mary Warren, letter to Minnie Nickell, 12 November 1936(?), Whyte Museum of the Canadian Rockies, M8.

11. Qtd. in Reichwein, *Guardians of a Rocky Mountain Wilderness*, 67.
12. Ibid.
13. Ibid., 68.
14. "Expedition to Maligne Lake," *Canadian Alpine Journal* 4 (1912), 77.
15. Ibid.
16. Ibid.
17. Mary Warren, letter to J. Monroe Thorington, 13 March 1924, Whyte Museum of the Canadian Rockies, M106: 36.
18. Ibid.
19. Mary Warren, letter to J. Monroe Thorington, 28 March 1924.
20. Ibid.

A New Beginning
1. Mary Warren, letter to Humphrey Toms, 24 June 1936, Whyte Museum of the Canadian Rockies, M429.
2. Mary Schäffer, letter to George Vaux Jr., 30 November 1911, Whyte Museum of the Canadian Rockies, M107.
3. Mary Schäffer, letter to George Vaux Jr., 20 September 1911.
4. Mary Schäffer, letter to Humphrey Toms, 13 December 1933.
5. Mary Schäffer, letter to George Vaux Jr., 10 October 1911.
6. Mary Schäffer, letter to George Vaux Jr., 16 December 1911.
7. Mary Schäffer, letter to George Vaux Jr., 4 November 1912.
8. Mary Schäffer, letter to George Vaux Jr., 10 October 1911.
9. Mary Schäffer, letter to George Vaux Jr., 30 November 1911.
10. Ibid.
11. Ibid.
12. Mary Warren, letter to Humphrey Toms, 25 May 1935.
13. Mary Warren, letter to Humphrey Toms, 13 December 1933.
14. Mary Warren, letter to Humphrey Toms, 24 June 1936.
15. Ibid.
16. Ibid.
17. Note on Mary S. Warren, "Palliser's Expedition: Some Intimate Glimpses," *Calgary Herald*, clipping, n.d., Whyte Museum of the Canadian Rockies, M79: 8.
18. Mary S. Warren, "The Byways of Banff," *Canadian Alpine Journal* 10 (1919), 78.
19. "The Late Dr. Charles Schäffer..." *The Nation* (3 September 1908), 217.
20. Mary Warren, letter to Humphrey Toms, 26 November 1937.
21. Mary Warren, letter to Humphrey Toms, 11 September 1933.
22. Mary Warren, letter to Humphrey Toms, 2 December 1933.
23. Mary Warren, letter to Humphrey Toms, 28 March 1935.
24. Panzer, *Philadelphia Naturalistic Photography*, 6.
25. "Mrs. Shaefer Tells of Rocky Mountains," clipping, 1907, Whyte Museum of the Canadian Rockies, M70: 91.

A True Banffite
1. Mary Schäffer, "Tepee Life in the Northern Hills," unpublished manuscript, Whyte Museum of the Canadian Rockies, M79: 6, 3.
2. Qtd. in Cavell and Whyte, *Rocky Mountain Madness*, 7.
3. Mary Warren, letter to Raymond Zillmer, 28 February 1928, Whyte Museum of the Canadian Rockies, M8.
4. Mary Schäffer, letter to Cousin Lottie, 4 December 1912, Whyte Museum of the Canadian Rockies, M8.
5. Mary Warren, letter to Humphrey Toms, 16 November 1937, Whyte Museum of the Canadian Rockies, M429.
6. Ibid.
7. Ibid.

8. Mary Warren, letter to Humphrey Toms, 2 December 1933.
9. Mary Warren, letter to Charles Reid, 3 March 1935, Whyte Museum of the Canadian Rockies, M413:2.
10. Mary Warren, letter to Minnie Nickell, 12 November 1936(?), Whyte Museum of the Canadian Rockies, M8.
11. Mary Warren, letter to George Vaux Jr., 11 June 1917, Whyte Museum of the Canadian Rockies, M107.
12. Qtd. in Mary S. Warren, "In the Heart of the Canadian Rockies with Horse and Camera, Part I," unpublished manuscript, Whyte Museum of the Canadian Rockies, M189: 7, 14.
13. Mary Warren, letter to George Vaux Jr., 7 October 1915(?).
14. Mary Warren, letter to George Vaux Jr., 9 May 1915.
15. Mary Warren, letter to George Vaux Jr., 30 September 1916.
16. Mary Warren, letter to George Vaux Jr., 30 March 1919.
17. Ibid.
18. "Interesting Lecture," Banff Crag and Canyon (15 August 1914), 8.
19. "Banff and the I.O.D.E.," Banff Crag and Canyon (28 October 1927), 1.
20. Mary Warren, letter to Humphrey Toms, 26 November 1937.
21. Mary Warren, letter to Lillian Gest, n.d., Whyte Museum of the Canadian Rockies, M67:8.

Ever the Traveller
1. Mary Schäffer, "The Story of Revelstoke," unpublished manuscript, Whyte Museum of the Canadian Rockies, M79: 6, 7.
2. Ibid., 16.
3. Ibid., 20-1.
4. Mary Warren, letter to Minnie Nickell, 11 April 1937(?), Whyte Museum of the Canadian Rockies, M8.
5. Mary Warren, letter to Charles Reid, 29 March, n.y., Whyte Museum of the Canadian Rockies, M413: 12.
6. Mary Warren, letter to Charles Reid, 3 March 1935.
7. Mary Warren, letter to Humphrey Toms, 28 March 1935, Whyte Museum of the Canadian Rockies, M429.
8. Mary Warren, letter to Humphrey Toms, 9 April 1937.
9. Mary Warren, letter to Minnie Nickell, 11 April 1937(?).
10. Ibid.
11. Ibid.
12. Ibid.
13. Mary Warren, letter to Humphrey Toms, 17 April 1935.
14. Mary Warren, letter to Charles Reid, March 29, n.y.
15. Mary Warren, letter to Minnie Nickell, 11 April 1937(?).
16. Mary Warren, letter to Humphrey Toms, 6 March 1938.
17. Mary Warren, letter to Lillian Gest, 6 September, n.y., Whyte Museum of the Canadian Rockies, M67: 8.
18. Mary Warren, letter to Humphrey Toms, 24 June 1936.

Opinions, Opinions!
1. Mary Schäffer, "The Heart of a Child," unpublished manuscript, Whyte Museum of the Canadian Rockies, M79: 7, 16.
2. Mary Schäffer, "A New Year in the Wilds," unpublished manuscript, Whyte Museum of the Canadian Rockies, M79: 6, 12-3.
3. Schäffer, A Hunter, 94.
4. Mary S. Warren, "In the Heart of the Rockies with Horse and Camera, Part I," unpublished manuscript, Whyte Museum of the Canadian Rockies, M189: 7, 3.
5. Schäffer, A Hunter, 60.
6. Ibid.

7. Mary Schäffer, "The Heart of a Child," 9.
8. Mary Warren, letter to Minnie Nickell, 21 September 1936(?), Whyte Museum of the Canadian Rockies, M8.
9. Schäffer, *A Hunter*, 125.
10. Mary Schäffer, "A New Year in the Wilds," 4.
11. Schäffer, *A Hunter*, 70.
12. Schäffer, *A Hunter*, 90.
13. Schäffer, *A Hunter*, 73.
14. Herman Sharpless, letter to George Vaux Jr., 3 October 1914, Whyte Museum of the Canadian Rockies, M107.
15. Mary Schäffer, "A New Year in the Wilds," 7.
16. Ibid.
17. Schäffer, *A Hunter*, 72.
18. Ibid.
19. Ibid., 71.
20. Ibid.
21. Ibid.
22. Ibid., 94.
23. Mrs. Charles Schäffer, "The Valleys of the Saskatchewan with Horse and Camera," *The Bulletin of the Geographical Society of Philadelphia* (April 1907), 42.
24. Schäffer, *A Hunter*, 69.
25. Ibid., 134.
26. Ibid., 135.
27. Ibid., 136.
28. Mary Schäffer, "Tepee Life in the Northern Hills," unpublished manuscript, Whyte Museum of the Canadian Rockies, M79: 6, 32.
29. Schäffer, *A Hunter*, 140.
30. Ibid.
31. Ibid.
32. Ibid., 139.
33. Ibid.
34. Ibid., 140.
35. "The Right Angle," *Canada West Monthly*, clipping, n.d., Whyte Museum of the Canadian Rockies, M79: 9A.
36. Mary Warren, letter to Humphrey Toms, 25 May 1935, Whyte Museum of the Canadian Rockies, M429.
37. Mary Warren, letter to Humphrey Toms, 27 June 1937.
38. Mary Warren, letter to Charles Reid, 18 March 1936, Whyte Museum of the Canadian Rockies, M413: 2.
39. Mary Warren, letter to J. Monroe Thorington, 13 March 1924, Whyte Museum of the Canadian Rockies, M106: 36.
40. Mary Warren, letter to J. Monroe Thorington, 28 March 1924.
41. Mary Warren, letter to Humphrey Toms, 26 November 1937.
42. Ibid.
43. Mary Warren, letter to Raymond Zillmer, 2 January, n.y., Whyte Museum of the Canadian Rockies, M8.
44. Mary Warren, letter to Humphrey Toms, 26 November 1937.
45. Ibid.
46. Ibid.
47. Mary Warren, letter to Raymond Zillmer, 12 April, n.y.
48. Ibid.
49. Mary Warren, letter to Minnie Nickell, 12 November 1936(?).
50. Mary Warren, letter to Lillian Gest, 23 May 1938(?), Whyte Museum of the Canadian Rockies, M67: 8.
51. Mary Warren, letter to Minnie Nickell, 13 December, n.y.

52. Ibid.
53. Ibid.
54. Ibid.
55. Mary Warren, letter to Humphrey Toms, 2 April 1938.
56. Mary Warren, letter to Humphrey Toms, 14 May 1938.
57. Mary Warren, letter to Humphrey Toms, 3 December 1934.
58. Mary Warren, letter to Humphrey Toms, 16 November 1936.
59. Mary Warren, letter to Humphrey Toms, 27 June 1937.
60. Mary Warren, letter to J. Monroe Thorington, 7 April 1924.
61. Mary Warren, letter to Charles Reid, 2 February, n.y.
62. Mary Warren, letter to Humphrey Toms, 1 February 1934.
63. Mary Warren, letter to Humphrey Toms, 27 June 1937.
64. Mary Warren, letter to Humphrey Toms, 9 April 1937.
65. Mary Warren, letter to Humphrey Toms, 16 November 1936.
66. Ibid.
67. Ibid.
68. "Consider Well Before You Vote," *Banff Crag and Canyon* (16 August 1935), 2.
69. "Mr. Aberhart…" *Banff Crag and Canyon* (30 April 1937), 2.

Legacy of a Mountain Lover
1. Ward, *Lady Merton, Colonist*, 58.
2. Ibid., 132-3.
3. Mary Warren, letter to Humphrey Toms, 24 June 1936, Whyte Museum of the Canadian Rockies, M429.
4. Mary Warren, letter to Humphrey Toms, 7 July 1934.
5. Mary Warren, letter to Humphrey Toms, 20 July 1935.
6. Ibid.
7. Mary Warren, letter to Humphrey Toms, 6 September 1938.
8. Mary Warren, letter to Humphrey Toms, 27 April 1938.
9. Mary Warren, letter to Lillian Gest, 6 September, n.y., Whyte Museum of the Canadian Rockies, M67: 8.
10. Mary Warren, letter to Lillian Gest, 23 May 1938(?).
11. Mary Warren, letter to Humphrey Toms, 26 November 1937.
12. Mary Warren, letter to Humphrey Toms, 16 November 1937.
13. Mary Warren, letter to Humphrey Toms, 26 November 1937.
14. Mary Warren, letter to Humphrey Toms, 6 March 1938.
15. Mary Warren, letter to Humphrey Toms, 27 April 1938.
16. Mary Warren, letter to Minnie Nickell, 12 November 1936(?), Whyte Museum of the Canadian Rockies, M8.
17. "Mrs. Wm. Warren Banff Oldtimer and Explorer of Rockies Passes," *Banff Crag and Canyon* (27 January 1939), 1.
18. Elsie Park Gowan, *Jasper Story*, unpublished manuscript, University of Alberta Archives: 87-123, Box 1, Items 1-12, 1.
19. Ibid., 40.
20. Ibid., 39.
21. Ibid., 41.
22. Ibid., 40.
23. Ibid., 41.

Index